Yankees
TO
FIGHTING IRISH

Yankees
TO
FIGHTING IRISH

What's Behind Your
Favorite Team's Name

MICHAEL LEO DONOVAN

Foreword by
DICK ENBERG

TAYLOR TRADE PUBLISHING
Dallas • Lanham • Boulder • New York • Toronto • Oxford

Copyright © 2004 by Michael Leo Donovan

This Taylor Trade Publishing paperback edition of *Yankees to Fighting Irish: What's Behind Your Favorite Team's Name* is an original publication. It is published by arrangement with the author.

Published by Taylor Trade Publishing
An imprint of The Rowman & Littlefield Publishing Group, Inc.
4501 Forbes Boulevard, Suite 200
Lanham, Maryland, 20706

Distributed by National Book Network

Donovan, Michael Leo, 1954–
   Yankees to fighting Irish : what's behind your favorite team's name / Michael Leo Donovan.
      p. cm.
   ISBN 1-58979-034-0 (pbk. : alk. paper)
   1. Sports teams—United States—Names—History. 2. Sports teams—Canada—Names—History. 3. Sports teams—United States—History. 4. Sports teams—Canada—History. I. Donovan, Michael Leo, 1954– Yankees to fighting Irish. II. Title.
   GV583.D65 2004
   796'.06073—dc22

2004013745

♾™ The paper used in this publication meets the minimum requirements of American National Standard for Information Sciences—Permanence of paper for Printed Library Materials, ANSI/NISO Z39.48-1992.
Manufactured in the United States of America.

To Kathleen and Aileen
Some had sisters, I had guardian angels

Contents

What Might Have Been xv
Name Change xvi
Foreword by Dick Enberg xviii
Acknowledgments xx
Introduction xxi

Part 1
MAJOR LEAGUE BASEBALL

Anaheim Angels 3
Arizona Diamondbacks 3
Atlanta Braves 3
Baltimore Orioles 4
Boston Red Sox 4
Chicago Cubs 5
Chicago White Sox 6
Cincinnati Reds 6
Cleveland Indians 7
Colorado Rockies 7
Detroit Tigers 7
Florida Marlins 8
Houston Astros 8
Kansas City Royals 9
Los Angeles Dodgers 9
Milwaukee Brewers 10
Minnesota Twins 10
Montreal Expos 10
New York Mets 11
New York Yankees 11
Oakland Athletics 12
Philadelphia Phillies 12
Pittsburgh Pirates 13
St. Louis Cardinals 13
San Diego Padres 13
San Francisco Giants 14
Seattle Mariners 14
Tampa Bay Devil Rays 14
Texas Rangers 15
Toronto Blue Jays 15

Part 2
NATIONAL BASKETBALL ASSOCIATION

Atlanta Hawks 19
Boston Celtics 19
Charlotte Bobcats 20
Chicago Bulls 21
Cleveland Cavaliers 21
Dallas Mavericks 21
Denver Nuggets 22
Detroit Pistons 22
Golden State Warriors 23
Houston Rockets 23
Indiana Pacers 24
Los Angeles Clippers 24
Los Angeles Lakers 25
Memphis Grizzlies 25
Miami Heat 26
Milwaukee Bucks 26
Minnesota Timberwolves 27
New Jersey Nets 28
New Orleans Hornets 28
New York Knickerbockers 29
Orlando Magic 29
Philadelphia 76ers 30
Phoenix Suns 30
Portland Trail Blazers 31
Sacramento Kings 32
San Antonio Spurs 32
Seattle Supersonics 33
Toronto Raptors 33
Utah Jazz 34
Washington Wizards 34

Part 3
NATIONAL FOOTBALL LEAGUE

Arizona Cardinals 39
Atlanta Falcons 39
Baltimore Ravens 40
Buffalo Bills 40
Carolina Panthers 41
Chicago Bears 41
Cincinnati Bengals 42
Cleveland Browns 42
Dallas Cowboys 43
Denver Broncos 44
Detroit Lions 44

Green Bay Packers 44
Indianapolis Colts 45
Houston Texans 46
Jacksonville Jaguars 46
Kansas City Chiefs 47
Miami Dolphins 47
Minnesota Vikings 48
New England Patriots 49
New Orleans Saints 49
New York Giants 50
New York Jets 50
Oakland Raiders 51
Philadelphia Eagles 51
Pittsburgh Steelers 52
St. Louis Rams 52
San Diego Chargers 53
San Francisco 49ers 54
Seattle Seahawks 54
Tampa Bay Buccaneers 55
Tennessee Titans 55
Washington Redskins 56

Part 4
NATIONAL HOCKEY LEAGUE

Anaheim Mighty Ducks 59
Atlanta Thrashers 59
Boston Bruins 59
Buffalo Sabres 60
Calgary Flames 61
Carolina Hurricanes 61
Chicago Blackhawks 61
Colorado Avalanche 62
Columbus Blue Jackets 63
Dallas Stars 63
Detroit Red Wings 64
Edmonton Oilers 64
Florida Panthers 65
Los Angeles Kings 66
Minnesota Wild 66
Montreal Canadiens 67
Nashville Predators 67
New Jersey Devils 68
New York Islanders 69
New York Rangers 69
Ottawa Senators 70
Philadelphia Flyers 71
Phoenix Coyotes 71
Pittsburgh Penguins 72

St. Louis Blues 73
San Jose Sharks 73
Tampa Bay Lightning 74
Toronto Maple Leafs 74
Vancouver Canucks 75
Washington Capitals 75

Part 5
COLLEGES

Air Force Falcons 79
Akron Zips 79
Alabama-Birmingham Blazers 80
Alabama Crimson Tide 80
Alaska-Anchorage SeaWolf 81
Alaska-Fairbanks Nanooks 81
Arizona State Sun Devils 82
Arizona Wildcats 82
Arkansas Razorbacks 83
Arkansas State Indians 83
Arkansas Tech Wonder Boys 84
Auburn Tigers 84
Ball State Cardinals 85
Baylor Bears 85
Boise State Broncos 86
Boston College Eagles 86
Boston Terriers 87
Bowdoin Polar Bears 87
Bowling Green Falcons 87
Brigham Young Cougars 88
California Golden Bears 88
California State Maritime Keelhaulers 89
California State Northridge Matadors 89
Central Florida Knights of Pegasus 90
Central Michigan Chippewas 90
Chaminade Silverswords 91
Cincinnati Bearcats 91
Clemson Tigers 91
Coastal Carolina Chanticleers 92
Colby White Mules 92
Colorado Buffaloes 93
Colorado State Rams 93
Connecticut Huskies 94
Delaware Fighting Blue Hens 94
Dickinson Red Devils 94
Duke Blue Devils 95
East Carolina Pirates 95
Eastern Michigan Eagles 96
Endicott Power Gulls 96

Florida Gators 97
Florida State Seminoles 97
Fresno State Bulldogs 98
Georgetown Hoyas 98
Georgia Bulldogs 99
Georgia Tech Yellowjackets 99
Harvard Crimson 100
Hawaii Rainbow Warriors 101
Houston Cougars 101
Idaho Vandals 102
Illinois College Blueboys 102
Illinois Fighting Illini 102
Indiana Hoosiers 103
Iowa Hawkeyes 104
Iowa State Cyclones 104
Irvine Anteaters 105
Kansas Jayhawks 105
Kansas State Wildcats 106
Kent Golden Flashes 106
Kentucky Wildcats 107
Louisiana State Fighting Tigers 107
Louisiana Tech Bulldogs 108
Louisville Cardinals 108
Maryland Terrapins 108
Memphis Tigers 109
Metropolitan State College of Denver Roadrunners 109
Miami Hurricanes 110
Miami (Ohio) Redskins 111
Michigan State Spartans 111
Michigan Wolverines 112
Minnesota Golden Gophers 112
Mississippi Rebels 113
Mississippi State Bulldogs 113
Missouri-Kansas City Kangaroos 114
Missouri Tigers 114
Navy Midshipmen 115
Nebraska Cornhuskers 115
Nevada-Las Vegas Runnin' Rebels 116
Nevada Wolf Pack 117
New Mexico Lobos 117
New Mexico State Aggies 118
New Orleans Privateers 118
North Carolina State Wolfpack 118
North Carolina Tar Heels 119
North Florida Ospreys 120
North Texas Eagles 120
Northeast Louisiana Indians 120
Northern Illinois Huskies 121
Northern Kentucky Norse 121

Northwestern Wildcats 122
Notre Dame Fighting Irish 122
Ohio Bobcats 123
Ohio State Buckeyes 123
Oklahoma Sooners 124
Oklahoma State Cowboys 124
Oregon Ducks 125
Oregon State Beavers 125
Pacific Tigers 126
Penn State Nittany Lions 126
Pepperdine Waves 127
Pittsburgh Panthers 127
Pomona Sagehens 127
Purdue Boilermakers 128
Rice Owls 128
Richmond Spiders 129
Rutgers Scarlet Knights 129
St. John's Red Storm 129
St. Louis Billikens 130
San Diego State Aztecs 130
San Jose State Spartans 131
Santa Barbara Gauchos 131
Santa Cruz Banana Slugs 132
Scottsdale Artichokes 132
South Carolina Fighting Gamecocks 133
South Dakota Tech Hardrockers 133
Southern California Trojans 134
Southern Colorado Thunderwolves 134
Southern Illinois Salukis 135
Southern Methodist Mustangs 135
Southern Mississippi Golden Eagles 136
Southwestern Louisiana Ragin' Cajuns 136
Stanford Cardinal 137
Stetson Hatters 137
Syracuse Orangemen 138
Tarleton State Texans 139
Temple Owls 139
Tennessee Volunteers 140
Texas A&M Aggies 140
Texas Christian Horned Frogs 141
Texas-El Paso Miners 141
Texas Longhorns 141
Texas Tech Red Raiders 142
Toledo Rockets 142
Trinity Christian Trolls 143
Tulane Green Wave 143
Tulsa Golden Hurricane 144
UCLA Bruins 144
Utah State Aggies 145

Utah Utes 145
Vanderbilt Commodores 145
Virginia Cavaliers 146
Virginia Tech Hokies 146
Wake Forest Demon Deacons 147
Washington Bears 147
Washington Huskies 148
Washington State Cougars 148
West Point Black Knights 149
West Virginia Mountaineers 149
Western Kentucky Hilltoppers 150
Western Maryland Green Terrors 150
Western Michigan Broncos 150
Wichita State Shockers 151
Wisconsin Badgers 151
Wyoming Cowboys 152

Part 6
THE BEST OF THE REST

Abilene Prairie Dogs 155
Acadia Axemen 155
Altoona Curve 155
Arsenal Gunners 156
Asheville Tourists 156
Aston Villa Villans 157
Atlanta Knights 157
Bishop Gaitors 157
Bolton Wanderers 158
British Columbia Lions 158
Brooklyn Cyclones 159
Calgary Dinosaurs 160
Charleston Riverdogs 160
Chattanooga Lookouts 160
Chicago Wolves 161
Chillicothe Paints 161
Cincinnati Cyclones 162
Cleveland Lumberjacks 162
Dallas Burn 162
Durham Bulls 162
Everton Toffeemen 163
Fort Wayne Komets 164
Fort Wayne Wizards 164
Frederick Keys 164
Grand Rapids Mackers 165
Hamilton Tiger-Cats 165
Hershey Bears 166
Houston Aeros 166
Indiana Legends 166

Indianapolis Ice 167
Johnstown Chiefs 167
Kalamazoo Kingdom 167
Kansas City Blades 168
Kansas City Knights 168
Kansas City Wizards 169
Kissimmee Cobras 169
Lansing Lugnuts 170
Las Vegas 51s 170
Los Angeles Galaxy 171
Louisville Riverbats 171
Louisville Riverfrogs 171
Macon Whoopee 172
Manchester United Red Devils 172
Manitoba Moose 172
McGill Redmen 173
Medicine Hat Rattlers 173
Michigan Battle Cats 174
Michigan K-Wings 174
Milwaukee Admirals 175
Minnesota Arctic Blast 175
Montreal Alouettes 175
New Britain Rock Cats 176
Newcastle United Magpies 176
Norfolk Tides 177
Nottingham Forest 177
Peoria Rivermen 178
Piedmont Boll Weevils 178
Quad City River Bandits 179
Rancho Cucamonga Quakes 179
Roanoke Express 180
San Bernardino Stampede 180
San Jose Clash 181
Saskatchewan Roughriders 181
Savannah Sand Gnats 182
Sheffield Wednesday 182
Shreveport Swamp Dragons 183
Tampa Bay Mutiny 183
Tehran Peruzee 183
Toledo Mud Hens 184
Toronto Argonauts 184
Tottenham Hotspurs 185
Trent Excalibur 186
West Ham United Hammers 186
Winnipeg Blue Bombers 186
Winston-Salem Warthogs 187

What Might Have Been

Many of the nicknames sports fans have grown accustomed to were not the only, or even the first choice of some organizations. The fan base for the NFL's Oakland Raiders had selected the Señors — until a last minute change by management. Some other suggested and considered franchise names might surprise you: imagine the NFL's Falcons, Cowboys, and Dolphins being cheered on as the Atlanta Peaches, Dallas Steers, or Miami Moons. Or the NHL's Flyers, Coyotes, and Sharks wearing the colors of the Philadelphia Mohawks, Phoenix Phreeze, and San Jose Ice Breakers. Baseball might've enjoyed the fragrant Tampa Bay Fruit Blossoms, and basketball the Torontosaurus Rex, Boston Unicorns, and Washington Jam-A-Rama.

Name Change

How about name changes? It's hard to imagine that the Chicago Cubs were first called the Chicago White Sox, but they were. Other name changes include baseball's Detroit Creams, Pittsburgh Innocents, and Brooklyn Bridegrooms becoming the Tigers, Pirates, and Dodgers. Football's Philadelphia Eagles were once called the Yellowjackets, and the NHL's Toronto Maple Leafs skated as the Iron Dukes.

Some Other Name Changes

(BASEBALL)

CLEVELAND INDIANS; NAPS
DETROIT TIGERS; CREAMS
BROOKLYN DODGERS; BRIDEGROOMS
PITTSBURGH PIRATES; INNOCENTS
CHICAGO CUBS; WHITE SOX (ORPHANS)
NEW YORK YANKEES; BALTIMORE ORIOLES

(NFL)

PHILADELPHIA EAGLES; YELLOWJACKETS
ARIZONA CARDINALS; CHICAGO NORMALS

(NHL)

OTTAWA SENATORS; SILVER SEVEN (1900-07)
ST. LOUIS BLUES; EAGLES (1934-35)
TORONTO MAPLE LEAFS; IRON DUKES (pre-1900)
VANCOUVER CANUCKS; CREAMERY KINGS (pre-1900)

(COLLEGE)

ARKANSAS STATE INDIANS; GORILLAS
KANSAS STATE WILDCATS; FARMERS

NEBRASKA CORNHUSKERS; BUGEATERS
NORTH CAROLINA STATE WOLFPACK; RED TERROR
NOTRE DAME FIGHTING IRISH; RAMBLERS
OKLAHOMA SOONERS; ROUGH RIDERS
OREGON DUCKS; WEBFOOTS
PURDUE BOILERMAKERS; PUMPKIN SHUCKERS
SAN DIEGO STATE AZTECS; PROFESSORS
SOUTHERN METHODIST MUSTANGS; PARSONS
SYRACUSE ORANGEMEN; PINK-AND-BLUEMEN
TEXAS TECH RED RAIDERS; MATADORS
VIRGINIA CAVALIERS; WAHOOS
WASHINGTON HUSKIES; SUN DODGERS

Names That Might Have Been

(COLLEGE)

BALL STATE CARDINALS; SCRAPPIN' TEACHERS
BUFFALO BEARS; BOOKWORM
FLORIDA STATE SEMINOLES; FLEAS
IDAHO VANDALS; WRECKING CREW
NORTH CAROLINA STATE WOLFPACK; PINEROOTERS
SOUTHERN MISSISSIPPI GOLDEN EAGLES; WAR LORDS
TEXAS CHRISTIAN HORNED FROGS; CACTUS
TOLEDO ROCKETS; TURTLES

(NFL)

ATLANTA FALCONS; PEACHES
CAROLINA PANTHERS; RHINOS
CINCINNATI BENGALS; BUCKEYES
DALLAS COWBOYS; STEERS
MIAMI DOLPHINS; MOONS
SAN DIEGO CHARGERS; CABALLEROS
SEATTLE SEAHAWKS; ASPARAGUS

(NHL)

BUFFALO SABRES; EAGER BEAVERS
COLORADO AVALANCHE; ROCKY MOUNTAIN EXTREME
PHILADELPHIA FLYERS; MOHAWKS
PHOENIX COYOTES; PHREEZE
SAN JOSE SHARKS; ICEBREAKERS

Foreword

I have been a passionate sports fan all my life. Growing up, I attended games, listened to broadcasts, memorized record books, and devoured the sports pages. I couldn't get enough, consuming all I could about all sports, never with the intent of one day becoming an announcer. In fact, while attending Central Michigan University, my studies were geared toward becoming a teacher and possibly a coach. One of my early fascinations was the nicknames of certain teams. How did the Los Angeles (formerly Brooklyn) Dodgers earn their name? Why is the hockey team in Detroit called the Red Wings? And, just what is a Kansas Jayhawk?

I did teach and coach baseball at California State Northridge before being hired full-time by Gene Autry's radio (KMPC) and television (KTLA) stations in Los Angeles. There I became the "voice" of UCLA Bruins basketball during the majority of Coach John Wooden's remarkable national championship run. I was also the play-by-play announcer for the California Angels and the Los Angeles Rams, teams, incidentally, with interesting origins behind their nicknames.

In *Yankees to Fighting Irish*, you have a carefully researched book that reveals the origin of a team's nickname (who, when, why), how the name might have changed through the years, and other entertaining information about the team or its mascot. I especially enjoyed learning more about the monikers behind the schools and professional teams with which I have been associated.

Consider my alma mater, Central Michigan University. The original nicknames were the Dragons, and then the Bearcats, before becoming the Chippewas in 1942. Likewise, I did not know that the Rams (originally in Cleveland) were named by the franchise's first general manager, Buzz Wetzel, who admired the Fordham University Rams — thus making the Cleveland (Los Angeles, St. Louis) Rams the first pro franchise to take its name from a college team.

As you read through the pages that follow, you'll encounter such nicknames and mascots as the Banana Slugs, the Excalibur, the Lumberjacks, the Yellowjackets, and the Zips. Should you need a name for your son or daughter's little league team . . . reading the history of the

Billikens, Kangaroos, or Wolverines might spark an idea. Regardless, *Yankees to Fighting Irish* offers great history, terrific trivia, and wonderful fun for fans of all the teams!

After reading these stories, maybe we can borrow the famous "Lions and tigers and bears" line from *The Wizard of Oz* and change it to, Hatters and Sand Gnats and Chippewas . . . *oh my!*

Dick Enberg

Acknowledgments

First and foremost I wish to thank my wife Jane, the best thing that could ever happen to a writer, and our children Kayleigh and Matthew. I would also like to acknowledge the hundreds of individuals who responded to my inquiries about their team names—from college sports info departments to media relations officers, sportswriters to retired athletes — many of whom didn't know the answers themselves and had to search out hundred-year-old files for long-forgotten origins. This book is for their team effort, and for all of us who love to cheer out loud.

Introduction

The idea for this book came about the day I heard sports paraphernalia had become a billion-dollar-a-year industry. I started to wonder about the team nicknames I'd always taken for granted. Today we sports fans watch as merchandisers select names and design logos with a fervor verging on propaganda, with nothing but T-shirt sales in mind. Was it always thus? After all, do Browns, Reds, and White Sox have the aggressive cash register cachet of Raptors, Diamondbacks, and Avalanche? And how about Hoosiers, Hoyas, and Buckeyes? What do they even MEAN?

So began my research, and three years later, this book.

Think about it — no one who was there when the decision was made to call the Brooklyn baseball team the Dodgers is even alive today. But that storied moniker, and countless others like it, will survive even those of us who cheer them aloud today, more than one hundred years after they were first christened. So, was there a clever marketing scheme in place when Detroit's baseball team was anointed the Tigers, or when hockey's Chicago Blackhawks skated into the hearts of a city?

The fast answer is 'no.' It could be said that the value of merchandising a sports name came about by accident, when the Notre Dame Fighting Irish realized entrepreneurs were cashing in on their fabled moniker. When the university moved to protect the name, it was told it couldn't be done — Fighting Irish was part of the public domain. Leave it to the dogged Irish to rectify the situation of course, and now ALL nicknames are jealously guarded by their proper teams, from the New York Yankees to the Central Florida Knights of Pegasus.

That said, have you ever wondered why, with more than a million words in the English language, someone would call their team the Packers? (Football, page 44) If your answer is yes, then you will enjoy reading this book as much as I did researching it. You might also be interested to learn that some clubs have NEVER changed their moniker — the Philadelphia Phillies (Baseball, page 12) have the longest continuous nickname in pro sports — or that Chicago fielded more than a dozen

xxi

monikers, including Orphans and Spuds, before settling on Cubs. (Baseball, page 5) Did you know that when Washington christened its ball club the Bullets in 1946, the local munitions factory was a source of civil pride? Then times changed, and with them came a new reality where fantastical Wizards (Basketball, page 34) would replace old allegiances. And though it might be obvious WHAT inspired Louisiana Tech to call themselves the Bulldogs (College, page 108), WHY might surprise you — maybe even move you to tears. Then there's the English Premier League team, worth a billion dollars today, so named Sheffield Wednesday (The Best of the Rest, page 182) in the early 19th (!) century because THAT was the only day these otherwise employed soccer fanatics could get together for a game.

This book contains as all-encompassing gathering of sports franchise nicknames as exists anywhere — pros AND college — and all provided directly from the source. The NBA, NFL, MLB, and NHL are here in their entirety, plus almost two hundred of your favorite college teams — including all of Division I (football). For pure entertainment you will also enjoy the chapter called Best of the Rest, containing teams that don't fit into any of the above categories, but belong because they are simply too interesting not to be discussed. They come from everywhere, including minor league baseball, junior hockey, the Canadian Football and English Premier soccer leagues. This way we are able to present not only the Lions, Tigers, and Bears, but also the Riverfrogs, Banana Slugs, and Christian Trolls. And let's not forget the Macon Whoopee, Durham Bulls, and Toledo Mud Hens.

This book exists because no nickname is an accident. And every nickname has a story.

Part 1

Major League Baseball

ANAHEIM ANGELS

Radio, recording, movie, and television star Gene Autry rekindled an old flame of his when he acquired the ANGELS franchise at an American League expansion meeting late in 1960. The club was named the Los Angeles ANGELS to preserve and continue the legacy of a popular Pacific Coast League team that had departed Los Angeles when the DODGERS arrived from Brooklyn in 1957. To escape the DODGERS, whose park they shared during the 1962 through 1965 seasons, the team moved to suburbia. Anaheim Stadium was erected within the shadow of Disneyland, and the team first became known as the California ANGELS, then the Anaheim ANGELS.

NICKNAME: "HALOS"

ARIZONA DIAMONDBACKS

A popular name-the-team contest for this new Major League Baseball expansion team in Phoenix was finally reduced to these names in late 1995 — Arizona COYOTES, SCORPIONS, DIAMONDBACKS, RATTLERS, and even the Arizona PHOENIX! Team ownership was looking for a name that evoked local color, a moniker that would draw attention to the Arizona desert made famous in legend and lore. Also, marketing strategy informs contemporary sports franchises that animals make good copy. Therein came the Diamondbacks, a local poisonous snake with a diamond pattern on its back. Team owner Jerry Colangelo said, "We wanted to put a little bite into our name, and I think we've done that." Coincidentally, sports fans in the state of Arizona were busy looking for a new name for the Winnipeg JETS National Hockey League franchise moving to Phoenix in 1996. A virtually simultaneous name-the-team contest attracted 10,000 entries, with the front-runners including SCORPIONS, MUSTANGS, POSSE, OUTLAWS, and DRY ICE. But COYOTES beat the other finalist, the Phoenix PHREEZE. Now the NHL and Major League Baseball have to watch out for two desert predators — the COYOTES and DIAMONDBACKS.

NICKNAME: "D-BACKS"

ATLANTA BRAVES

This team originated in Boston as the BEANEATERS. After that, the franchise was known as the Boston RED STOCKINGS until 1907. When they dropped that moniker, the American League Boston PILGRIMS snatched it up, becoming the Boston RED SOX. The National League team from Boston took on their new name, the BRAVES, in 1911. James E. Gaffney, nicknamed the "political brave from Tammany Hall," had bought the RED STOCKINGS and named them after himself. From 1936 until 1940, the team was known as the Boston BEES. The Boston BRAVES became the Milwaukee BRAVES in 1953, the first major-league franchise shift in half a century. And, in 1966, the Milwaukee BRAVES moved to Atlanta, where they remain today.

BALTIMORE ORIOLES

The first franchise in Baltimore, from 1872 to 1874, was called the LORD BALTIMORES. Lord Baltimore founded the city in the 1600s. In 1875 until 1881, there was no pro ball in Baltimore. In 1882, the six-club American Association was formed, and Baltimore was a last-minute substitute for Brooklyn. The Baltimore BASEBALL CLUB was its name at that time. In 1883, there was a call for new owners, a manager, and a ballpark. The Von der Horst family, famous as beer brewers, took over ownership of the team with Bill Barney as manager. A new field called Oriole Park was built. The park was named after the Order of the Oriole Parade, which was a Northern autumnal Mardi Gras. There used to be a specific bird that nested in Baltimore, and it was called the Baltimore ORIOLE. The bird, unfortunately, no longer exists. Everything connected with the franchise, the park, and the parade was named for that bird. In January of 1903, this club left town to establish a franchise in the Northeast — the New York YANKEES. Today's Baltimore ORIOLES began their major-league lives as the St. Louis BROWNS. As the BROWNS, they won the American League pennant in 1944, then played the St. Louis CARDINALS in the World Series, losing four games to two. All games were played in the same stadium, Sportsman's Park, the only time this has ever occurred in World Series history. In 1954, the St. Louis BROWNS became the Baltimore ORIOLES, in remembrance of a bird that had long ago left town.

NICKNAMES: "BIRDS"
                "O'S"

BOSTON RED SOX

As one of four new ball clubs to enter into the newly formed American League in 1901, the RED SOX were then known as the Boston

AMERICANS. Previous to that, the club had been called the SOMER-
SETS, after original owner Charles W. Somers, the PLYMOUTH
ROCKS, the SPEED BOYS and the PURITANS. For a while they settled
on the PILGRIMS. When the Boston PILGRIMS won the American
League pennant in 1903, they challenged the National League champion
Pittsburgh PIRATES in the first true World Series. The PILGRIMS won
the best-of-nine series, five games to three! No World Series was played
in 1904 because of a dispute between the leagues, but by 1905 the annual fall classic was here to stay. Various names were applied to the
Boston club until 1907 when the current name RED SOX was adopted.
The origin of this name is traced to the Boston RED STOCKINGS, a
powerful club of the National League in the 1870s and '80s. In 1907 the
RED STOCKINGS abandoned the red hosiery they customarily wore
because manager Fred Tenney believed that the red dye in the socks could
possibly cause infection in spike wounds. So, they changed their name to
the BRAVES. That's when the owner of the Boston PILGRIMS in the
American League, John I. Taylor, said, "From now on we'll wear red
stockings, and I'm grabbing that name RED SOX!"

NICKNAME: "BOSOX"

CHICAGO CUBS

They were originally named the Chicago WHITE STOCKINGS by
owner William Hulbert, and kept that moniker for almost 20 years. But the
flurry of names that followed make the modern-day CUBS the most
nicknamed in baseball. Most of these nicknames were the result of the
Chicago newspapers, each with their own idea as to what name best
suited "their" team. So, at various times, the *Chicago Tribune*, the *Daily
News*, the *Journal*, and the *Interocean* referred to the club as the COLTS
(1887-1906), BLACK STOCKINGS (1888-1889), EX-COLTS (1898),
RAINMAKERS (1898), ORPHANS (1898-1902), COWBOYS (1899),
ROUGH RIDERS (1899-1900), DESERT RANGERS (1899), REM-
NANTS (1901-1902), RECRUITS (1902), PANAMAS (1903),
ZEPHYRS (1905), NATIONALS (1905-1907), SPUDS (1906), the
TROJANS (1913), and, again, the Chicago WHITE STOCKINGS — a
moniker later lifted and still in use by the CUBS' cross-town rivals in
the American League, the Chicago WHITE SOX. In 1902, a sports
columnist for the *Chicago Daily News* (George Rice or Chris Sinsa-
haugh) referred to the team's newest players as CUBS. Sports editor Fred
Rayner liked the name and so he continued to use it. The name stuck.
While every other club had succumbed to night games by 1946,
Chicago's Wrigley Field didn't turn on the lights until 1988. Nineteen

hundred and eight was the club's last championship year.

NICKNAME: "CUBBIES"

CHICAGO WHITE SOX

In the 1890s, the onetime player and manager after whom Comiskey Park was named, Charles Comiskey, invested in an eight-team circuit called the Western League. For reasons that remain unclear, Comiskey decided to purchase the ailing Sioux City club and transfer it to St. Paul. There, the newly baptized SAINTS prospered enough to attract the attention of Chicago CUBS owner James Hart. Hart was looking for a "farm" club, but Comiskey would have nothing of it — he had his eyes on a move to Chicago and the big leagues where his club could challenge the CUBS themselves. In 1900, an enterprising young journalist named Ban Johnson, with Charles Comiskey, created the American League. The winners of the American League pennants in 1900 and 1901 were Comiskey's former St. Paul SAINTS, now the Chicago WHITE STOCKINGS, having lifted the very same moniker the Chicago CUBS had dropped a few years earlier. In 1906 the Chicago WHITE STOCKINGS won the American League pennant, three games ahead of the New York HIGHLANDERS, later to be known as the YANKEES. The STOCKINGS then met and defeated their crosstown rivals, the National League Champion Chicago CUBS, four games to two in the World Series. Comiskey's dream had been fully realized.

NICKNAMES: "SOX"
                "CHISOX"
                "THE HITLESS WONDERS" (affectionately in 1906)
                "PALE HOSE"
                "GO GO SOX" (1959 A.L. Champions)

CINCINNATI REDS

In 1869 the team was called the Cincinnati RED STOCKINGS because they wore red stockings. In the early 1900s the name was shortened to the Cincinnati REDS. Major League Baseball's first night game was played in Cincinnati's Crosley Field on May 24, 1935, with the hometown REDS besting the Philadelphia PHILLIES, 2-1. In the 1950s, Cincinnati's team became the RED STOCKINGS again because of the McCarthy era, when REDS and communism became synonymous, and there was a fear about the association. After two seasons with this old moniker, they were re-christened as the RED LEGS. In 1959 the club felt secure enough to return to their REDS nickname.

NICKNAME: "REDLEGS"
                 "REDS"

CLEVELAND INDIANS

The team was originally called the NAPS, after a player on the team, Napoleon Lajoie. When Napoleon was cut in 1915, the Cleveland club had to unload its moniker. A local newspaper, the *Plain Dealer*, had a naming contest. It was decided to honor a Penobscot Indian, Lewis Sockarlexis, who starred on the club in 1898-99. Since then, the INDIANS have changed leagues — from the National to the American in the late 1800s — but not their name. This team has the added distinction of bringing the first black player into the American League, Larry Doby in 1947. The team mascot is named "Slider."

NICKNAME: "TRIBE"

COLORADO ROCKIES

There were few teams in professional sports that could make the claim that Colorado did when they were awarded their Major League Baseball franchise; they were the only baseball team within a 1,000-mile radius to the north, south, and west! (The closest Major League team is the American League's Kansas City ROYALS at nearly 600 miles to the east.) Marketing and management obviously took this fact into consideration when they called their club the ROCKIES, after North America's largest mountain range, therefore appealing to the entire region and generating more interest across the state borders. The region sure loves its mountain nicknames, as the 1995 Denver entry into the National Hockey League, the Colorado AVALANCHE, can attest.

NICKNAME: "ROX"

DETROIT TIGERS

In its early years, the team was simply called DETROIT, THE DETROITS, sometimes the WOLVERINES, and, at other times, the CREAMS. The CREAMS broke into print in 1894, when a new owner from Los Angeles arrived with an aggregation "purported to be the

CREAM of California baseball players." Baseball historians long credited Philip J. Reid, city editor of the *Detroit Evening News*, with first using the TIGERS moniker in print in 1896. But George Stallings, manager of the Detroit team which was then a member of the Western League, took credit for the nickname. He had put his players in black-and-brown-striped stockings that, he said, reminded fans of tiger stripes. But, still later evidence makes it appear that an unidentified headline writer at the *Detroit Free Press* actually originated the TIGERS nickname in 1895, a year before Stallings became manager, and before the team was wearing striped stockings. From then on, the *Free Press* regularly called them the TIGERS. In May of 1895, the *Sporting Life* began using TIGERS in its dispatches from Detroit. Thus, it seems that the *Detroit Free Press* must get credit for originating the TIGER nickname in 1895.

FLORIDA MARLINS

Though a number of minor league clubs in 1956 and 1970, 1982 and 1988 had MARLIN in their name, it wasn't until owner H. Wayne Huizenga, founder of the Blockbuster Video rental chain, chose the name for his Florida team that it appeared in the major leagues. For years Mr. Huizenga had enjoyed the sport of deep sea fishing, appreciating especially the spirit of one particular dweller of the deep. Here's the metaphor that became his reason for the name, "I chose MARLIN because the fish is a fierce fighter and an adversary that tests your mettle."

HOUSTON ASTROS

Houston's major league team was originally called the COLT .45s after their first home field, Colt Stadium. When a new stadium was built, the team name changed to the ASTROS because of the area's association with astronauts and the aerospace industry. The new stadium, the Astrodome, was the Major League's first domed stadium. Originally, grass grew under the Texas dome bathed in brilliant sunlight. However, ballplayers complained about the glare, and the dome was painted opaque — and the grass stopped growing! Thus emerged "Astroturf," the fake "grass" that revolutionized baseball.

NICKNAME: "STROS"

KANSAS CITY ROYALS

A citywide contest was held in 1968 to select the name of the new Kansas City baseball club. The team's board of directors took the fans' choices into a meeting and emerged with a winner — the ROYALS. The moniker was a nod in the direction of the state's billion dollar livestock industry, and its livestock parade. Kansas City is very proud of the annual event with its western theme, the famous American Royal Parade. Long before the ROYALS, the Negro National League and the American Negro League had teams all over the country, including the Kansas City MONARCHS. Other clubs playing in the Black Leagues included the Philadelphia STARS, New Orleans SECRET NINE, Pittsburgh CRAWFORDS, Chicago AMERICAN GIANTS, Cuban STARS, Homestead GRAYS, New York BUSHWICKS, and Newark EAGLES.

NICKNAME: "K.C."

LOS ANGELES DODGERS

In 19th-century America, plenty of amateur clubs were playing the East Coast circuit, and many with inspired nicknames. Consider the Hartford WIDE AWAKES — so eager to play, they got up at dawn to get in a game before work! But it was in 1890 that a professional team from Brooklyn first stepped out onto legendary Ebbets Field. Because of the overwhelming number of streetcars at that time, and the need to stay alive by avoiding — or dodging — them, the good citizens of Brooklyn became known as TROLLEY DODGERS. It seemed only natural then to call the team representing the area the Brooklyn TROLLEY DODGERS, a label that was shortened just before the turn of the century to Brooklyn DODGERS. Then in 1936, Jimmy Powers of the *Daily News* decided the basement-dwelling DODGERS needed a new name and appealed to his readers. Out of the 7,000 responses he chose 10, all of which he submitted to the team's players. From the 10, they selected the ACES. But more than 2 million Brooklynites disagreed, and the team has remained the DODGERS even after its move to Los Angeles in 1957. The Brooklyn DODGERS also had the distinction of using the Major Leagues' first black player, a first baseman brought up from the Montreal ROYALS, named Jackie Robinson.

NICKNAMES: "BROOKS"
           "DAFFINESS BOYS"
           "DEM BUMS" (with affection)
           "BIG BLUE WRECKING CREW"

MILWAUKEE BREWERS

In 1968, the city of Seattle fielded an American League team called the PILOTS. That team was named by Dewey Sariano, a former ship pilot with the Coast Guard (not, as generally believed, a nod in the direction of the huge Boeing air industry that was located in Seattle) and a minority owner of the new franchise. After a disastrous season on the field and at the box office, the American League demanded that the PILOTS meet three conditions — including the groundbreaking of a new proposed stadium. When none of the conditions were met after that first season, a battle erupted over a new home for the Seattle PILOTS. Though bitterly fought until the end, Texas lost, and the BREWERS were born in Milwaukee. The BREWERS took to the field just two years after the Milwaukee BRAVES had left town for Atlanta. New Milwaukee owner Allan H. (Bud) Selig called his team the BREWERS because of the city's long association with the brewing industry.

NICKNAME: "THE BREW CREW"

MINNESOTA TWINS

This team originated in the nation's capital as the Washington SENATORS. When the franchise was moved to the state of Minnesota in 1961, new owner Calvin Griffiths baptized them the Minnesota TWINS. By embracing the twin cities of Minneapolis and St. Paul in this manner, he hoped to attract fan support from both. Bloomington, a suburb of both cities, was the home of Metropolitan Stadium, where the TWINS played from 1961 until 1981. They now play in Minneapolis, 15 miles from the old park, in the Hubert H. Humphrey Metrodome. The old Metropolitan Stadium is now the site of a shopping mall.

MONTREAL EXPOS

In 1967 the country of Canada celebrated its 100th birthday with two outstanding events in Montreal. It started by hosting one of the most outstanding World Fairs ever. Fifty million people made their way through the Expo turnstiles in 1967, enjoying the award-winning architecture of the international pavilions. Much of this enormously successful fairground still exists today as the "Man and His World" complex. The second major event occurred with the introduction of Major League Baseball to Canada, the first franchise ever granted outside of the United States. Taking to the field in 1968, the Montreal EXPOS name was, and continues to be, a celebration of this dual "centennial" occurrence. Selected from the thousands of contest submissions sponsored by the new club by then-owner Charles Bronfman, the moniker is also consistent with all the pro sport names that come out of bilingual Montreal — it is both a French and English word. Previously, the Montreal ROYALS of the semipro International League had fed the majors with such high-profile players/managers as Jackie Robinson, Tommy Lasorda, and actor Chuck Connors.

NICKNAME: "SPOS"

NEW YORK METS

In 1961, Mrs. Joan Payson, the owner of the National League's newest entry, had five stipulations for a name for the New York team. The stipulations were that the name must: 1 — have public press acceptance; 2 — be closely related to team corporation name "Metropolitan Baseball Club Inc."; 3 — be descriptive of the metropolitan area; 4 — be a brevity that will delight copyreaders; and 5 — be historically related to the Metropolitans of the 19th century American Association. The METS came closest to filling the bill. Other names considered at the time: the REBELS, the SKYLINERS, the NYB'S, the BURROS, the CONTINEN-TALS, the AVENGERS, the JETS, and the ISLANDERS.

NICKNAME: "AMAZIN' METS" (1969 World Champions)

NEW YORK YANKEES

There have been four National League franchises in the Big Apple: the MUTUALS (1876), GIANTS (1883-1957), Brooklyn DODGERS (1890-1957), and METS (1962 to present). In 1903, a team moved to New York from Baltimore, and has stayed through 38 American League pennants and 26 world championships. The most successful franchise in all professional sports began its storied existence at Hilltop Park as the New York HIGHLANDERS. When a fire forced the team to accept an invitation from the GIANTS to play at the Polo Grounds, a name change seemed necessary. Sports editors, weary of attempts to fit HIGHLANDERS into headlines, had aleady started to call the team the YANKEES. YANKEES they remain. The YANKS played in the big Harlem Horseshoe for 10 years until, in 1920, they outdrew their hosts by 350,000 fans. YANKEE Stadium was then built, and at the home opener on April 18, 1923, Babe Ruth took the dimensions of the new stadium by hitting one out of the park.

NICKNAMES: "HILLTOPPERS" (from the Hilltop Park days)
"INVADERS" (used by the GIANTS and other
HIGHLANDER detractors)

"BRONX BOMBERS"
"BOMBERS"
"YANKS"
"PINSTRIPES"

OAKLAND ATHLETICS

In the late 1800s, sports enthusiasts from various men's Athletic Clubs in Philadelphia got together and decided to form a professional baseball team. They called themselves the ATHLETICS — as did many different sports clubs around that time. They became part of the National Associat-ion, baseball's first professional league, which was formed on St. Patrick's Day, 1871, in New York. Along with the Philadelphia ATH-LETICS, other charter member teams were the Boston RED STOCK-INGS, Chicago WHITE STOCKINGS, Cleveland FOREST CITYS, Fort Wayne KEK-IONGAS, Brooklyn ECKFORDS, New York MUTUALS, Rockford FOREST CITYS, Washington NATIONALS, Washington OLYMPICS, and the Troy HAYMAKERS. The Philadelphia ATHLET-ICS won the first National Association Championship. The League fold-ed in 1875. In 1957, the Philadelphia ATHLETICS moved to Kansas City. Charles Finley purchased the Kansas City ATHLETICS in December 1960, and moved the franchise to Oakland in 1968. Once there, he short-ened the team name to the A's.

PHILADELPHIA PHILLIES

The PHILLIES weren't the first or only pro baseball team to play in Philadelphia. The ATHLETICS started in the "city of brotherly love" before making their way west to Oakland. Also, the Negro Baseball League had a team in Philadelphia, the STARS. Other clubs playing in the black leagues included the Baltimore ELITE GIANTS, New York BLACK YANKEES, Chattanooga WHITE SOX, Memphis RED SOX, Cincinnati TIGERS, and the St. Louis GIANTS. The Philadelphia PHILLIES franchise came into the league in 1883, having moved from Worcester, Massachusetts, where the baseball club was known as the BROWN STOCKINGS. The National League club was immediately dubbed the PHILLIES — a takeoff on the city name of Philadelphia — by owner Alfred Reach. In 1944 and 1945 the club was known as the BLUE JAYS, but the nickname was never "officially" changed from the PHILLIES. So, it remains the longest-running nickname in pro sports.

NICKNAMES: "WHIZ KIDS"
                "FIGHTING PHILS"

PITTSBURGH PIRATES

In the 1800s, the pro ball club out of Pittsburgh was called the ALLEGHENIES, a geographical reference to the Allegheny Mountain range of the Appalachian system that runs through Pennsylvania. When another pro league, the Players League, folded in 1890 after just one year, players were expected to return to the team they played for before the new league folded. Second baseman Lewis Bierbauer was to return to Philadelphia, but was stolen — or "pirated" away — by the Pittsburgh team. In 1891 he took to the field with the newly christened Pittsburgh PIRATES.

NICKNAME: "BUCS"

ST. LOUIS CARDINALS

This club was first named the BROWNS, and then briefly the PER-FECTOS. The St. Louis franchise became permanently known as the CARDINALS in 1899. Legend has it that *St. Louis Republic* newspaper reporter Willie McHale overheard a female fan react to the color on the uniforms, "Oh, what a lovely shade of cardinal!" From then on, McHale called the team the CARDINALS, and the nickname stuck. Never under-estimate the power of the press! It was only after the need arose to find an insignia for the club uniform that the bird was born.

NICKNAMES: "CARDS"
                "REDBIRDS"
                "THE GASHOUSE GANG" (1930s)

SAN DIEGO PADRES

This franchise on the West Coast settled on its name as the result of a local newspaper contest. PADRES is a geographical reference to the Catholic missions that were built in early California. Mexican settlers had established their first mission in San Diego, bringing with them their own religious leader, or father — padre, in Spanish. The moniker was also a nod in the direction of the hugely popular Pacific League PADRES that had entertained San Diego baseball enthusiasts in the early 1950s before the Major Leagues came to town in 1969.

NICKNAME: "PADS"

SAN FRANCISCO GIANTS

During the 1883-1885 seasons, the team out of the Big Apple was called the New York GOTHAMS. In 1886 the name was changed to GIANTS when Jim Mutrie, the manager at the time, shouted at his players in victory, "My big fellows! My giants! We are the people!" In 1957 the New York GIANTS left the Polo Grounds in the Big Apple to be reborn out west as the San Francisco GIANTS. They brought with them a grand old winning tradition, and more than a half-century's worth of healthy competition with their crosstown, and now cross-state rivals, the Los Angeles DODGERS, another team that made the trip from back east the same year.

NICKNAME: "JINTS"

SEATTLE MARINERS

The American League Seattle PILOTS were moved after only one season to Milwaukee, where they became known as the BREWERS. That was in 1969. Seattle, upset with the demands put on its PILOTS by the American League, sued. The A.L. promised to deliver another franchise. But it wasn't until eight years later, in 1977, that Seattle had its next taste of professional baseball. The Seattle MARINERS were introduced in the Kingdome, a stadium originally meant for the PILOTS. A local newspaper held a name-the-team contest, and the new ownership picked the club's moniker from the 15,000 entries and 1,600 different names. MARINERS is a response to the team's Pacific Northwest location, and the marine history of Seattle. The team mascot is called "Moose."

TAMPA BAY DEVIL RAYS

It was actually the neighboring city of St. Petersburg, Florida, that first flirted with the game way back in 1914 at a field near Coffee Pot Bayou when the St. Louis BROWNS lost 3-2 to the Chicago CUBS in the city's first spring training game. But it was Tampa Bay that was granted a major league franchise on March 9, 1995. During the weeks surrounding that date, fans submitted more than 7,000 names for a possible team name. Suggestions included such creative choices as FRUIT BLOSSOMS, PTERODACTYLS, BIGFEET, BACKCRACKERS, SNOWBIRDS, and TOADS. The largest percentage included the word "rays," an order of large, graceful fish that live primarily in the tropical waters off Florida's coast. In a telephone contest, more than 50,000 calls supported DEVIL RAYS over MANTA RAYS. Both names are actually used to describe the same fish. Devil Rays are the largest member of the ray family, measuring 19 feet long. They are found in Florida waters, the Gulf of Mexico, and along the Atlantic coast of the southern United States. They are massive but gentle creatures, harmless to humans. The Devil Ray got its name from the cephalic fins on the head that looked like a devil's horns to the early explorers who first saw the bat-shaped creatures. Although they are quite large, Devil Rays are known to leap from the water and can sail up to 20 feet in the air! The Tampa Bay managing general partner, Vince Naimoli, wanted a name and colors which reflected the geographical area.

TEXAS RANGERS

Shortly after the original Washington SENATORS left the nation's capital for Minnesota in 1960, baseball opted for expansion and a new SENATORS team took to the Washington field at the start of the 1961 season. Then, despite the efforts of such luminaries as Richard Nixon and Bowie Kuhn, the second SENATORS team left town 10 years later in 1971, this time for Arlington, Texas, much to the pleasure of Mayor Tom Vandergriff, who had been pursuing a major league franchise for the Dallas/Fort Worth area for 13 years. He'd already failed in his earlier bid for the Seattle PILOTS franchise, which had gone to Milwaukee to become the BREWERS. The new Major League Baseball franchise had the distinction of being the second team to honor the legendary Texas Rangers law agency. (The first was the New York RANGERS hockey team!) The Texas RANGERS baseball club was named by Robert Short, the SENATORS/RANGERS owner. In 1994, RANGERS ownership opened a new stadium in Arlington, simply known as "The Ballpark."

TORONTO BLUE JAYS

In 1976 the city of Toronto held a "name the team" contest. Thirty thousand entries were submitted, and of those, 4,000 were different. One hundred and fifty-four fans submitted the name BLUE JAYS. After management narrowed down the selection to 10 possibilities, BLUE JAYS came out on top. In 1944-45, the Philadelphia PHIILLIES were known as the BLUE JAYS but the name didn't stick. The Toronto BLUE JAYS were the second franchise granted outside of the United States (after the Montreal EXPOS), and the first non-American club to win a World Series, which they accomplished twice in the 1990s.

NICKNAME: "JAYS"

Part 2
National Basketball Association

ATLANTA HAWKS

A banjo box gymnasium called Wharton Field House seating 6,000 on hardwood benches in a city, or rather, three cities, straddling the Mississippi River, is where the ATLANTA HAWKS have their roots. They were known as the Tri City BLACKHAWKS, one of the original members of the NBA after a midsummer merger in 1949 of the 12-year-old National Basketball League and the four-year-old Basketball Association of America formed the new league. The Illinois cities of Moline and Rock Island, plus Davenport, Iowa, across the river formed the neophyte BLACKHAWKS, coached by Roger Potter. Potter was replaced by Red Auerbach, who led them into the playoffs only to drop out in the first round to the ANDERSON DUFFY PACKERS. Auerbach left for the CELTICS, and after two years and a grammatical change to Tri-Cities, the BLACKHAWKS packed their bags and moved to Milwaukee. There, they shortened the nickname to the Milwaukee HAWKS. In 1955 they moved again, this time to St. Louis. There, led by Bob Pettit, the HAWKS won their lone World Chanpionship by beating the formidable Boston team. The St. Louis HAWKS turned sour during the 1961-62 season, and if not for the expansion CHICAGO PACKERS, would've dropped from first to last in just one year. Nineteen hundred and sixty-eight was the best year in franchise history, and then came the shocker. During the broadcast of an Atlanta BRAVES baseball game announcer Milo Hamilton told Atlanta fans the city was going to have a professional basketball team. It was, of course, the HAWKS, a perennial NBA powerhouse, moving from St. Louis to Atlanta. After finishing last in 1976, changes came fast, starting with the hiring of Hubie Brown, who coached the Kentucky COLONELS to the 1975 American Basketball Association Championship. Still, rumors abounded that another move was imminent, and that a new owner was soon to purchase the team. But when R. E. "Ted" Turner bought the club, he promised the HAWKS would stay in Atlanta. Despite some disappointing seasons, so far Turner has held true to that promise.

BOSTON CELTICS

The Boston CELTICS and the National Basketball Association came into being on the same day, June 6, 1946. According to the arena owners of the time, the idea behind professional basketball was to create tenants that would fill empty dates in their respective buildings — between the popular hockey and boxing matches. The original owner of the Boston CELTICS franchise was Walter Brown — a man who uniquely would be elected to both the hockey and basketball halls of fame. He owned the team from 1947 to 1964. He and publicity staff member Howie McHugh, a captain and star goaltender of Dartmouth College's 1934 Ivy League hockey champions, took it on themselves to come up with a nickname. Among the suggestions were the WHIRLWINDS, OLYMPICS, and UNICORNS. Then Brown thought of CELTICS, and McHugh balked. Brown reminded him that the name already had a wonderful tradition. The New York CELTICS were a successful basketball franchise in the 1920s. And, Brown continued, Boston is full of Irish. "We'll put them in green uniforms and call them the Boston CELTICS!" McHugh was skeptical, telling his boss, "No team with an Irish name has ever won a damned thing in Boston — including a pro football team named the SHAMROCKS that fell flat." The CELTICS lost their first home game to the Chicago STAGS, a game delayed when the glass backboard was shattered by a CELTIC who would make an even greater impression elsewhere — Chuck Connors of "The Rifleman" television show fame. The CELTICS also lost to the Providence STEAMROLLERS, and then the St. Louis BOMBERS. Other teams in the new 11-franchise league included New York, Philadelphia, Pittsburgh, Washington, Cleveland, Detroit, and Toronto. Only Boston, New York, and Philadelphia would survive five years. Despite their early losses, the Boston CELTICS went on to become the winningest team in all of basketball.

CHARLOTTE BOBCATS

Robert L. Johnson, the billionaire founder of BET, paid $300 million for an expansion team to replace the HORNETS, who had moved to New Orleans in 2002. Seven thousand fans flooded the center of the city to see Johnson unveil the name and logo of his new NBA team. Nickname finalists included FLIGHT, DRAGON, and BOBCATS — with the owner saying BOBCATS had always been his choice. "The name represents the pride, enthusiasm, courage and commitment of Charlotte," Johnson said. "And the name has to symbolize the team, it is from the cat family so it is strong and a predator and agile. It has to have merchandising capability, and the owner has to like it," Bob said of his BOBCATS. Charlotte's team will be the first in professional sports to use the BOBCAT for its logo. BOBCAT ORANGE, unique to the NBA, is its primary color. Blue, silver, and black are also used in the logo. Utilizing fan feedback, legal reviews, creative analysis, and input from Johnson, "Rufus Lynx" was chosen as the name of the team mascot.

CHICAGO BULLS

According to the media relations department of the Chicago BULLS there is no official written documentation available that gives the history of the team nickname — one of the three best-selling logos in all of sports. There are two theories offered, however. One is that the team used to play in the Amphitheater; and live bulls were regularly led through the stockyard next door — Chicago is known for its stockyards, the Packingtown heritage. Dick Klein, the team owner in 1966, wanted a "ferocious" name for his club, and thought BULLS to be apropos. The other theory is that Klein's son came up with the nickname in response to his father's suggestions of MATADORS and TROUBADOURS. Young master Klein called these choices a load of BULL.

CLEVELAND CAVALIERS

Cleveland was granted a National Basketball Association franchise, along with the Portland TRAIL BLAZERS and the Buffalo BRAVES (now the Los Angeles CLIPPERS), to begin the 1970-71 season. The *Cleveland Plain Dealer* newspaper had a contest to name the team. The winning name, CAVALIERS, was chosen by more than one-third of the 6,000 voters. The other finalists were the JAYS, FORESTERS, TOWERS, and PRESIDENTS. Jerry Tomko, who was the contest winner, wrote that "the CAVALIERS represent a group of daring fearless men, whose life's pact was never surrender, no matter what the odds." In the mid-1980s, CAVALIERS was shortened to CAVS for marketing purposes and the two nicknames are now interchangeable. The team's colors were wine and gold through the 1982-83 season, and were changed to burnt orange, white, and royal blue for the 1983-84 season. Then, in 1994, a new logo and yet another color change occurred. The CAVS' new colors are orange, blue, and black.

DALLAS MAVERICKS

In March 1980, radio station WBAP conducted a name-the-team contest for the new National Basketball Association franchise. More than 4,600 entries were received and turned over to a five-person committee. The committee narrowed the choices to MAVERICKS, WRANGLERS, and EXPRESS, ultimately recommending MAVERICKS to owner Donald Carter. This moniker actually began its life as a personal name.

Samuel MAVERICK, a Texas rancher who died in 1870, refused to brand his cattle. This nonconformist attitude made the rancher's name a word firmly embedded in the English language. A MAVERICK is defined as a person who takes an independent stand, refusing to conform to that of his party or group. That is to say, unbranded. All 41 persons who suggested the name MAVERICKS were given two tickets to the charter season opener. In a drawing of those 41, Carla Springer was awarded a pair of season tickets.

NICKNAME: "THE MAVS"

DENVER NUGGETS

The American Basketball Association was established in 1967, with 11 teams. When J. W. "Bill" Ringsby brought an ABA team to Denver in 1967, he named it after his truck company, ROCKET. Under new owners, team president and general manager Carl Scheer changed the ROCKETS nickname to the NUGGETS in 1974-75 — feeling it was more in keeping with the mining tradition of Colorado, and was the name of Denver's original N.B.A. team in 1949-50. (Also, at the time, there was a National Basketball Association team called the San Diego ROCKETS — later, the Houston ROCKETS.) In 1976-77, 4 of the ABA's 11 teams merged with the NBA. The Denver NUGGETS was one of the clubs invited to change leagues at that time. The NUGGETS won the Midwest Division Title their first year in the NBA. The NUGGETS mascot is called "Rocky the Mountain Lion."

DETROIT PISTONS

Fred Zollner lived in Fort Wayne, Indiana, and it was there that the factory he owned manufactured PISTONS for the engines of automobiles and tractors. And it was there, in the war-stricken and prosperous 1940s, that Zollner founded his basketball team. He named them in reference to his company (Zollner Machine Works), the Fort Wayne Zollner PISTONS, and played in an industrial conference called the National Basketball League. Then, another group of adventurers with larger venues available to them formed the Basketball Association of America. They introduced teams with names like the KNICKS of New York, the CELTICS in Boston, the WARRIORS in Philadelphia — and such other clubs as the Pittsburgh IRONMEN, the Toronto HUSKIES, the Cleveland REBELS, the Detroit FALCONS, and the Providence STEAM

ROLLERS. Zollner saw his club's future in the BAA, joining with another NBL team, the Chicago American GEARS, who became the Minneapolis LAKERS. By the 1956-57 season, Zollner started considering transferring his club out of Fort Wayne. The last NBA Championship the Fort Wayne PISTONS would challenge for they lost to the Philadelphia WARRIORS, 4-1, in 1956. The Detroit auto companies were Zollner's major customers for the pistons manufactured in his plant. Detroit was a town with a large, sports-orientated population and a rich sporting heritage. The LIONS and RED WINGS were winning championships, and the struggling TIGERS were one of the most valuable franchises in baseball. On February 15, 1957, Fred Zollner signed the deal to switch his beloved basketball team's base to red-brick Olympia Stadium, the new home of the Detroit PISTONS.

GOLDEN STATE WARRIORS

The Golden State WARRIORS are descendants of an original National Basketball Association team. In 1946-47 they were known as the Philadelphia WARRIORS — a team that won the first NBA Championship ever, 4-1 over the Chicago STAGS. That Philly team got its name from a pro basketball franchise that played in the City of Brotherly Love in the 1920s also called the Philadelphia WARRIORS, and there was some fan recognition involved. The last NBA Championship played by the Philly WARRIORS was in 1955-56, 4-3 over the Fort Wayne PISTONS (later the Detroit PISTONS). In 1962-63, the team moved to San Francisco, bringing the nickname along with it. The San Francisco WARRIORS took a much shorter trip in 1971-72, across the bridge to Oakland, becoming the Golden State WARRIORS. Before the WARRIORS came to town, Oakland had played host to another pro club, the Oakland OAKS of the American Basketball Association. That franchise left town in 1970, becoming the Washington CAPITOLS (a name soon adopted by a National Hockey League franchise). The team that originated in Oakland moved once more before folding in 1977, as the Virginia SQUIRES. Meanwhile, the city of Oakland didn't have to wait long after its ABA OAKS left, to capture an even bigger prize with the WARRIORS.

HOUSTON ROCKETS

The American Basketball Association had a team in Houston in 1967 called the MAVERICKS. That team moved to North Carolina, becoming the Carolina COUGARS. In 1974 the COUGARS left for Missouri, and became the SPIRITS of St. Louis. But Houston didn't have to wait long after the MAVERICKS left before pro ball returned to that Texas city. Sometimes a sports franchise nickname is moved from one part of the country to another and makes just as much sense at its new location as its last! Take the Houston ROCKETS, which began their National Basketball Association life as an expansion team from San Diego. On January 4, 1967, the nickname was chosen in a contest that attracted 10,000 entries. The San Diego ROCKETS moniker was in keeping with the city's theme of a "City in Motion," and reflected the tremendous growth of the space industry in San Diego — Atlas rockets were being built there. When they moved to Houston in 1975, the ROCKETS nickname took on even greater relevance, and, with NASA, Houston Control took on a second meaning.

INDIANA PACERS

When professional basketball came to Indianapolis in 1967, one of the key decisions would be what to call the new American Basketball Association franchise. According to Indianapolis attorney Richard D. Tinkham, the nickname PACERS was decided on through a collective decision of the orignal investors. Tinkham, one of those investors, recalled that the nickname was a combination of the state's rich history with the harness-racing PACERS and the pace car used for the running of the Indianapolis 500. Tinkham said the PACERS decision was an easy one, but the real debate was whether the team should be called the Indiana PACERS or the Indianapolis PACERS. Since one of the original ideas for the team was to have it playing throughout the state with its base in Indianapolis, the official team name became the Indiana PACERS. In 1976 the PACERS changed leagues, joining the National Basketball Association.

LOS ANGELES CLIPPERS

In 1970 the National Basketball Association expanded, introducing the Buffalo BRAVES, a nickname chosen through a contest. In 1978 the team moved to San Diego, and renamed themselves the CLIPPERS. The new nickname was in reference to the ships that frequented the sea port in the city's 19th century. Plus, to this day, there is always a working CLIP-PER ship in the harbor. The CLIPPERS were not the first pro team in town. The San Diego CONQUISTADORS played for the American Basketball Association in 1972. In 1975 they changed their name to the San Diego SAILS. That team folded 12 games into its fourth season. The

NBA franchise hung around until it sailed up the coast to Los Angeles. In 1984-85 they became known as the Los Angeles CLIPPERS.

NICKNAME: "CLIPS"

LOS ANGELES LAKERS

They started playing in the National Basketball League as the Chicago American GEARS. When they jumped to the Basketball Association of America they also changed cities. Minneapolis was their new hometown where they became the LAKERS. Choosing their state rather than their city to baptize the franchise, the team was called the Minnesota LAKERS in 1948-49. The franchise was named after the team's close vicinity to the Great Lakes. A LAKER is also the word used to describe one of those big, ocean going-sized cargo carriers that used to travel the Great Lakes and St. Lawrence Seaway in large numbers. They carried coal, iron ore, bauxite, wheat, corn, and numerous other mining and agricultural products. There was a time when a major portion of the U.S. economic output was shipped on these waters, and the LAKERS were a symbol of the upper Midwest's strength and vitality. The last NBA Championship in Minneapolis was in 1953-54, 4-3 over the Syracuse NATIONALS (later the Philadelphia 76ERS). In 1960, the franchise moved to Los Angeles, becoming the Los Angeles LAKERS. It is assumed that the new L.A. team wanted to cash in on an established name because there are no lakes to speak of in the area. By the way, former LAKERS star Jerry West is the model for the NBA logo.

MEMPHIS GRIZZLIES

In 1994, during the NBA All-Star Weekend in Minneapolis, Vancouver Basketball Management Inc. had its Vancouver MOUNTIES bid unanimously endorsed. By April, the Royal Canadian Mounted Police had informed the Vancouver club that using their famous MOUNTIES moniker was not an option. So the owners, Arthur R. Griffiths and John E. McCaw Jr., went looking for a new name that would include something powerful to reflect the nature of the team and of basketball, a cultural or geographical association with Canada, especially British Columbia, an indigenous species or spirit, longevity and durability, and a positive emotional appeal with fans and players. The trend in pro sports was toward team identities based on animate subjects, such as living people or animals, so it was not surprising that a name such as GRIZZLIES was a frontrunner from the beginning along with DRAGONS, ORCAS, and RAVENS. It was decided that the franchise would adopt the name and identity associated with the GRIZZLY bear, which was highly prominent in northwestern native culture and mythology and was a leading icon of Canadiana. Team colors include Naismith Red, in honor of Dr. James A. Naismith, the Canadian who invented basketball in 1891 while studying at the YMCA International Training School in Springfield, Massachusetts. The GRIZZLIES joined the Toronto RAPTORS, their first Canadian expansion cousins, in memorializing the Naismith legacy — the RAPTORS carry Naismith Silver in their dinosaur moniker. On May 16, 1995, the National Basketball Association officially made the Vancouver GRIZZLIES and Toronto RAPTORS its 28th and 29th teams. The franchise moved from Vancouver to Memphis in the 2001-2002 season, deciding to keep the same nickname as many transplanted NBA franchises have done in the past. Who knows, maybe Grizzlies in Memphis make as much sense as Lakers in Los Angeles and Jazz in Salt Lake City. And how about Hawks in Illinois's Tri-Cities, then in Milwaukee, in St. Louis and for now Atlanta!

MIAMI HEAT

Billy Cunningham and Lewis Schaffel, who had both been associated with the National Basketball Association in various capacities for many years, had thought for some time about pursuing an NBA franchise. In 1986, Cunningham and theatrical producer Zev Buffman announced plans to bring an NBA expansion team to South Florida. Schaffel, then vice president of the New Jersey NETS, resigned to officially join the ownership. In October of 1986 the Miami franchise selected the name HEAT from over 20,000 entries, submitted by Stephanie Freed — a moniker in reference to the notorious climate of southern Florida. And it wasn't until March of 1988 that Mark Henderson's flaming basketball was selected from 1,000 entries as the HEAT's official logo. The HEAT's mascot is called "Burnie."

MILWAUKEE BUCKS

Milwaukee's first professional basketball team was the Milwaukee HAWKS, who played in the Milwaukee Arena from 1951 through 1956 before moving to St. Louis, where a fellow by the name of Bob Pettit led them to great prominence and an NBA Championship in 1958. On that original Milwaukee team, one of the HAWKS' backcourt aces was 5'10" guard William "Red" Holzman, who went on to coach the New York KNICKER-BOCKERS to NBA Championships in 1970 and 1973. On January 22, 1968, the National Basketball Association awarded a second franchise to a Milwaukee group headed by Wesley D. Pavalon and Marvin L. Fishman. The group, called Milwaukee Professional Sports and Services, Inc., named Pavalon its president and Fishman as the executive vice president. More than 14,000 fans participated in a team-naming contest. According to the 1969-70 Milwaukee BUCKS yearbook, R. D. Trebilcox of Whitefish Bay, Wisconsin, was one of 45 persons who suggested the name BUCKS. His reasoning — "BUCKS are spirited, good jumpers, fast and agile." Mr. Trebilcox won a new car for his efforts in helping to position Milwaukee's entry into the professional sports world with an enduring nickname. In 1992 a new logo and team colors were introduced. According to Creative Director Tom O'Grady, the "contemporary but not trendy" logo design represents the theme of solidarity, strength, and focused determination. The colors of hunter green, purple, and silver display a regal spirit of character.

MINNESOTA TIMBERWOLVES

Four months before the N.B.A. awarded Minnesota a franchise for the 1989-90 season, a contest drew 6,076 entries with a total of 1,284 different nicknames. Among the intriguing suggestions were FAT CATS, KILLER KARPS, PURPLE COWS, and ZIPS. The Minnesota climate seemed to be on the minds of many voters as well with DEEP FREEZE, DRIZZLERS, FRIGID FIVES, FROST-BITE, SNOWBOUNDERS, SNOWPLOWERS, THERM O STATS, and WEATHERMEN. Fish or fowl? How about the BURBOTS, FISHER PRACTICES, DUCKSTERS, GOERS, and FIGHT-ING WALLEYES? And what exactly are LUCUSTRIANS, MAEL-STROMS, and YUAAS? Though the most popular submission was BLIZ-ZARDS, the contest was reduced to two finalists, the POLARS and the TIMBERWOLVES, because "We didn't want to be associated with blizzards, and both reflect the state's strong orientation toward outdoor recreation, and both have excellent mascot potential." The final decision was left to the 842 city councils throughout the state. They went with TIMBER-WOLVES, reflecting the animal's presence in the state. Seventeen people submitted the winner, and a drawing awarded Tim Pope of Brooklyn Center, Minnesota, first prize: a trip to the 1987 NBA All-Star weekend in Seattle.

NICKNAME: "THE PACK"
"T - WOLVES"
"WOLVES"

NEW JERSEY NETS

In 1967-68 the New Jersey AMERICANS were born into the American Basketball Association. One year later the franchise moved to New York. There they became known as the New York NETS in reference to the silken ropes commonly referred to as a basketball net. Rhyming with both the METS and the JETS just seemed like a New York thing to do. In 1976 the team changed leagues, joining the National Basketball Association. Another move the following year prompted another name change. In 1977-78 they became the New Jersey NETS. Other clubs invited to leave the American Basketball Association for the NBA were the Indiana PACERS, the San Antonio SPURS, and the Denver NUGGETS.

NEW ORLEANS HORNETS

For five years the home of the JAZZ before they departed for Salt Lake City in 1979, New Orleans has been the home of the HORNETS since 2002-2003. The HORNETS were also migrators, and since 1988 had previously been creating a buzz in Charlotte, where they received their moniker. When George Shinn selected the HORNETS nickname for his NBA franchise, he knew that Charlotte's affiliation with the aggressive, pain-inflicting insect had implications of historical significance dating back to the American Revolution. After one especially bitter skirmish, British General Charles Cornwallis discovered that his expected push through the Carolinas was to end in Charlotte. Though there were few soldiers to oppose him, his troops were harried on all sides, and soon the British were running out of provisions. Patrols sent out to obtain supplies were fired upon. "There's a reb behind every bush," Cornwallis declared in a letter. "It's a veritable nest of HORNETS." At a two-story log home seven miles from Charlotte, the British were fired upon by a group of 14 youthful Americans. So much confusion followed that the pillaging soldiers overturned several beehives in the yard, which added considerably to the confusion. This skirmish, locally famous, came to be known as the "Battle of the Bees." Shinn first tried to launch a local entry of the United States Football League, but as the fledgling league fell upon hard times, he turned his attention to a sport for which expansion was imminent, the NBA. The effort to "Bring the NBA to Basketball Country" caused the community to explode with civic pride. The original name for the team was the SPIRIT, selected by a committee from a pool of suggested names. But due to popular demand, Shinn held another "Name the Team" campaign, soliciting suggestions from the community via the *Charlotte*

Observer newspaper. An overwhelming number of votes for HORNETS poured in and Charlotte's NBA team had a new name.

NEW YORK KNICKERBOCKERS

The term KNICKERBOCKERS traces its origins back to the Dutch settlers who came to the New World and especially to what is now New York in the 1600s. Until a British change of name in 1664, New York used to be called New Amsterdam. Specifically, it refers to the style of pants the settlers wore . . . pants that rolled up just below the knee, which became known as KNICKERBOCKERS, or KNICKERS. Through history, the Dutch settler KNICKERBOCKER character became synonymous with New York City. The city's most popular symbol of the late 19th and early 20th centuries was "Father KNICKERBOCKER," complete with cotton wig, three-cornered hat, buckled shoes, and, of course, KNICKERED pants. The KNICKERBOCKER name had its first use in the world of sports in 1845: Alexander Cartwright's Manhattan-based baseball team — the first organized team in baseball history — was named the New York KNICKER-BOCKERS or the KNICKERBOCKER NINE. The KNICKERBOCKER name stayed with the team even after it moved its base of operations to Elysian Fields at Hoboken, New Jersey, in 1846. Thus the KNICKER-BOCKER name was an integral part of the New York scene when the Basketball Association of America granted a charter franchise to the city in the summer of 1946. As can be best determined, the final decision to call the team the KNICKERBOCKERS was made by the club's founder, the legendary Ned Irish. Irish's longtime righthand man, Fred Podesta, was present at the Knicks' birth and recalls that the name selection was easy, quick, and uncomplicated. "The name came out of a hat," he says. "We were all sitting in the office one day — Irish, PR Director Lester Scott, and a few others on staff. We each put a name in the hat, and when we pulled them out, most of them said KNICKERBOCKERS, after Father KNICKERBOCKER. It soon was shortened to KNICKS."

NICKNAME: "KNICKS"

ORLANDO MAGIC

The Orlando MAGIC was a National Basketball Association expansion team, arriving in 1989. They are not the first pro club in Florida, however. Among the original teams in the American Basketball Association in 1967 was the Minnesota MUSKIES (a fish). The MUSKIES moved to Miami in

1968, becoming the Miami FLORIDIANS. In 1970, the franchise changed their location name, becoming the Florida FLORIDIANS. They folded after five years in 1973. In 1986, Orlando Mayor Bill Frederick presented a check for $100,000 and a set of Mickey Mouse ears to NBA commissioner David Stern, officially entering the race to bring a franchise to Orlando. One month later, former 76ERS general manager Pat Williams announced that the Orlando franchise would be named the MAGIC. The name was chosen from 4,296 entries submitted in a contest held by the *Orlando Sentinel* newspaper. The NBA MAGIC nickname is a nod in the direction of the entertainment giant in Orlando, Walt Disney World and its famous MAGIC Kingdom. Team mascot is "STUFF, the MAGIC dragon."

PHILADELPHIA 76ERS

Professional basketball in its modern phase has had two stages in this city. The first section comprised the career of the WARRIORS between 1946 and 1962 with two titles, 1947 and 1956. The WARRIORS were transferred to San Francisco after the 1961-62 campaign. The Philadelphia 76ERS franchise actually began in 1949, when six teams from the Midwest-based National Basketball League joined the Basketball Association of America to form the 17-team National Basketball Association. One of those teams was the Syracuse NATIONALS. The NATS were very successful in Syracuse, reaching the finals in 1951 and 1953, losing both times to the Minneapolis LAKERS — the team that left for Los Angeles in 1960. The NATS won their first and only NBA title in 1954, defeating the Fort Wayne PISTONS, 92-91, to take the series, four games to three. Philadelphians Irv Kosioff and Ike Richman teamed up to purchase the Syracuse NATS in the spring of 1963 and brought the franchise to Philadelphia with league approval on May 22, 1963. These NATIONALS had their nickname changed to the 76ERS, in appreciation of the national association of Philadelphia with American independence. Ironically, it was the ex-Philly San Francisco WARRIORS that the Wilt Chamberlain-led 76ERS beat in 1967 for their first NBA Championship.

NICKNAME: "SIXERS"

PHOENIX SUNS

Although a contest to name the team generated an impressive 28,000 entries, the name SUNS — the Star of the Solar System — wasn't just picked out of a hat. Considerable thought went into the selection of not only the name but also the colors of Arizona's National Basketball Association franchise. In fact, the SUNS' young general manager, Jerry Colangelo, was on the cutting edge of a marketing science that integrated a team's logo, nickname, colors, and merchandise with the character of the team's city. "The purpose is to develop a strong bond, a two-way sense of identity, between the fans and their team." The idea for the SUNS' purple and orange came from those spectacular Arizona sunsets. The name SUNS not only identified with the city and state, it was also short. "When thinking in terms of newspapers and headline space, editors like team names with three, four, or five letters," Colangelo said. "Since the exposure of our team through the media is vital to a new club, a short name was a must." Of course, with 28,000 entries, SUNS was not the only name suggested. Some were too long, some were inappropriate, and some were downright strange. The more creative Phoenix rejects included the GRANDSUNS, UNICORNS, PRICKLY PEARS, CACTUS COWBOYS, EAGER BEAVERS, DESERETTES, FABLES, SINNERS, DUST DEVILS, THUNDERBELTERS, ARIZONIACS, POOBAHS, DOMINATORS, MERRY MEN, BASKETEERS, BOYS, MULESKINNERS, TIPINEERS, BABY STATERS, LARIATS, BOX CARS, HOT SHOTS, PACKRATS, and the PRIDE. Phoenix itself is nobly named after a beautiful, lone bird, which lived in the Arabian desert for 500 or 600 years and then consumed itself in fire, rising renewed from the ashes to start another long life, becoming a symbol of immortality.

NICKNAMES: "THE PURPLE GANG"
"SUNDERELLA SUNS" (1975-76 playoffs)

PORTLAND TRAIL BLAZERS

In 1970, the National Basketball Association granted expansion franchises to Buffalo, Cleveland, and Portland. Within a month, a contest was held in the West Coast city, asking Oregonians to submit nominations for the new team's name. The contest attracted more than 10,000 entries, and TRAIL BLAZERS was identified by many as synonymous with the rugged individualism, exploration, and pioneering spirit of Oregon, and of the Pacific Northwest corner of the United States. The term TRAIL BLAZING comes from the act of chopping BLAZE-type notches in tree trunks at eye level with axes to mark new TRAILS made through the wilderness. Hence, TRAIL BLAZERS was recognized as a perfect fit for a basketball team from Oregon finding a successful path for itself in major league basketball. Local media support for the selected name was strong for several reasons, not the least of them being that it was easily shortened to BLAZERS, making it fit nicely into headlines.

NICKNAME: "BLAZERS"

SACRAMENTO KINGS

The Sacramento KINGS began their lives as an original team in the National Basketball Association, but as the Rochester ROYALS. They played in Rochester from 1946 to 1957, when they moved to Cincinnati. The last NBA Championship the ROYALS of Rochester won before leaving town was in 1950-51, when they defeated the New York KNICKS, four games to three. The Cincinnati ROYALS played for 14 years in Ohio before packing their bags for Kansas City. But they didn't bring the nickname with them. They became the Kansas City-Omaha KINGS — intentionally maintaining a royal-like moniker, but one with more alliteration for Kansas City. The name changed to the Kansas City KINGS in 1975-76, and stayed that way until 1986. Then the team moved to the capital of California, becoming the Sacramento KINGS.

SAN ANTONIO SPURS

In 1967-68 the Dallas CHAPARRALS (a roadrunner-type bird) joined the American Basketball League. They changed their name in 1970-71 to the Texas CHAPARRALS, to help the CHAPS draw more fans statewide. For some reason, in 1972 they went back to the Dallas CHAPARRALS. It was announced late in this season that the team would be sold to New Jersey. That didn't happen. In 1973-74 the team moved to San Antonio, picking up a new nickname, the SPURS. This was in reference to the famous western horseback riding accessory — and its kick-butt, get-up-and-go connotation. The dictionary defines SPUR as anything that can urge, incite, or stimulate to action and a greater effort. In 1976-77 the SPURS changed leagues, joining the National Basketball Association, winning the Central Division Title in their first year. Teams that played alongside the SPURS in the ABL that were not invited to join the NBA in 1976 were the Pittsburgh CONDORS, Florida FLORIDIANS, Kentucky COLONELS, Baltimore CLAWS, SPIRITS of St. Louis, Utah STARS, Virginia SQUIRES, and San Diego SAILS.

SEATTLE SUPERSONICS

After poring over about 25,000 entries in a weeklong name-the-team contest, franchise general manager Don Richman announced that Seattle's new National Basketball Association club would be called the SUPERSONICS. "We think the name best expresses Seattle's people and its present and future," Richman said. Howard E. Schmidt, an economics and history teacher of Seattle, submitted the winning entry. The nickname was suggested by Boeing's proposal to build a Concorde-style commercial airplane during the late 1960s. The new plane was to be known as the SST, for SuperSonic Transport. Although the transport never got off the ground, the name had a lasting effect, as the Schmidts' entry (with son, Brent, 10) was one of many using a variation of SUPER or SONIC. The father-and-son team's contribution to Seattle history won them a weekend trip to Palm Springs and two season tickets for the 1967-68 season. Richman said 162 other persons also entered the name SUPERSONICS and 278 entries listed either SUPERS or SONICS. All received two tickets to a SONICS game.

NICKNAME: "SONICS"
 "SUPES"

TORONTO RAPTORS

This franchise, which took to the court for the 1995-96 season, was the second Toronto entry in professional basketball. The HUSKIES played in the pre-NBA Basketball Association of America League, for only one season in 1946. HUSKIES became the most enthusiastically suggested nickname when word first got out about the new franchise. But concern over the difficulty finding a logo that didn't look like that of the TIMBERWOLVES in Minnesota provoked a name search. The entire Canadian nation was invited to suggest franchise names, and more than 40,000 were received — the record at that time in all of professional sports. The top 10 names were culled from a reduced list of 189 by a panel of celebrity judges, including two-time Lillehammer Olympic gold medal biathlete Myriam Bedard, and hockey great Wayne Gretzky. This list of potential names was made up entirely of animals: DRAGONS, BEAVERS, HOGS, TERRIERS, RAPTORS, SCORPIONS, TARANTULAS, TORONTOSAURUS-REX (T-REX), GRIZZLIES, and BOBCATS. The finalists were the BOBCATS, the DRAGONS, and the eventual winner, RAPTORS — which was chosen by team ownership. Marketing the dinosaur had much to do with the final decision. In 1995, NBA merchandising pulled in 75 million dollars in Canada alone, and 14 billion worldwide. The top sellers worldwide were the Chicago BULLS, Charlotte HORNETS, and Orlando MAGIC, giving RAPTORs president John Bitove Jr. two out of three good reasons to pick an animal as his team's logo.

UTAH JAZZ

Pro ball existed in Utah once before the JAZZ came to town. In 1967-68 a team called the Anaheim AMIGOS entered the American Basketball Association. The following year the name changed to the Los Angeles STARS — a reference to all of Hollywood's STARS. In 1970-71 that ABA team moved to Utah, but kept the STARS nickname. It's generally believed that a nickname and logo define a professional sports team, because both are chosen at a team's inception. A bad nickname could mean bad publicity. That's why, while a team's home city might change, the logo most likely will not. It made perfect sense to name the New Orleans basketball team the JAZZ and the Minneapolis team the LAKERS. But when these teams moved to another city (as both eventually did), the nickname and the logo followed, even though it didn't make much sense. Fans just had to get used to it. It was in 1974 that a National Basketball Association team took to the court in New Orleans. A public contest brought the very appropriate JAZZ moniker to the attention of team ownership — in appreciation for the famous musical element of the city's heritage. When the franchise moved to Salt Lake City, Utah, in 1979, it somewhat mysteriously decided to bring the nickname along.

WASHINGTON WIZARDS

The Washington WIZARDS have changed cities and nicknames many times since their Baltimore beginnings as one of the original National Basketball Association teams in 1946. The Baltimore BULLETS received their moniker because the team practiced near the Old Shot Tower, a munitions factory, and also played some of their games near an armory. Owner Stan Behrend said his nickname reasoning was hope that the BULLETS would utilize their "significant explosive talents and speed in humbling the opposition." These BULLETS folded in 1954, then were reborn as an expansion team in 1961 — the Chicago PACKERS. In 1962 they changed the nickname to the ZEPHYRS. When this franchise packed its bags back to Baltimore, they resurrected the old Baltimore BULLETS name. In 1973-74 the BULLETS took to the road once again, this time down the road to nearby Washington. For one season, they were known as the Capital BULLETS, before changing to the Washington BULLETS. Then in November of 1995, Abe Pollin, who'd owned the team since 1964, decided to change the nickname because of its street violence connotation. "I've thought about it for 31 years," he said, "because BULLETS connote killing, violence, death. Our slogan used to be 'Faster than a speeding bullet,' but that is no longer appropriate." On February 22, 1996, it was announced that the team would be called the WIZARDS, the result of a fan phone contest that attracted 500,000 suggestions, including 2,996 different names. From ACCELERATORS to ZULUS, other considered monikers included DRAGONS, SEADOGS, STALLIONS, MONUMENTS, WOLVERINES, AURA, COBRAS, COURT MARSHALLS, CUCKOOS, DEAL MAKERS, DODECAHEDRONS, DUNKIN' DONKEYS, ENCHANTERS, FURY, GLORY, JUSTICE, RAVENS, JAM-A-RAMAS, LIGHT OF FLOWERS, POWER, POWER ATS, RIVERDAWGS, SAVAGE, and WIPEOUTS.

Part 3

National Football League

ARIZONA CARDINALS

The CARDINALS, a charter member of the National Football League, boast the distinction of being the oldest continuously run pro football franchise in the nation. Founded in 1898, the team began as a neighborhood group that gathered to play football in a predominantly Irish area of Chicago's South Side, playing under the name MORGAN ATHLETIC CLUB. When its playing site changed to nearby Normal Field, so did the nickname — to the NORMALS. In 1901, team owner Chris O'Brien bought used jerseys from the University of Chicago. When attempting to fade them to a maroon color, O'Brien declared, "That's not maroon, it's CARDINAL red!" The club's permanent nickname was born. The jersey color and the location of the field on a Chicago street called Racine led to a new name, the RACINE CARDINALS. Two years after joining the American Football League in 1920, a team from Racine, Wisconsin, joined the National Football League, forcing the Illinois club to change their name to the CHICAGO CARDINALS. In 1944 the CARDINALS and Pittsburgh STEELERS combined to form one team called CARD-PITT (nicknamed the CARPETS). In 1960 the team moved and became the ST. LOUIS CARDINALS. After 28 years in St. Louis, the CARDINALS relocated to Arizona in the spring of 1988 and made Sun Devil Stadium on the campus of Arizona State University their new home. At that time they became the PHOENIX CARDINALS. On March 17, 1994, team president William Bidwill announced his intention to broaden the team's horizons, and changed the name from the PHOENIX to the ARIZONA CARDINALS.

NICKNAME: "THE BIG RED"

ATLANTA FALCONS

As fast as the flight of a FALCON the new National Football League team got its name. On June 30, 1965, the NFL won a battle with the American Football League to place a pro football franchise in Atlanta and play at the Atlanta Stadium, the new home of the Atlanta BRAVES (from Milwaukee). Local radio station WSB began a name-the-team campaign with a deadline of August 15 for entries. Fans were asked to give them a name and a reason in 25 words or less. As thousands of entries poured in, a panel of five persons was selected to choose the winner. Fan submissions included such monikers as PEACHES, REBELS, CONFEDER-ATES, GEORGIANS, CRACKERS, BOMBERS, KNIGHTS, FIRE-

BIRDS, LANCERS, THRASHERS, WILDCATS, and many more. More than 40 entries offered the FALCONS. The winner, high school teacher Julia Elliot, wrote, "The FALCON is proud and dignified with great courage and fight. It never drops its prey. It is deadly and has a great sporting tradition." The raptor is also a native Georgian species, as one newspaper columnist pointed out, "How many LIONS do you see running around Detroit, how many REDSKINS do you see in Washinton, and how many GIANTS do you see walking around New York?"

BALTIMORE RAVENS

In 1995 Cleveland Browns' owner Art Modell announced he was moving his team to Baltimore to fill the void in that city left by the Colts, who had departed in 1984. Quarterback Vinny Testaverde started the rumor that the new team in Baltimore would be called the MUSTANGS. But 12 years to the day that the COLTS bolted from Baltimore in the dark of night and left a gaping hole in the hearts of area football fans, the name RAVENS was picked for the city's new National Football League team. Modell announced the name before a crowd of officials and fans huddled under umbrellas at Baltimore's Inner Harbor. RAVENS, named after the famous poem by Edgar Allan Poe, who died in 1849 and is buried in Baltimore, beat out AMERICANS and MARAUDERS in a phone-in poll fans used to choose the team's name. Modell's team was temporarily nameless after he agreed to leave the BROWNS' moniker and colors behind in Cleveland — which landed an expansion team in 1999.

BUFFALO BILLS

Bob Curran of the *Buffalo News* had to do some digging to get this one. He discovered that Jim Breuil, the owner of the Buffalo franchise in the All-American Football Conference, had organized a contest for fans who would be interested in trying to pick a name for the new club that would start playing in 1946. The impetus behind the contest was the desire to break away from "the unimaginative Buffalo BISONS name that all prior or existing professional teams were named." Breuil's company was called the Frontier Oil Company, and a young employee of that organization had it in the front of his mind when he was thinking of a name for the new team. An entrant had to accompany his proposed name with a 25-word explanation of his choice. Jimmy Dyson wrote about Buffalo BILL, the famous Western hero, being part of the American frontier and the new team that was being supported by Frontier Oil opening a new frontier in sports in Western New York. Hence the name the Buffalo BILLS. The officials liked the name so Jimmy won the contest. No one was more pleased than Jimmy, who passed away in 1975, when Buffalo kept the moniker even after it changed leagues in 1959. Owner Ralph Wilson said of his new National Football League BILLS, "The old team was a proud team. Its fans had been very loyal. I could not see any reason why we should change the name and so a change was never considered."

CAROLINA PANTHERS

The Richardson family of Charlotte, North Carolina, had been contacted about possibly buying the New England PATRIOTS, Seattle SEAHAWKS and — before Jerry Jones emerged — the Dallas COWBOYS. "But we always came back to one simple thing," said Mark Richardson, director of business operations, "We were only interested in a National Football League team in the Carolinas." It was Mark who first suggested the PANTHERS nickname and the team colors of black, blue, and silver. "I told my father (Jerry Richardson, whom his sons Mark and Jon call the "Boss") I thought it needed to all work together. There needed to be a synergy between the name, the color scheme, the logo and the image the team portrays." Mark suggested the power colors, and had always liked the PANTHER animal. It wasn't a cinch, though. Mark and his father discussed the nickname COUGARS, while NFL Properties offered COBRAS and RHINOS, and the color purple, for consideration. PANTHERS stuck as did the colors — a nod in the direction of Mark's favorite childhood teams, the Oakland RAIDERS and Pittsburgh STEELERS. In the long history of the NFL, only one other team has had the nickname PANTHERS — the Detroit PANTHERS of 1925-26. Detroit fans had their interest centered on the Michigan WOLVERINES in nearby Ann Arbor, and failed to support the team — they moved, becoming the Providence STEAM ROLLER. In 1995 the Carolina PANTHERS made NFL history, becoming the first expansion team to ever beat the reigning Super Bowl champs (San Francisco 49ERS) while in their inaugural season.

CHICAGO BEARS

On September 17, 1920, George S. "Papa Bear" Halas met with representatives from 12 other football teams in Canton, Ohio, and formed the American Professional Football Association, which later became the

National Football League. He originally named his team the Decatur STALEYS, after A. E. Staley, a starch manufacturer and enthusiastic sports fan who sponsored a semipro baseball team and commissioned Halas to organize the team. In 1920 the Decatur STALEYS moved to Chicago where they played in Wrigley Field, the same park as baseball's Chicago CUBS. Halas decided that he wanted to keep his club's nickname in the same family as the CUBS, so he chose BEARS. The Chicago BEARS and Green Bay PACKERS enjoy the oldest rivalry in pro football. The jersey colors have always been blue and orange, the same colors as the University of Illinois.

NICKNAME: "MONSTERS OF THE MIDWAY"

CINCINNATI BENGALS

Why BENGALS? Owner Paul Brown picked the name BENGALS for Cincinnati's football team "to give it a link with past professional football in Cincinnati." From 1937 through 1941, the BENGALS were a famous unit in the Cincinnati area. In 1938 they played three teams from the National Football League. They beat the Chicago BEARS 17-14 and the Pittsburgh STEELERS 38-0, and tied the Chicago CARDINALS 7-7. "If we can pick up a thread of tradition, we think it's good," said Brown when he named the team. Fans suggested hundreds of names in an effort to name the new Cincinnati team and the most popular was BUCKEYES, but they kept searching for the obvious reason. "The owners rejected it becanse we didn't want it to be confused with the Ohio State BUCKEYES and wanted something to embody four states rather than just the one," he said. "We feel at home with the name BENGALS."

CLEVELAND BROWNS

Named after a boxer? That's right. In 1945 the Cleveland RAMS shocked the National Football League by winning the championship. But they did it in a near-empty Cleveland Stadium, and the team owner decided he'd had enough of the town. On January 12, 1946, the RAMS moved to Los Angeles and suddenly Cleveland's new team in the All-American Conference had the town to itself. But it didn't have a name. Team owner Mickey McBride offered a $1,000 war bond to the fan who could pick an appropriate nickname. The winner, PANTHERS, came from a Navy sailor named John J. Hartnett. PANTHERS was fine with McBride and coach Paul Brown, both of whom wanted a name that "could be animated for promotional use and around which a symbol could be formed." But soon after, McBride received a visitor in his office claiming the name PANTHERS already had prior ownership. Brown ordered some inquiries and discovered that it was the name of a semipro football team near Cleveland, a franchise that was apparently a chronic loser. This provoked another contest, one that was to actively pursue names of championship caliber. "Joe Louis was the best known champion at the time, and we received a lot of entries suggesting we name the team after him," Brown said. Everyone liked the idea. So the Cleveland franchise was named the BROWN BOMBERS after the heavyweight champion of the world, Joe Louis. Soon after, the name was shortened to the BROWNS. Of course it didn't go unnoticed that the name also coincided with that of its coach-general manager and chief architect, but there weren't many who blamed Paul Brown if he might want a familiar name close by. In 1995, after 45 years of NFL tradition in Cleveland, owner Art Modell signed a 30-year lease to play in Baltimore. As a part of the deal, the city of Cleveland kept the name BROWNS, while Modell called his team the RAVENS. Before the end of the decade, a new Cleveland BROWNS team was re-born.

DALLAS COWBOYS

When the Dallas expansion team was looking for a nickname in 1960, the job fell to General Manager Texas E. Schramm. Some of the first names considered were RANGERS, LONGHORNS, and STEERS. The RANGERS name at that time had been associated with minor league baseball. The University of Texas had a lock on LONGHORNS. When STEERS was brought up, Schramm tossed it aside commenting that when you consider what a STEER is, that's not a very macho image for a pro football team. So, "Tex" began asking people what they thought of when the state of Texas was mentioned. The word COWBOYS kept coming back to him. The COWBOYS "Star" emblem was just a logical extension of the COWBOYS name, since Texas is the Lone Star State. Schramm must have made the right choices — the COWBOYS have a vast worldwide following, the COWBOYS Star is recognized everywhere, and Schramm was the first general manager inducted into the Pro Football Hall of Fame.

NICKNAMES: "AMERICA'S TEAM"
    "COWPOKES"
    "BOYS"

DENVER BRONCOS

The Denver BRONCOS arrived on the scene in 1960, and the search for a nickname went public. Fans were invited to submit names, with the suggestion that any new moniker would have to be symbolic of the region. But Denver is an area with many personalities. (Remember, this is the city that sports the NHL's Colorado AVALANCHE and the NBA's Denver NUGGETS.) The original name for the football franchise was the Denver BRONCOS — a nod in the direction of the wild horses once associated with the wild west. These wild BRONCOS, an English translation derived from the Mexican word for ROUGH, had a reputation for being tough to break.

NICKNAME: "THE BRONCS"

DETROIT LIONS

Detroit welcomed the LIONS in 1934, but it was not the area's first look at professional football. In 1920, the Detroit HERALDS were a charter member of the American Professional Football Association. They folded after two years as did their replacements, the Detroit PANTHERS. In 1928 the Detroit WOLVERINES were formed, but they failed after just one year. In 1930, the then 10-year-old National Football League added a franchise from Portsmouth, Ohio, called the SPARTANS. After four seasons, the team was purchased by Detroit radio executive George A. Richards and moved to the Motor City. A 1934 *Detroit Times* article announced the team's new nickname. "Inspired by the spirited fight the Detroit TIGERS are making for the American League baseball championship, sponsors of the Detroit professional football team have decided to call their entry in the National Football League the Detroit LIONS. They would call this team the TIGERS, but that might create confusion." Cy Huston, the team's GM, explained that the LION is monarch of the jungle, and he hoped to be monarch of the league. "It is our ambition to make the LION as famous as the Detroit ball club has made the TIGER." The blue and silver LIONS won the NFL Championship in 1935, their second year.

NICKNAME: "THE PRIDE"

GREEN BAY PACKERS

On the evening of August 11, 1919, a score or more of husky young athletes, called together by Curly Lambeau and George Calhoun, gathered in the dingy editorial room of the old *Green Bay Press-Gazette* building on Cherry Street and organized a football team. They didn't know it, but that was the beginning of the Green Bay PACKERS. First they talked Lambeau's employer at the Indian Packing Company into putting up some money for equipment. Because the team's jerseys had been provided by the packing company — which also permitted the use of its athletic field for practice — the club was identified in its early publicity as a project of the company. With this tie-in the name PACKERS was a natural, and PACKERS they have been ever since, although the corporation had practically faded out of the picture before that first season was half over. After two years of 'passing the hat,' the team was so successful that Lambeau was backed by two officials of the packing plant in obtaining a franchise in the new national pro league that had been formed in 1920. But it wasn't until the Green Bay Football Corporation was formed in support of the team that the PACKERS overcame their enormous financial troubles. From those modest and somewhat tenuous beginnings, the PACKERS have gone on to earn national stature and virtual worldwide recognition by winning more championships (11) over the intervening 70-plus years than any other team in professional football. The fact that these achievements have come while representing a city of only 96,000 inhabitants in competition with the country's population giants has endeared them to all fans of the David versus Goliath concept. The Green Bay PACKERS-Chicago BEARS rivalry is the oldest in pro football.

NICKNAME: "THE PACK"

INDIANAPOLIS COLTS

Follow the bouncing ball. The roots of the Indianapolis franchise go back to December 28, 1946, when the bankrupt Miami SEAHAWKS of the All-American Football Conference were purchased and relocated in Baltimore. As a result of a contest in Baltimore won by Charles Evans, the team was renamed the COLTS. The AAFC and the National Football League merged in 1950. After being a member of the NFL for two years, the Baltimore franchise was dissolved because of its failing financial condition. Now, rewind. In 1943, a man named Ted Collins was granted a National Football League franchise that he called the Boston YANKS. In 1944, Boston and the Brooklyn DODGERS merged into a team that played home games in both cities and was known simply as the YANKS. When the Brooklyn franchise withdrew from the NFL, the YANKS went back to Boston. In 1949, the Boston YANKS moved, becoming the New York BULLDOGS, and shared the Polo Grounds with the GIANTS. In

1950, they became the New York YANKS. Ted Collins sold the team to the NFL in 1952, and a group from Dallas purchased the assets. But those Dallas TEXANS were not to be, and the franchise cancelled at the end of that season was the last time an NFL team failed. But in 1953, a Baltimore group headed by Carroll Rosenbloom was granted a franchise and was awarded the holdings of the defunct Dallas organization. So it was this Dallas team that became the second NFL franchise in Baltimore where, keeping the COLTS nickname, the Texas team colors of blue and white were inherited. Thirty years later the franchise left Baltimore for the Hoosier Dome in Indianapolis. And that's how the Miami SEAHAWKS, Dallas TEXANS, Boston YANKS, and original Baltimore COLTS ended up the Indianapolis COLTS in 1984.

HOUSTON TEXANS

Hardly a well-kept secret was revealed the day Houston owner Bob McNair announced that the nickname of the National Football League's 32nd franchise would be the TEXANS. The name won out over the STALLIONS and APOLLOS. The TEXANS nickname has been used extensively over the years in virtually every local sport, including the long-gone Dallas TEXANS football club (now the Kansas City CHIEFS), but once the OILERS left town, it was meant to be. "Are you ready for football?" McNair shouted to a downtown crowd estimated at 16,000 that turned out to learn the team's name, logo, and colors. The colors of the first new team of the third millennium are battle-red, steel-blue, and liberty-white, with a bulls-head logo, that includes a Texas Lone Star on one side. McNair paid $700 million for the franchise in a lengthy battle with Los Angeles, a favored place for the NFL because of the size of its media market. But according to the decision-makers, Los Angeles never presented a unified plan, virtually handing McNair his franchise.

JACKSONVILLE JAGUARS

In 1995, a new breed of cat pounced onto the National Football League playing field, although the name wasn't chosen because the animal is indigenous to the area. Even though jaguars in the U.S. are found mainly in the Southwest, mostly they are found in Central and South America. "We liked JAGUARS because no other professional sports team has it," said Rick Catlett, the executive vice-president of Touchdown Jacksonville! Ltd. "Plus, we do have the oldest living

JAGUAR in North America at the Jacksonville Zoo — it's a 24-year-old female." Three other names were finalists in the contest: SHARKS, PANTHERS, and STINGRAYS. Ownership liked the animal's reputation, considered by many to be more dangerous than the LION (sorry, Detroit) or leopard. Maya Indians worshiped it as a god, a symbol of strength and courage. They believed it was a sacred animal and that the sun hid inside the jaguar at night. And maybe most important for Jacksonville fans — considering the movement of professional franchises of late — the JAGUAR is not known to migrate. Pete Prisco of the *Florida Times Union* suggested that if the team lived up to its nickname, the NFL should look out, because "The *Encyclopedia Americana* says a JAGUAR is the most powerful, most feared carnivorous animal in Latin America."

NICKNAME: "JAGS"

KANSAS CITY CHIEFS

Lamar Hunt did more than bring the Dallas TEXANS into the big leagues in 1959. He established and organized the whole American Football League with six original cities — Dallas, New York, Houston, Denver, Los Angeles, and Minneapolis (Buffalo and Boston were added later and Oakland replaced Minneapolis). "Without him," said Boston's Billy Sullivan, "there would have been no AFL." In 1961, the AFL's Dallas TEXANS and NFL's Dallas COWBOYS both drafted E. J. Holub, described by many scouts at the time as "the best football player in America." Holub, much to the benefit of the fledgling league, went with the TEXANS and a Hall of Fame career. On May 14, 1963, Hunt announced he was moving the franchise to Kansas City and renaming it the CHIEFS. Kansas City mayor H. Roe Bartle had promised to enlarge Municipal Stadium and guaranteed Hunt three times as many season ticket sales as the TEXANS had in Dallas. The mayor's nickname? The CHIEF.

MIAMI DOLPHINS

MARINERS, MARAUDERS, MUSTANGS, MISSILES, MOONS, SHARKS, SUNS — none of these other names suggested to the American Football League expansion franchise in 1965 could raise a fin to the swim-away winner. DOLPHINS was submitted by 622 entrants in a contest which attracted 19,843 entries and more than a thousand different names. The dozen finalists were delivered to a seven-member screening committee of local media. The beloved dolphin has inspired wonder for centuries. A philosopher named Plutarch observed 1,900 years ago that the dolphin "is the only creature who loves man for his own sake." Every trainer will have a tale of the dolphin's cleverness and ingenuity, and scientists are fascinated by a dolphin's natural equipment, which far surpasses the range of Navy sonar equipment. "The dolphin is one of the fastest and smartest creatures of the sea," Joe Robbie said in announcing the team name on October 8, 1965. "Dolphins will attack and kill a shark or whale. Sailors say bad luck will come to anyone who harms one of them." Mrs. Robert Swanson of West Miami was selected from the 600 winning entries, and won two lifetime passes to Dolphin games. The tiebreaker was naming the winner and score of the 1905 game between the University of Miami and Notre Dame — it ended in a scoreless tie.

NICKNAME: "THE FISH"

MINNESOTA VIKINGS

Minnesota was granted a National Football League franchise in 1960 and fielded a team in 1961. When Bert Rose was selected general manager in 1961, one of the first steps he took was to recommend to the Board of Directors that the club be nicknamed the VIKINGS. A nickname should serve a dual purpose, he said. First, it should represent an aggressive person or animal imbued with the will to win. Secondly, if possible, it is desirable to have it connote the region that the particular team represents. The VIKINGS score well on both points. Certainly, the Nordic VIKINGS were a fearless race. Following many years of victories against the British Isles and France, under Erik the Red, they sailed in open boats across the North Atlantic, seeking new peoples to conquer. Their entire history is punctuated with the aggressive desire and will to win. While Minnesota is populated by the descendants of settlers from many nations, the area has a rich Nordic lore, perhaps due to the mythology of Paul Bunyan and his Blue Ox, perhaps due to the preponderance of the "sons" and "sens" in the phone book. Karl Hubenthal, sports cartoonist for the *Los Angeles Times*, did the original drawing of the VIKING logo. Marking the entrance to Winter Park — home of the Minnesota VIKINGS — is an authentic replica of a VIKING coastal raider ship, patterned after relics that have been discovered in Scandinavian countries. Incidentally, Bert Rose passed away in October 2001, at the age of 83.

NEW ENGLAND PATRIOTS

In the late 1950s, the National Football League's Chicago CARDI-NALS were looking for a new home and Boston opened its doors. But that franchise decided on Missouri instead and became the St. Louis CARDINALS. William Sullivan, who had pursued the CARDINALS for Boston, decided then to join the fledgling American Football League in 1959. The first promotion was to name the club. A contest was held and the various names were submitted to a panel of sportswriters. Seventy-four fans suggested the name PATRIOTS, which the panel agreed best personified the New England region. So the PATRIOTS were born in 1960, as were their colors of red, blue, and white. The original Patriot logo was designed by local cartoonist Phil Bissel — it was in the *Boston Globe* where William Sullivan saw it, and Pat PATRIOT was born. The team started play as the Boston PATRIOTS, changing finally to the New England PATRIOTS to help attract a broad-er fan base. For a team without any change of locale in 40 years, the PATRIOTS sure have called a lot of stadiums their home field. The PATRIOTS have played home games on five different gridirons, includ-ing Boston University Field (1960-62), Fenway Park in Boston (1963-68), Boston College Alumni Stadium in Chestnut Hill (1969), and Harvard Stadium in Cambridge (1970), before leaving the hub for per-manent residence in Schaefer (1970-82)/Sullivan (1983-89)/Foxboro Stadium (1990-present) in Foxboro.

NICKNAME: "THE PATS"

NEW ORLEANS SAINTS

The merging of the American Football League with the National Football League allowed for expansion into New Orleans. Art dealer Dave Dixon, one of the visionaries who brought the franchise to town, said, "My wife and I were sitting in a little cafe in Paris in 1961, and all of a sudden this three-piece band played 'When the Saints Go Marching In.' I was flabbergasted and realized that this song had universal appeal. I said to my wife, 'By God, the SAINTS would be a perfect name for the New Orleans football team,' but later when it came to decision time, some people felt that the name might have an improper religious connotation. That was dispelled by Archbishop Phillip Hannan when he first arrived in town. I asked him what he thought of the name SAINTS for the football team. He replied, 'I think it would be wonderful. Besides, I have a premo-nition we are going to need a 12th man on our side for several years to come.'" Ownership at the time didn't consider it a coincidence when New Orleans received news of its franchise on November 1, 1966 . . . All-Saints Day, a holiday significant to the religious history of the city. There was a name-the-team contest, but it was only a formality. New Orleans had an NFL football team with a heavenly nickname. So it was September 17, 1967, opening day in the NFL, and a throng of 80,879 fans witnessed rookie John Gilliam take the opening kickoff and return it 94 yards for a touchdown against the Los Angeles RAMS. That's how the SAINTS came marching in.

NEW YORK GIANTS

Tim Mara purchased a National Football League franchise in 1925 for $500. And it was Mara, as owner and founder, who picked the GIANTS nickname. The GIANTS originally played their games at the Polo Grounds, which was also home to the very successful Major League Baseball GIANTS. The football team felt that they might be able to attract some attention by sharing the name. Therefore they were named the GIANTS in the year of their inception, with no other nicknames considered at that time. According to the football GIANTS information, the baseball GIANTS got their name from the large buildings that compose New York City. But the baseball GIANTS claim their name was changed from the New York GOTHAMS in 1886 when Jim Mutrie, the manager at the time, shouted at his players after a victory, "My big fellows! My GIANTS! We are the people!" The baseball GIANTS left for San Francisco in 1957, leaving the NFL GIANTS alone to carry on their names in New York.

NICKNAMES: "THE BIG BLUE WRECKING CREW"
            "MARA TECH"

NEW YORK JETS

On March 28, 1963, a five-man syndicate composed of David A. (Sonny) Werblin, Leon Hess, Townsend B. Martin, Donald C. Lillis, and Philip H. Iselin purchased the New York TITANS of the American Football League for the price of one million dollars. Less than a month later, on April 15, Warblin, the team's president and CEO, renamed the club the JETS. The reasons, he said, were twofold. At the time, the United States was entering the "space" or "JET Age." Commercial airlines were filling the air and soon there would be men walking on the moon. Also, the JETS' new facility, Shea Stadium, would be located in Flushing

Meadows, New York, between the LaGuardia and Idlewild (later renamed John F. Kennedy) Airports. Hence the name, the New York JETS.

OAKLAND RAIDERS

The RAIDERS were added to the American Football League as an afterthought and subsequently had to draft from the other teams' rejects. At first, they were named the SEÑORS, the name picked by a raffle winner. After throwing a celebration for the winner, team officials quietly changed the name from SEÑORS to RAIDERS the following day! The new nickname was a tip of the pirate's hat to Oakland's proximity to the Pacific and its rich history of sea robbers — much like the Spanish that terrorized the East Coast, and are remembered by Tampa Bay's BUCCANEERS. It was probably the Dutch who were the RAIDERS on the West Coast, however. In 1963, Al Davis left his assistant coaching job in San Diego to become head coach of the RAIDERS. He changed the team colors from orange and black to silver and black and led the club to their first-ever winning season. In 1982 the franchise moved, becoming for the next 12 years, the Los Angeles RAIDERS. They returned to Oakland in 1995.

PHILADELPHIA EAGLES

In 1902, baseball's Philadelphia ATHLETICS and Philadelphia PHILLIES formed football teams. It was the first attempt at a pro gridiron league, and was named the National Football League. The first World Series of pro football was played with a team made up of players from both the ATHLETICS and the PHILLIES, but for some reason named NEW YORK! They lost to the Syracuse ATHLETIC CLUB, and soon the league itself failed. In 1922 another league started up with the same NFL name and it soon included a club from a section of Philly called Frankford. When the Frankford YELLOWJACKETS won the NFL Championship in 1926, no one in the 22-team league had played more games — and that included the Philadelphia QUAKERS, playing in the renegade American Football League. When the YELLOWJACKETS went into bankruptcy, a syndicate bought it from the NFL. The new owners named their team the EAGLES in honor of President Franklin Roosevelt's New Deal, whose symbol was the American EAGLE. Roosevelt's "thunderbird" was meant to symbolize the nation's industrial rebirth. At first blue and yellow were adopted because they were Philadelphia's city colors, but owner Bert Bell decided to use Kelly green, a hue that has survived to this day. In 1943, because of the World

War II manpower shortage, Philadelphia and Pittsburgh were granted permission to merge for one season. The Phil-Pitt STEAGLES were dissolved after the last day of the season.

NICKNAME: "THE BIRDS"

PITTSBURGH STEELERS

The fifth oldest franchise in the National Football League (behind the Chicago (Arizona) CARDINALS, Green Bay PACKERS, Chicago BEARS, and New York GIANTS), the Pittsburgh football team was founded in 1933 by Art Rooney. The gridiron club has experienced a number of name changes, including the MAJESTIC RADIOS ATHLETIC CLUB pre-1933 and Pittsburgh PIRATES from 1933 to 1939. But the STEELERS nickname in 1940 was the result of a name-the-team contest, and was in tribute to the livelihood of the town that hosted it. The name was suggested by the wife of Joe Carr, who was the ticket manager. In 1943, because of the World War II manpower shortage, the Philadelphia EAGLES and Pittsburgh STEELERS were granted permission to merge for one season. The Phil-Pitt STEAGLES were dissolved after the last day of the season — the same season the National Football League made the wearing of helmets mandatory. In 1944 the STEELERS merged with the Chicago CARDINALS. The CARDS-PITTS (or CARPETS as they were known) didn't win a single game. In 1945 they were once again the Pittsburgh STEELERS. The colors on the hypercycloid — the extruded diamond shape found on the STEELERS helmet — represent the three materials used to make steel: yellow for coal, orange for ore, and blue for scrap STEEL. In 1952 the men from steel city became the last club to move from the single wing to the T-formation, which is now recognized as the standard in football. In 1962, Republic Steel of Cleveland, Ohio, suggested that the STEELERS use the national Steel Industry's logo because of their long association with the industry. The STEELERS accepted, and the Steel logo is now worn only on the right side of the helmet.

NICKNAME: "STEEL CITY"

ST. LOUIS RAMS

This franchise, which started in Cleveland, is responsible for a number of interesting firsts in pro sports. They were the first and probably the only pro club to ever take its name from a college football team! It was

1937 and the football team's first general manager, Buzz Wetzel, admired a college team known as the Fordham University RAMS. The pro squad's first owner, Homer Marshman, also liked the name, and so baptized their NFL team the CLEVELAND RAMS. In 1946, new owner Dan Reeves, heir to a 600-store grocery chain that was sold to Safeway for $11 million in 1940, felt the future of his franchise was in the West. The RAMS became the first major professional sports team on the Pacific coast, forging the way west for the National Football League. Another first — in 1947 halfback Fred Gehrke, an art major in college, made a pen-and-ink sketch of a ram's horns. Head Coach Bob Snyder could not visualize the artwork on a helmet till Gehrke transferred the design onto his teammate's leather headgear. The following season, the RAMS became the first pro team with a helmet insignia. Ironically, of the 28 NFL clubs playing today, only the team that took root back in Ohio after the RAMS left, the Cleveland BROWNS, does not have helmet insignia. In the 1995-96 season, the RAMS packed their bags and moved back east to become the St. Louis RAMS. Also, the RAMS win hands-down for most cleverly nicknamed cheerleading squad — those Embraceable Ewes.

SAN DIEGO CHARGERS

No sooner had the American Football League been formed than on October 14, 1959, Frank Leahy, former University of Notre Dame football coach, was named general manager of the Los Angeles-based team. The club held its own name-the-team contest and received a number of considered monikers including FRONTIERSMEN, CABALLEROS, CHALLENGERS, RANCHEROS, JETS, TOWNSMEN, and BRACEROS. Leahy liked the sound of a name submitted by Gerald Courtney of Hollywood, the CHARGERS. The AFL club shared the Coliseum with the college football USC TROJANS until the Greater San Diego Sports Association made an offer the CHARGERS couldn't refuse. In 1961 construction finished to enlarge Balboa Stadium, and the CHARGERS took to their own home field. It was in 1960 and while still in Los Angeles that owner Barron Hilton unveiled the CHARGERS uniform — blue and gold with lightning bolts on the sides of helmets and trousers. It was at his Santa Monica residence, and one of the players who modeled the new nickname and uniform was none other than Republican Congressman Jack Kemp.

NICKNAMES: "THE LIGHTNING BOLTS"
                     "THE BOLTS"

SAN FRANCISCO 49ERS

The San Francisco 49ERS have the distinction of being the first major league professional sports franchise on the West Coast. Beginning play in 1946 as a member of the All-American Football Conference, the 49ERS were also the first professional sports team to "originate" on the West Coast. They were later joined by the National Football League's Los Angeles RAMS, who moved from Cleveland (and then left LA for St. Louis in 1995), and baseball's Los Angeles DODGERS and San Francisco GIANTS, who migrated from Brooklyn and New York, respectively — bringing their East Coast nicknames along with them. The San Francisco 49ERS franchise was founded in 1946, which was very close to the 100th anniversary of the Gold Rush of 1849. In 1849, San Francisco experienced an influx of settlers, adventurers, risk-takers, and hell-raisers from all over America. These newcomers brought with them a spirit that defines Frisco to this day. The team's 49ERS nickname is in honor of those gold miners of San Francisco legend, as is the gold helmet they have always worn. The 49ERS name is the only one with which the team has been affiliated and San Francisco is the only city in which they have resided.

NICKNAME: "NINERS"

SEATTLE SEAHAWKS

In 1975, Seattle team management selected the nickname SEA-HAWKS following a fan competition that attracted 20,365 entries and 1,741 different names. "Our new name shows aggressiveness, reflects our soaring Northwest heritage, and belongs to no other major league team," said John Thompson, SEAHAWKS general manager. Other fan suggestions included the Seattle ASPARAGUS, SWARTHY SWANS, Washattle WHOPPERS, and Milltown MAULERS. The more popular suggestions included the MARINERS, SKIPPERS, PIONEERS, LUM-BERJACKS, SPACERS, SOCKEYES, SEAGULLS, and SPIN-NAKERS. Listen to some fans' reasons for selecting their names: "The UFOs. People will come from everywhere to see a UFO." "The Seattle SEPTICS is easy to say, and has a certain air about it." "Seattle SEM ANON. That's NO-NAMES spelled backwards." "Seattle SAMS, from SOUND and MOUNTAINS and SEA. Play it again, Sam." And how about "The Seattle FIRE, because fire leaves total destruction in its path, boys have a 'burning desire' to become pro football players, and most of us girls carry a 'torch' for a pro football player," offered Sue Simon of Coupeville.

NICKNAME: "HAWKS"

TAMPA BAY BUCCANEERS

The BUCCANEERS was originally the nickname of a local Florida semipro football team. Tampa Bay was granted its National Football League franchise in 1974, and the team played its first game in the fall of 1976. It was February of 1975 when the club got its moniker. They were nicknamed by a panel of local newspaper sportswriters and members of the new NFL organization. There had been a local name-the-team competition, which was nonbinding. That is to say, the authorities were not obligated to use the winning name. But, coincidentally, BUCCANEERS was the unanimous choice of the panel as well as the winning entry. The nickname is a nod in the direction of the Florida coastline and its history. It was the BUCCANEERS, the pirates or sea robbers, who raided the Spanish coasts of America in the 17th century.

NICKNAME: "THE BUCS"

TENNESSEE TITANS

When Houston OILERS owner K. S. "Bud" Adams Jr. signed a contract to move his National Football League team from Texas to Tennessee, he announced a statewide name-the-team contest. Among the more interesting suggestions included the Nashville SOUND, ELVISES, HOUND DOGS, HILLBILLIES, TWANG, HEEHAWS, MOUNTAIN CATS, BANJOS, KNIGHTS, and the Tennessee SOUTH STARS, TORNADOES, PIONEERS, WRANGLERS, MOUNTAINEERS, and VOLUNTEERS. Thankfully, TITANS was picked as the new nickname of the National Football League's Tennessee franchise. "We wanted a new nickname to reflect strength, leadership and other heroic qualities," Adams said in making the announcement. "TITANS come from early Greek mythology and the fact that Nashville is known as the Athens of the South makes the TITANS name very appropriate." The team was the Houston Oilers from 1960 until it relocated to Tennessee in 1996, when it became the Tennessee OILERS. TITANS was the original nickname of the New York JETS in the old American Football League. JETS officials have indicated they had no problem letting Adams, who helped found the AFL, take the name TITANS. Because it didn't have a stadium arrangement yet in Nashville, the team temporarily settled in Memphis. Tennessee fans had a hard time warming up to the OILERS, who drew an NFL-worst average crowd of 28,028 in Memphis' Liberty Bowl in 1997. They opened in their new Adelphia Stadium in Nashville to 65,729 — the largest crowd in franchise history.

WASHINGTON REDSKINS

The Washington REDSKINS were originally located in Boston and were named the Boston BRAVES by team owner George Preston Marshall. They were renamed in 1933 to differentiate between the Boston BRAVES baseball team of the National League, and the Boston BRAVES of the National Football League. The team retained the name when it relocated to Washington in 1937. Over the long history of the Washington REDSKINS, the name has reflected positive attributes of the American Indian such as dedication, courage, and pride. The RED-SKINS have become an institution in the nation's capital and the team's popularity brings the community together. Because of the respect that goes with the name REDSKINS, the team has never been referred to by any other name. In the 1970s, when head coach George Allen brought in a plethora of veterans, the team became known as the "Over the Hill Gang." During the 1980s, when the REDSKINS went to three Super Bowls, several nicknames were born to describe certain aspects of the team. The team's offensive line became known as the "Hogs," a moniker that remains today and is well known by all NFL fans.

NICKNAMES: "SKINS"
             "OVER THE HILL GANG"
             "HOGS"

Part 4

National Hockey League

ANAHEIM MIGHTY DUCKS

The film that became a hockey club! *The Mighty Ducks* was a successful feature film released by the Walt Disney Studios in 1992. This film was followed by an equally successful sequel, *Mighty Ducks 2* in 1994. In between these two pictures Disney released a National Hockey League club which it called the MIGHTY DUCKS of Anaheim. Early in the 1992 movie hit we are introduced to the main character, played by actor Emilio Estevez. The character's name? Ducksworth. You got it. The ragamuffin bunch of inner-city kids he leads to national hockey prominence was named the Mighty Ducks — after himself. When it was learned that Disney had purchased an NHL team, word quickly spread that the film moniker was being considered as the franchise nickname. Fans of the rough-and-tumble sport held their collective breath, for good reason — MIGHTY DUCKS they became. It was Disney CEO Michael Eisner who named the team. The DUCKS team colors are purple, yellow, white, and green. The mascot is named Wild Wing. Between-period entertainment is supplied by the NHL's first ice-skating cheerleaders, an all-female squad called the "Decoys"!

NICKNAME: "DUCKS"

ATLANTA THRASHERS

In a time when most teams have marketing firms select their nicknames to maximize retail sales of hats and T-shirts, you've got to hand it to maverick owner Ted Turner and the suggestion he made for his new NHL club. Turner decided to name his team after the Georgia state bird, the THRASHERS, and that was that. No name search, no fan considerations, no staff meetings. You don't mess with a billionaire who challenged rival media mogul Rupert Murdoch to a boxing match. Besides, THRASHERS is a tough enough-sounding name, considering it does come from a small bird known for its song (the brown thrasher is a close relative of the mockingbird.) Atlanta first joined the NHL with the New York ISLANDERS in 1972-73 as the FLAMES, but that franchise moved to Calgary in 1980. The THRASHERS set a record for an NHL expansion team by averaging 17,205 fans per home game their first season.

BOSTON BRUINS

After Charles F. Adams acquired the National Hockey League franchise for Boston and hired Art Ross as the first general manager and coach, it became necessary to acquire an appropriate name for the new entry into the hockey wars. Adams' ground rules for the selection of a name at that time were based largely on color. The team's basic colors would be brown with yellow trim (brown eventually became black). This color scheme was selected primarily because Adams was then president of Brookside Stores, all of which had a color combination of brown and a yellow trim. The name chosen should preferably relate to an untamed animal whose name was synonymous with size, strength, agility, ferocity, and cunning, and in the color brown category. Dozens of names were submitted from various sources like news media, sportsmen, and fans, none of which proved entirely satisfactory. It remained for Ross's secretary — Ross ran a sporting goods store part-time in Montreal — to submit the name BRUINS. Adams accepted the team's bearlike nickname, because he appreciated the animal's combined qualities of speed, strength, agility, ferocity, and animal cunning. The bear logo was replaced by the letter "B" in a wheel, which comes from the city's nickname, "The Hub."

NICKNAMES: "BIG BAD BRUINS"
              "THE B'S"
              "BEANTOWNERS"

BUFFALO SABRES

Awarded its National Hockey League expansion franchise on December 2, 1969, Buffalo SABRES management worked on the matter of getting a name by sponsoring a contest. There were 13,000 entries submitted, suggesting 1,047 different names. Some of the nicknames that didn't reach the finals included the FLYING ZEPPELINS, MUGWUMPS, MOGULS, BUZZING BEES, BANDITS, BORDER WEAVERS, FLASHES, JESTERS, EAGER BEAVERS, and STREAKS. Five people came up with SABRES, and Robert Sonnelitter Jr. of Williamsville, New York, won a drawing of those five for a pair of season tickets. It's probably a good thing the club's management didn't go with one of the other nickname suggestions: the Buffalo BABOONS. The Knox brothers, owners of the team, explained that the sabre is a symbol of authority, a weapon carried by a leader. Team colors were taken from the polo club where the Knox brothers' father was a member.

CALGARY FLAMES

The Calgary FLAMES nickname comes from the team's original home, Atlanta, and the infamous burning of that southern city during the Civil War — remember that thrilling scene from *Gone With the Wind*? The team played in Georgia beginning with the 1972-73 season until 1979-80. They arrived in Alberta for the 1980-81 season. Despite fans wanting to change the nickname when the franchise moved north to Canada, a media panel decided that the FLAMES moniker would still be appropriate for an oil town like Calgary, with its population hovering around half a million. The red and gold trim on the uniforms was also retained after the move, while a new flaming red "C" replaced Atlanta's "A." The new millennium brought pro hockey back to Atlanta with the THRASHERS.

CAROLINA HURRICANES

HURRICANES are to the Carolinas what bluegrass is to Kentucky — a seasonal given. Although other names were considered, none were considered seriously. Team management made the Carolina hockey club the only HURRICANES in pro sports, sharing it with the NCAA's University of Miami team. These National Hockey League Carolina HURRICANES swept into Greensboro, North Carolina, (and now Raleigh) in 1998. Originating as the World Hockey Association's New England WHALERS, the team played in Boston from 1972 to 1974, West Springfield from 1974 to 1975, Hartford from 1975 to 1978, then Springfield in 1979. The team moved back to Hartford when it joined the National Hockey League in 1979-80. Other teams that played in the defunct WHA include the Ottawa NATIONALS, who moved to Toronto; the Ottawa CIVICS; the Philadelphia BLAZERS, who moved to Vancouver and stayed the BLAZERS; the Phoenix ROADRUNNERS; the Quebec NORDIQUES (now the NHL's Colorado AVALANCHE); the Toronto TOROS, who moved to Birmingham and became the BULLS; and the Winnipeg JETS, now the NHL's Phoenix COYOTES.

NICKNAME: "CANES"

CHICAGO BLACKHAWKS

The man behind the creation of the name for this Chicago club was Major Frederick McLaughlin, the first owner of the team. When Major

McLaughlin initially purchased the NHL franchise from Portland (Oregon) in 1926, it was known as the Portland Rosebuds. McLaughlin adopted the name BLACKHAWK in memory of the Blackhawk Field Gun Battalion, a unit with which he served during World War I. The battalion was named after a famous Indian Chief who headed the Sauk tribe in the early 1800s. And it is Chief Blackhawk himself who rides proudly on the Chicago team's jersey. It is believed that the colors red, white, and black also have some military connection. The uniform was designed in 1954 by then-GM Tommy Ivan's wife. Tomahawks were added to the shoulders and the Indian head was made more prominent. By the way, Major McLaughlin's pride in his battalion reached beyond the ice surface. He also owned an eatery in Chicago called the BLACK HAWK, and for some time it was believed the team was named after it — which wasn't the case. Originally spelled as two words, BLACK HAWKS, in 1988 the two words were officially merged into one, the BLACK-HAWKS.

NICKNAME: "HAWKS"

COLORADO AVALANCHE

The National Hockey League was founded on a chilly November day in 1917, inheriting six teams from a seven-year-old circuit, the National Hockey Association, where the Quebec BULLDOGS were two-time Stanley Cup winners. The team was formally renamed the Quebec ATHLETICS, a fact that has been almost entirely forgotten. Still, the BULLDOG name remained popular with the club's fans. The team became the Hamilton TIGERS in 1920-21, folding in 1925. With the formation of the NHL's rival World Hockey Association in 1971 came the rebirth of pro hockey in Quebec. The name NORDIQUES was chosen from 1,500 contest entries, illustrating the team's geographical location as the most northerly franchise in professional sports. The NORDS were swallowed by the NHL, and then the team moved to Denver for the 1995-96 season, becoming the Colorado AVALANCHE. Even the location name was contested in-house: Denver, Rocky Mountain, or Colorado? Selected by the team's new owners, COMSAT, rejected names included the ROCKY MOUNTAIN EXTREME, the ICE, the STORM, RAPIDS, OUTLAWS, COUGARS, RENEGADES, WRANGLERS, and briefly, the ROCKY MOUNTAIN AVALANCHE. COMSAT even filed copyright protection for the name BLACK BEARS. Why AVALANCHE? A press release mentioned Colorado's Rocky

Mountains, and the strength required to succeed in the NHL. Also, the AVALANCHE-on-a-puck logo represents the power and speed of the skating, passing, and shooting in the game. It's not the first local use of the moniker, however. In the late 1970s and early '80s, the Denver AVALANCHE played in the Major Indoor Soccer League. The AVALANCHE are not the first NHL team in Colorado, either. In 1976 the Kansas City SCOUTS moved to Denver to become the Colorado ROCKIES. In 1982 the ROCKIES left Denver, becoming the New Jersey DEVILS and winning their first Stanley Cup in 1994-95. In 1996, the first-year AVALANCHE won the Cup.

NICKNAMES: "LANCHE"
                  "AVS"

COLUMBUS BLUE JACKETS

Ohio's latest NHL franchise (remember the Cleveland BARONS?) is called the Columbus BLUE JACKETS — a nod in the direction of local military history. The name BLUE JACKETS recognizes the contributions by Ohio and the city of Columbus to the Union Army during the Civil War. The state of Ohio made a larger contribution of its population to the Union Army than any other state in the union. The blue coats of the Union Army were manufactured in Columbus. The BLUE JACKETS' colors are capital blue, red, and white. Capital Blue is similar to the Union Army's blue coats. The blue conveys stability and tradition. The red conveys pride. There are white stars on the end of the sleeves wrapped with a red ribbon. The stars signify patriotism, with the number 13 representing the original Union. Owners of the franchise that began play in 2000 decided on STINGER as a mascot — a red-eyed, snarling bug with a thick stinger, clad in a federal blue jacket with stars on the collar and a cocked Union Army hat, and carrying a florescent green hockey stick. The logo features a swirling red banner dotted with white stars forming the letters C and B — for Columbus and BLUE. A hockey stick in the middle forms a green J for JACKETS.

NICKNAME: "JACKETS"

DALLAS STARS

Three months into their inaugural 1967 season, the California SEALS were renamed the Oakland SEALS. In 1970 they became the California

GOLDEN SEALS, then were re-christened with their original name in 1975, the California SEALS. In 1976 the SEALS left the coast for Cleveland. In 1978 the Cleveland BARONS merged with the Minnesota NORTH STARS — Star of the North is the Minnesota state nickname, and fans chose it in a contest — becoming the Minnesota NORTH STARS. The team color of green came from Dartmouth College in New Hampshire, where Walter Bush, Jr., a club founder, attended college. In 1993, after 26 seasons, the Minnesota NORTH STARS moved to Dallas, and had their moniker shortened to the STARS — a nod in the direction of the Lone Star State, along with the rich Texas history of lawmen, wearers of the sheriff's star. Under the new ownership of Norman N. Green, the uniform and team logo were redesigned. Team colors became blue, yellow, red, and white.

DETROIT RED WINGS

Pro hockey arrived in Detroit on September 25, 1926, when a group of Detroit businessmen purchased a National Hockey League franchise and stocked it with players from the Victoria COUGARS of the Western Hockey League. The club was called the Detroit COUGARS but played its inaugural season across the Detroit River in Canada at Windsor's Border Cities Arena. In 1930, the Detroit COUGARS were getting blitzed by the fans and media, who wanted to see some changes. The team missed the playoffs in 1929-30, and had only made the playoffs once in their four-year existence — a rather unimpressive record, considering there were only six teams in the league. The owners renamed the team the Detroit FALCONS, hoping a facelift would give the club new life. Unfortunately, the FAL-CONS — like the COUGARS — missed the playoffs in their first year. In 1932, with the nation still recovering from the Great Depression, James Norris bought the FALCONS. In 1933 the team's new president changed the FALCON nickname to the RED WINGS in memory of the Winged Wheelers, the amateur Montreal Athletic Association team he'd played on in the 1890s. Of course it isn't a coincidence that the red jersey insignia has a wing protruding out of an automobile wheel, a nod in the direction of Motown's car industry.

NICKNAMES: "WINGS"
                "RED ARMY" (1996 team with 10 Russian players)

EDMONTON OILERS

The Edmonton OILERS was a charter member team of the World Hockey Association when the league was formed in 1972-73. During that first season the team was called the Alberta OILERS. The name was changed to Edmonton OILERS in 1973-74, and has remained that way ever since. In 1979-80, the OILERS, along with three other WHA teams, merged with the National Hockey League. The team's nickname is derived from the city of Edmonton's long history with the discovery of oil in the area. In 1949 a major oil field was discovered just south of Edmonton and the oil industry has been vital to the economic well-being of both the city and province since that time. The selection of the nickname OILERS was a decision made by team owner Dr. Charles Allard, and the first general manager, Bill Hunter — with Edmonton fans agreeing overwhelmingly. The OILERS logo employs a script style in which the letters appear to be sitting in a pool of oil. This is to symbolize depth of talent, and the flame is to demonstrate the eternal nature of the team. The teams that came and went with the WHA were the Los Angeles SHARKS, which became the Michigan STAGS, which became the Baltimore BLADES; the Minnesota FIGHTING SAINTS, which became the NEW FIGHTING SAINTS; the New Jersey KNIGHTS, which became the San Diego MARINERS; and the New York RAIDERS, which became the NEW JERSEY GOLDEN BLADES.

NICKNAME: "THE OIL"

FLORIDA PANTHERS

Felis concolor coryi, a subspecies of the North American cougar discovered in 1896 by naturalist Charles B. Cory, can be found only in Florida. Given that the protection efforts on the Florida Panther's behalf are somewhat recent developments, and the population growth of Florida in the latter half of the 20th century severely encroached on the animal's natural habitat, the panther is one of the most endangered mammals on Earth. In fact, it's estimated that only between 30 and 50 of these animals remain in the wild. Shortly after being granted an NHL expansion franchise, team owner H. Wayne Huizenga held a "name-the-team" contest. The organization received thousands of responses in little more than a week and the overwhelming favorite was PANTHERS. Because of the alarming problems that surround this beautiful animal, the Florida PANTHERS Hockey Club has made the commitment to raise to a higher plateau the awareness level of this animal's plight. To accomplish this goal, the entire hockey organization is committed to working with the groups and individuals who dedicate themselves to sharing the common desire to help sustain and replenish the population of the Florida Panther. The hockey club's "PANTHERS Saves help Save the Panther" program enlists individuals and corporations to help the creature's cause. The team and various support groups solicit pledges from people wishing to help: they may make a financial contribution for every save a PANTHERS goaltender makes at home games. Due to the high visibility of a professional sports team, it is hoped that this program will receive widespread exposure throughout North America and thus generate significant financial contributions to help save *Felis concolor coryi*, the Florida Panther.

NICKNAME: "CATS"

LOS ANGELES KINGS

This Southern California-based team's first owner, Jack Kent Cooke, named the team the KINGS himself. It was Cooke's idea to give his franchise a jump start by connecting it with established concepts, including naming his rink the Great Western Forum — a show of respect and appreciation for what the Russians call the Shrine of Hockey, the Montreal Forum. The crown is a natural logo and the original colors of purple and gold represented the traditional hues of royalty. With the addition of former Edmonton OILERS superstar Wayne Gretzky to the lineup in 1988, then-owner Bruce McNall wanted his team to stand on its own and not look like hockey's version of the Los Angeles LAKERS, owned by a former KINGS owner, Dr. Jerry Buss. New team colors were introduced as silver and black — similar to the National Football League RAIDERS, who were Los Angeles-based at the time.

MINNESOTA WILD

Would the Minnesota GNATS have struck fear into the hearts of NHL opponents? How about the St. Paul FROZEN EARS? In addition to the GNATS and FROZEN EARS fans from the fishing-crazy state suggested the FLYING WALLEYE, NINJA MUSKIES, and FIGHTING SMELT, a team spokesman said. Other suggestions included the CORN DOGS, TEN THOUSAND LAKERS, and PUCKEROOS. Team CEO Jack Sperling said this about the WILD nickname when it was introduced in 1998 after six months and thousands of fan submissions: "We think it best represents what Minnesota hockey fans hold most dear. Our rugged natural wilderness, the premier-brand hockey that's native to Minnesota and the great enthusiasm of all of our hockey fans." The area's previous NHL team, the Minnesota NORTH STARS, moved to Dallas after the 1992-93 season, becoming the STARS.

MONTREAL CANADIENS

When the *Sporting News* compiled a book entitled *Dynasty – The 12 Most Dominant Teams in Sports History*, the Montreal CANADIENS were there among basketball's CELTICS, football's PACKERS, college's SOONERS, and baseball's YANKEES. NOS GLORIEUX, French for "Our Glory," hold the hockey record for most consecutive championships — five. When J. Ambrose O'Brien founded the team on December 4, 1909, it was known as the CLUB CANADIEN, and for its first game at Jubilee Rink, the players wore jerseys of red, white, and blue, which were, at that time, the colors of the Canadian flag. In 1911-12 a "CAC" was placed in the center of the sweater, and the team was called the CANADIAN ATHLETIC CLUB. The CANADIENS introduced the famed CH sweater now in use in 1916 en route to their first Stanley Cup. The French influence has given LES CANADIENS their most endearing nickname, with partial credit going to American Tex Rickard, who had picked up a false rumor about the "H" (for Hockey) on the club's uniform. Camille Desroches recalled, "This guy told Tex that the French-speaking players were 'farmers,' and therefore HABITANTS." And HABS is derived from HABITANT, meaning "person of the land." Other clubs that have played out of Montreal for the Stanley Cup and won included the Montreal WANDERERS (nicknamed the RED-BANDS), the SHAMROCKS, the VICTORIAS, and the first-ever winner of Lord Stanley's trophy, the Montreal AMATEUR ATHLETIC ASSOCI-ATION. And a franchise that survived across town from the CANADIENS until 1938 — the Montreal MAROONS. Another Montreal club, the CRYS-TALS, never won the Cup.

NICKNAMES: "THE CANUCKS" (Pre-Vancouver Canucks)
"LES HABITANTS"
"THE HABS"
"NOS GLORIEUX"
"LES BOYS"
"BLEU-BLANC-ROUGE" (blue, white, and red)

NASHVILLE PREDATORS

The PREDATORS unveiled their logo, a saber-toothed tiger, in Nashville's downtown First American Center on September 25, 1997, 26 years after a fang and foreleg bone of a saber-toothed tiger were found in a cave just below the very same Center. In May of 1971 construction

workers drilled through 20 feet of solid rock before coming to a cave containing the nine-inch fang of the tiger, extinct for at least 10,000 years.
Possibly one of the last of its breed to exist, the discovery marked only the
fifth of its kind in North America. The cave is preserved under concrete
for historic and educational purposes. The naming of the PREDATORS is
a direct reflection of this find and the local fans. On September 27, 1997,
Nashville's NHL expansion team hosted the Ice Breaker Bash to launch a
season ticket campaign. During this celebration, plus through focus
groups and related surveys, the name PREDATORS won in an overwhelming two-to-one margin over the second choice. Country music sen-
sation and PREDATORS fan Garth Brooks sent the team a telegram after
their first win. Coach Barry Trotz said at the time, "Southern hospitality
isn't some myth. The people down here are more cordial than you might
find up north or on the East Coast." The PREDATORS were part of an
expansion that gave the NHL as many franchises at the turn of the century as both the National Football League and Major League Baseball. The
National Basketball Association had one less franchise at 29.

NEW JERSEY DEVILS

New Jersey DEVILS named after a baby? Well, this wasn't just any
kid. Starting out as the Kansas City SCOUTS, the club moved to
Colorado to become the ROCKIES, in Denver's pre-MLB days. The New
Jersey DEVILS were christened at the Byrne Meadowlands Arena on
June 30, 1982. The question at hand, however, is whether that date comes
within two centuries of the actual birth of the Jersey Devil. It was 1735,
or so the legend goes, that a farm woman named Mrs. Leeds gave birth to
her 13th child — the Jersey Devil, itself. In and out of hiding the Devil
seems to have appeared just often enough to remain a permanent fixture
in the minds of area inhabitants. He became so ingrained in people's
thoughts that in 1939, the Devil was appointed the "official state demon."
In statewide, name-the-team newspaper contests, familiar handles such as
BLADES, LIGHTNING, COLONIALS, MEADOWLANDERS, GEN-
ERALS, and AMERICANS found widespread support. But local folklore
was so pervasive that DEVILS couldn't miss. Team owner John
McMullen agreed, saying, "Webster's Dictionary defines devil as a person of notable energy, recklessness and dashing spirit — an excellent way
to describe what we're going to have with this new franchise." It's said
that Mrs. Leeds went into labor in the midst of a violent thunderstorm,
fueling rumors that the mother-to-be was involved in sorcery. That uneasi-

ness was transformed into horror as the child was born. With features described as those of a bat, a kangaroo, and a serpent, the newborn creature flew right out the window, destroying crops, and ravaging livestock, cutting the throats of hogs, cattle, sheep ... and people! The Devil has been "sighted" over the years by luminaries no less than politicians, military men, clergymen, and policemen. It has been exorcised, hunted, shot at by posses, and traced with electronic equipment. Or so they say.

NICKNAME: "THE DEVS"

NEW YORK ISLANDERS

The team is based in Uniondale, Long Island, New York. The New York ISLANDERS nickname came about from a suggestion made by co-owner Roy Boe's wife. Instead of naming the team the LONG ISLANDERS, she suggested calling the team the New York ISLANDERS, in an effort to win over some unhappy New York RANGER fans, a team that had not won the Stanley Cup in 50 years. The ISLANDERS colors of orange and blue are also the colors of Nassau County. Mrs. Boe, a dress designer, recommended the use of the map of Long Island as part of the logo. Long Island is in southeast New York, between Long Island Sound and the Atlantic. It is 1,411 square miles and has a population of over seven million. The ISLANDERS are one of only two clubs to win four successive Stanley Cups. The other is the CANADIENS.

NICKNAME: "ISLES"

NEW YORK RANGERS

In 1926 the New York AMERICANS took to the ice in spectacular "stars and stripes." They lasted 17 mostly uneventful seasons, their last in 1941 as the BROOKLYN AMERICANS. The 1926 birth of the RANGERS was something of a team effort that involved team president Lester Patrick, a successful hockey man from Toronto named Conn Smythe, and Madison Square Garden fight promoter Tex Rickard. Rickard, a Texan, had become fascinated with hockey, and was convinced the game would be enthusiastically supported in the Garden, the world's premier sports arena, which had opened its doors just a year earlier. As a nod to Rickard's home state and the famed police force that existed there, the team was jocularly called TEX'S RANGERS. As displaced as this moniker may have appeared in geography and tone, the latter part of the name stuck. The club soon became the toast of New York, attracting a formal "dinner-jacket" crowd to the games. These fans were headed to "the classiest team in hockey" by no less a personage than the mayor himself, the Honorable Jimmy Walker. The RANGERS have the distinction of ending one of the longest droughts in professional sports when they won the Stanley Cup in 1994. Not since 1940 had hockey's most prestigious banner been hung from the Garden rafters. The colors of blue, red, and white had nothing to do with the AMERICANS. Today the words "New York" are on the sweaters for road games while the home jerseys sport the nickname "RANGERS."

NICKNAMES: "BROADWAY BLUES"
                    "BLUESHIRTS"

OTTAWA SENATORS

As far back as the 1880s Ottawa fielded a team to contest the Stanley Cup named the CAPITALS. A lack of success drove the team away, but it returned at the turn of the century called the SILVER SEVEN, so named when Manager Bob Shillington handed over a silver nugget to each player in recognition of their winning season. The SEVEN was in reference to the fact that teams played seven a side then, not the six used now. In their three-year reign as Cup champions, they turned back the challenges of seven now long-gone teams: the Rat Portage (the city later changed its name to Kenora, thankfully) THISTLES, the Winnipeg ROWING CLUB, the Toronto MARLBOROUGHS, the Brandon WHEAT KINGS, and the fabled Dawson City KLONDIKERS. The SILVER SEVEN were the sport's first legitimate heroes, finally defeated in 1906 by the Montreal WANDERERS. Team nicknames were employed much more casually in the early days of hockey than they are today, and so it was in the season following the Ottawa club's defeat in Montreal that SILVER SEVEN began to be replaced by SENATORS, a reference to the Canadian capital city. In 1934, seven years after winning their last Cup, the SENATORS were gone. The team was gutted, the owners broke, the fans no longer supportive. The remnants moved to St. Louis, becoming the EAGLES — a team that folded in 1935. Incredibly, the man who scored the first goal of the game in which the Ottawa SENATORS won their last Stanley Cup in 1927, Frank Finnigan, lived long enough to be on hand when the Ottawa SENATORS were awarded their new NHL franchise in 1991. He died a hockey legend just after learning his old sweater, number eight, would be retired with glory. The team logo represents a SENATOR from

Roman times, and the colors are red, black, and gold.

NICKNAME: "THE SENS"

PHILADELPHIA FLYERS

The earliest Philadelphia hockey team arrived in 1930 by way of Pittsburgh. The PIRATES, the first franchise granted to Philadelphia, had their name changed to the QUAKERS. They played only one season, 1930-31. The FLYERS nickname was selected from a public contest that attracted 25,000 entries. Actually, the new team moniker had been reduced to two choices: the FLYERS and re-introducing the QUAKERS (some sources claim one entry, seriously considered, had the spelling PHLY-ERS). The idea of the FLYERS came down from Philadelphia's first general manager, Bud Poile, who once ran a pro team in Edmonton called the FLYERS. Many thought that the QUAKERS represented losing, which the orignal team did quite often, holding the second-worst record in league history (4-36-4). Thus, the FLYERS were born. A local artist designed the winged P, while orange and black were chosen as team colors. Among the other contest entries were names such as PIPERS and MOHAWKS.

NICKNAMES: "BROAD STREET BULLIES"
"PHILLY"

PHOENIX COYOTES

In 1896 the Winnipeg VICTORIAS played the Montreal VICTORIAS (imagination!) for the Stanley Cup. The Winnipeg goaltender put on a pair of goalie pads (the first ever) and shut out the club from the East. Winnipeg returned to the big leagues in 1972 with the formation of the World Hockey Association. Team owners attracted one of the biggest names in the National Hockey League at the time — Bobby Hull, from the Chicago Black Hawks — to help bolster the new league. The Golden JET, which was his nickname, signed the first million-dollar contract in pro hockey, and though it sounds like he lent his nickname to the club from Winnipeg, that's not the official story. Team owner Ben Hatskin developed the club's name. He originally picked the name to mirror Sonny Werblin's New York JETS of National Football League fame. Hatskin also said the nickname was chosen because of the city's growing air transport business. The Winnipeg JETS was one of four WHA clubs to be welcomed into the NHL when the upstart league folded in 1979. Other clubs that came and went in the WHA included the Baltimore BLADES; Birmingham BULLS; Calgary COWBOYS; Chicago COUGARS; Cincinnati STINGERS; Cleveland CRUSADERS, who moved to Minnesota; Denver SPURS, who moved to Ottawa; Houston AEROS; and Indianapolis RACERS. After a deal to move the Winnipeg franchise to Minnesota fell apart, an arrangement was struck with Jerry Colangelo, who owns the Phoenix SUNS of the National Basketball Association, for a move to the Southwest. A name-the-team contest attracted 10,000 entries, with the frontrunners including SCORPIONS, MUSTANGS, POSSE, OUTLAWS, JETS, and DRY ICE. But COYOTES beat the other finalist, the Phoenix PHREEZE. The word coyote is Spanish, and comes from the Aztec *coyotlinoult*. The wily coyote can be found in most of North and South America.

NICKNAME: "DESERT DOGS"

PITTSBURGH PENGUINS

Pittsburgh iced a team in 1925 called the PIRATES, built around an amateur club called the Pittsburgh YELLOW JACKETS. In 1930, this club moved to Philadelphia where it played one season as the Philadelphia QUAKERS, folding in 1931. The latest Pittsburgh franchise held a contest in 1967 to find a name and chose PENGUINS, partly because the first three letters match those in PENnsylvania. Milton Roberts, a steelworker who submitted the winning entry, won a pair of season tickets and a color television. Pennsylvania State Senator Jack MacGregor's wife also recommended the name. When the general manager of the time Jack Riley heard the decision of the judges, his response was to the point: "You're kidding." He then proceeded to design uniforms that did not contain the team nickname. Perhaps more upset than Riley was the Hornet Booster Club. One member called it a sacrilege to drop the name that other Pittsburgh hockey team had carried for 25 years. Coach Red Sullivan remarked at the time: "Detroit has a team called the RED WINGS. What's a RED WING, anyway? Is it a bird? Is it a flower? At least we have something that people recognize." Right. "A little fat man in a tuxedo," commented *Pittsburgh Press* journalist Roy McHugh. When looking for a connection between PENGUINS and Pittsburgh, fans were reminded that the Civic Arena where the home team would play was known as the Big Igloo. But when Riley and Sullivan were asked what the team should have been called they answered together, "The SHAMROCKS." Riley and Sullivan? It figured. The team color was originally light blue but was changed to a black and gold combination when the STEELERS and PIRATES were in the midst of winning six world titles in the 1970s.

NICKNAME: "THE PENS"

ST. LOUIS BLUES

In 1934 the Ottawa SENATORS, after winning six Stanley Cups, moved to St. Louis. The St. Louis EAGLES played one season in the National Hockey League in 1934-35, then folded. The city of St. Louis had to wait until 1967-68 for the birth of the BLUES. The name came unchallenged from Sid Saloman III, part-owner of the team, who drew his inspiration from the famous song written by W. C. Handy. Saloman also authorized use of the musical note for the logo. Team colors are blue, yellow, red, and white. In 1983 Harry Omest saved the BLUES from deportation to Saskatoon, which would have certainly required a nickname change. Meanwhile, the SENATORS have been reborn in Ottawa.

NICKNAME: "BLUE NOTES"

SAN JOSE SHARKS

Suggestions for the team name came in the form of sea creatures, fictional characters, and computer components. They included BLADES, BREAKERS, BREEZE, CONDORS, FOG, GOLD, GOLDEN GATERS, GOLDEN SKATERS, GRIZZLIES, ICEBREAKERS, KNIGHTS, REDWOODS, SEA LIONS, SHARKS, and WAVES. Although the most popular name submitted by San Jose fans was BLADES, management felt the word had too many negative connotations — as in weapons — and went with the second most popular suggestion. Good choice. The neighboring Pacific Ocean is home to seven different varieties of sharks, including the Great White, Leopard, Mako, Seven-gill, Blue, Soupfin, and Spiny Dog. A specific area of the Pacific in the Bay Area is called the "Red Triangle" because of its shark population. And, as stated by the team's vice president at the time, "Sharks are relentless, determined, swift, agile, bright and fearless. We plan to build an organization that has all these qualities." In its first year, the San Jose SHARKS took a 40 percent share of all NHL hockey merchandising sales. This was no accident. Many merchandising organizations believe that the SHARKS created the blueprint for sports merchandising later used successfully in all sports from basketball (Toronto RAPTORS) to football (Jacksonville JAGUARS and Carolina PANTHERS). The question asked in-house was, how aggressive could the moniker be and still be acceptable? Pretty aggressive it turns out, because this extensive research also gave the SHARKS their motto, "If looks could kill."

TAMPA BAY LIGHTNING

Over the years, professional sports team names have been determined through some rather unusual circumstances and procedures. But to the Tampa Bay hockey franchise's first general manager, Phil Esposito, the answer came to him like a lightning bolt out of the sky. Make that exactly like a lightning bolt. "I never expected to decide on the team name in the manner we did," said Esposito. "The story behind it is unique. When I first came to Tampa, everyone mentioned the frequent lightning storms that would hit the area. I didn't actually believe it until we were out on a deck that overlooks the bay one afternoon and a lightning storm hit." Too close for comfort, it turned out. Running for cover, "Someone said that LIGHT-NING would be a great name for the hockey team and I knew it was the perfect name." The Tampa Bay area is known as the lightning capital of the world as storms occur frequently throughout the year. Plus, the name relates closely to the sport. In fact, the theme line for the NHL's 75th anniversary season (1991-92) was "Lightning on Ice." The LIGHTNING colors of black, blue silver, and white are unique within the league. They are considered powerful, dynamic, and exciting, matching the approach and image of the team.

NICKNAME: "BOLTS"

TORONTO MAPLE LEAFS

Toronto teams that played for the Cup before and after the turn of the century included the BLUESHIRTS, the MARLBOROUGHS, and the WELLINGTONS, a Toronto railway powerhouse nicknamed the IRON DUKES. But the true bloodline to the MAPLE LEAFS started with the Toronto ARENAS, which then became the ST. PATRICKS. In 1926 Conn Smythe bought the club for $160,000. Smythe was not a follower. He was the sort of man to leave his imprint in the hardest of pavement, and it would not do to have the new team continue as the ST. PATRICKS. Among the teams he scouted for talent were a group of young men who called themselves the East Toronto MAPLE LEAFS — grammatically incorrect, but effective just the same. Smythe liked the name. He liked the fact that the maple leaf was something of a Canadian symbol, and that it was the logo of the 1924 Olympic team, the Toronto

GRANITES. Smythe had also worn the symbol proudly as a soldier in the Great War. It would be the symbol of his proud new team. Smythe designed new uniforms for the squad, but he kept the green color for one more season, as a sign of respect for the loyal supporters of the SAINT PATS team. So, on February 14, 1927, the Toronto MAPLE LEAFS were born wearing the blue color of the great Canadian skies, and white, representing the color of snow.

NICKNAME: "LEAFS"

VANCOUVER CANUCKS

Like many pro hockey cities, Vancouver had a team before the turn of the century, then lost it, only to return again to the National Hockey League decades later. The CREAMERY KINGS became the MILLION-AIRES, then the MAROONS. The inspiration for the latest Vancouver franchise nickname came from "Johnny Canuck," a term used to describe Canadian soldiers in World War II — and many Americans still believe it was meant as a put-down. Not true. Legend has it that the moniker Johnny Canuck was taken from a Canadian folk hero — a great logger who was a skater and hockey player in his spare time. The moniker actually began its professional life as the nickname for the Montreal CANADIENS hockey club. The Vancouver CANUCKS have gone through a number of changes since their 1970 debut, but all to do with costume. The original team color was Pacific Ocean blue. The logo was a hockey stick jutting into a rink. Known throughout the hockey world as the Vancouver UGLY SWEATERS, the club has worn an array of vulgar colors and uninspired designs on their jerseys. The CANUCKS made a radical change in 1978, introducing new team colors of yellow, red, and black with a stylized skate as their logo. So the team that played for the 1993-94 Stanley Cup looked good doing it.

WASHINGTON CAPITALS

Everyone knows that Washington D.C. is the capital of the U.S., so here's some history. Before the National Basketball Association's Golden State WARRIORS entered the Bay Area, Oakland had played host to another pro basketball club, the Oakland OAKS of the American Basketball Association. That franchise left town in 1970, however, becoming the Washington CAPITALS, which later folded. Management of the expansion National Hockey League Washington franchise knew this when they went looking for a nickname that would best represent the prominence of the region in which the team played. When Abe Pollin was awarded the NHL franchise in 1974, a contest was held from which the name CAPITALS was chosen.

NICKNAME: "CAPS"

Part 5
Colleges

AIR FORCE FALCONS

The Class of 1959, the first cadets to enter the Air Force Academy, selected FALCONS as the nickname and mascot of the Cadet Wing. The falcon's characteristics were believed to typify the Air Force as a combat service, including "high speed flight, powerful and graceful flight maneuvers, great courage, keen eyesight, alertness and noble bearing, and noble tradition." The Academy's first falcon mascot was named Mach 1 in October 1955, and this has been retained as the official name through the years, even though there usually are six to eight falcons in the mews at the Academy at any one time. They are cared for, trained, and flown by cadet handlers who volunteer their spare time to practice the ancient sport of falconry. The flying FALCON mascot can reach speeds exceeding 100 mph during dives upon its prey. Experts said falcons could not be trained to perform before large audiences, but Guinevere, the bird's pet name, has flown before more than 50,000 spectators at intercollegiate football games, soaring and diving throughout the stadium just above the crowd — the only demonstration of its type in college sports.

AKRON ZIPS

The association of the ZIPS with varsity sports began in 1925 when a University of Akron coed tried on a pair of Zippers. At the time, the University athletic teams were without a nickname but desired to fill the void. A contest was conducted on campus, and names were submitted by students, faculty, and alumni. Many suggestions were entered, including GOLDEN BLUE DEVILS, TIP TOPPERS, RUBBER-NECKS, HILLBILLIES, KANGAROOS, and CHEVALIERS, to name a few. The winner was decided on January 15, 1926, when Margaret Hamlin, a freshman, had found the answer with the ZIPPERS, and received a $10 prize. Hamlin's idea emerged from a $6 pair of rubber overshoes called Zippers, a brand name of the BF Goodrich Company — and the word went out to all concerned. On September 13, 1950, Athletic Director Kenneth "Red" Cochrane shortened the nickname to ZIPS. Some say this happened because of the opportunity for puns when the zipper became a popular addition to men's trousers. Others say the shorter name was easier to use. Whatever the case the nickname ZIPS has stuck. On May 1, 1953, ZIPPY the kangaroo was declared the official mascot.

ALABAMA-BIRMINGHAM BLAZERS

The University of Alabama-Birmingham became a full-fledged university in the late 1960s and began its athletic program in 1977. At that time a name-the-team contest was held in the *Kaleidoscope*, UAB's student newspaper. Among the thousands of entries received from students, faculty, and employees, nicknames such as BARONS (a tribute to the city's industrial heritage and the name of Birmingham's class AA baseball team), TITANS, and WARRIORS were finalists, as was the name BLAZERS. Whether it was a reference to the school's "trailblazing" in the medical field (UAB has a world-class medical center and is the home of one of the nation's top medical schools), the fact that UAB was blazing a new trail in the field of athletics, or the recent success of the Portland TRAIL BLAZERS, who had won the NBA title in 1977, BLAZERS won the contest and became the official nickname. The question "what is a BLAZER?" was a tricky one, however, and the question of how to represent the BLAZER concept would pose difficulties for many years. The original BLAZER mascot was a dragon, which was soon replaced by "Beauregard T. Rooster," who bore a striking resemblance to the famous San Diego Chicken. The Rooster character lasted until the advent of "Blaze," a fierce-looking Nordic Warrior, who lasted less than a year before succumbing to complaints about his violent image. In 1995 UAB unveiled the dragon again, still named "Blaze."

ALABAMA CRIMSON TIDE

Alabama's first football game was played in Birmingham on Friday afternoon, November 11, 1892, at the old Lakeview Park. The team beat opposition furnished by Professor Taylor's school and Birmingham high schools, 56-0. In early newspaper accounts of Alabama football, the team was simply listed as the VARSITY or the CRIMSON WHITE, after the school colors. The first nickname to become popular and used by the headline writers was the THIN RED LINE. This moniker was used until 1906. The name CRIMSON TIDE is supposed to have first been used by Hugh Roberts, former sports editor of the *Birmingham Age-Herald*. He used CRIMSON TIDE in describing an Alabama-Auburn game played in Birmingham in 1907, the last football contest between the two schools until 1948, when the series was resumed. The game, in which Auburn was a heavy favorite to win, was played in a sea of mud. But, evidently, the THIN RED LINE played a great game in the red mud and held Auburn to a 6-6 tie, thus establishing the name CRIMSON TIDE. Zipp Newman, former sports editor of the *Birmingham News*, probably popularized the name more than any other writer. Around 1930, an unusually large group of Alabama linemen earned the nickname the RED ELEPHANTS, a reference to their size and jersey color.

NICKNAMES: "RED ELEPHANTS"
     "THE TIDE"
     "BAMA"

ALASKA-ANCHORAGE SEAWOLF

Originally nicknamed the SOURDOUGHS, the University of Alaska-Anchorage adopted the SEAWOLF moniker in 1977. The name SEAWOLF represents a mystical sea creature whose origin is linked with the Tlingit (pronounced Clink-it) Indians of Southeastern Alaska. According to legend, anyone fortunate enough to view the SEAWOLF was subject to good luck. The exact nature or shape of the SEAWOLF, however, was left to the imagnation and thus the creature has been depicted in many forms throughout the years. The SEAWOLF of today was introduced in 1985. Created by Clark Mishler & Associates Company of Anchorage, in cooperation with a University committee, it represents an adaptation of a more traditional Alaskan totemic-like characterization of the mythical SEAWOLF. The most recent makeover of the SEAWOLF, a University-wide project, was taken on in order to update the look of the UAA mascot into a more recognizable and marketable image. The University has since trademarked the logo.

ALASKA-FAIRBANKS NANOOKS

The University of Alaska-Fairbanks was founded in 1917. During the early years, the athletic teams were called the POLAR BEARS, after the most dominant animal in the state of Alaska. When the basketball teams began traveling by air for their competitions (around 1970), the team's name was changed from POLAR BEARS to FLYING NANOOKS, which is the Athabascan Indian name for a Polar Bear. UAF believes that the FLYING part of the nickname was dropped within a couple of years as air travel became more prevalent. NANOOKS was chosen by a vote of the student body. Incredibly, each year the NANOOK athletic teams log more than 500,000 air miles, traveling to competitions throughout the

United States. The constant travel paid off in 1994 with the NCAA Rifle
Championship.

ARIZONA STATE SUN DEVILS

It was the summer of 1946 when someone uttered the words "SUN
DEVILS" for the first time. But who? That question has perplexed
Arizona State University historians for years. The nickname SUN DEV-
ILS is the third in the school's 110-year history. When the second Tempe
Normal football team opened play in 1889, the student body chose OWLS
for its moniker. And when Tempe Normal became Arizona State Teachers
College, OWLS became BULLDOGS. The *State Press*, the student newspaper, ran frequent appeals during the fall of 1946, urging the BULLDOG
be replaced by the new SUN DEVIL. On November 20, 1946, the student
body voted 819 to 196 to make the change. On November 20, says *The
Arizona Republic*, the student council made it official. The following day,
the first Arizona State team played as the SUN DEVILS. The problem of
drawing a SUN DEVIL was handed over to the late Bert Anthony, an artist
for Walt Disney. Anthony, creator of the defunct Stanford Indian symbol,
designed the current SUN DEVIL imp, Sparky. It is rumored that Sparky
was modeled after Walt Disney himself.

ARIZONA WILDCATS

Before 1914 the University of Arizona's teams were called the VAR-
SITY or Arizona RED AND BLUE. In 1914, a student correspondent for
the *Los Angeles Times*, covering the Arizona-Occidental football game on
the Occidental campus, penned the following phrase: "The Arizona men
showed the fight of wild cats." Back in Tucson, when the student body
read the dispatch of the game, a resolution was passed that henceforth,
Arizona athletic teams would be called the WILDCATS. The LA writer,
the late Bill Henry, was then a senior at Occidental and his reputation
grew as did the WILDCATS. He later became a columnist for the *Times*,
and a war correspondent and news analyst for NBC. Henry was honored
as the "Father of the Arizona WILDCATS" at the 50th Homecoming in
1964, when Arizona defeated Idaho, 14-7. Until the University fielded its
first football team in 1899, the school colors were sage green and silver.
However, the student manager that year, Quintus J. Anderson, was able to
strike a particularly good deal with a local merchant for game sweaters of
solid blue with red trim. He then wrote a request that the school colors be

changed, which was approved quickly. The colors have been cardinal red and navy blue ever since.

NICKNAME: "DESERT SWARM" (Football's Defense)

ARKANSAS RAZORBACKS

The history of Arkansas' athletic appearance began in 1894 when a contest was held on the University of Arkansas campus to select school colors, 23 years after classes were first held. Cardinal, a shade of deep red, was voted in over heliotrope, a shade of moderate purple. The school athletic teams carried the name of CARDINALS into battle for the next 15 years until the close of the 1909 season. Arkansas coach Hogo Bezdek referred to his team as "a wild band of RAZORBACK hogs" at a post-season rally following an unbeaten season. The name RAZORBACKS quickly caught on and the famous yell, "Whooo, Pig! Sooie!" was added in the 1920s. Arkansas didn't have a live mascot until the mid-1960s when some fans donated a pig, which was named Big Red I. That pig, and a second, Big Red II, were duroc hogs, each of which died of heart attacks. The Little Rock Zoo secured an Australian wild boar in 1975. Christened Big Red III, it served at games until it escaped from an animal exhibit near Eureka Springs in the summer of 1977. An irate farmer in Carroll County shot and killed Big Red III as it broke into an animal pen. Ragnar, a wild hog captured in South Arkansas by Leola farmer Bill Robinson, served as mascot in 1977. During Ragnar's reign it killed a coyote, a 450-pound domestic duroc and seven rattlesnakes. Ragnar died in 1978 of unknown causes, though no autopsy was performed. Big Red X currently serves as Arkansas' number one RAZORBACK. He makes the rounds before the games but no longer remains in the stadiums after kickoff.

ARKANSAS STATE INDIANS

The term INDIANS officially became Arkansas State's athletic nickname in 1931. The first nickname, in 1911, was the AGGIES, since Arkansas State University was the only agricultural school in Eastern Arkansas. For the same reason, FARMERS was also sometimes used as a moniker. In 1925 the name was changed to GORILLAS, but that one wasn't too readily accepted. WARRIORS was adopted in 1930, and it evolved to INDIANS one year later. INDIANS is taken from the heritage of the state of Arkansas — from the Osage tribe, which roamed northern Arkansas before the settlers arrived. During the 18th century, the Osage were at war with practically all other tribes of the plains, as well as with the woodland tribes. For that reason, ASUers look with pride to the fighting spirit which dwelled among the Indians of Northern Arkansas.

NICKNAME: "THE TRIBE"

ARKANSAS TECH WONDER BOYS

Founded in 1909 as the Second District Agricultural School, the name was changed to Arkansas Polytechnic College in 1925, and then to Arkansas Tech University in 1976. It was in 1919 that Arkansas Tech upset the highly favored Jonesboro AGGIES (now Arkansas State University) 14-0 behind a pair of 70-yard punt returns for touchdowns and two point-after kicks by 17-year-old quarterback John Tucker. The Jonesboro team had staked claim to the mystical state championship prior to the game. Henry Loesch, sports editor for the *Arkansas Gazette* in Little Rock, coined the name WONDER BOYS in complimenting the Tech team, then known as the AGGIES, in his post-game story. Tech's athletic teams have been known as the WONDER BOYS ever since.

AUBURN TIGERS

Through the years, Auburn teams have been known as both the WAR EAGLES and TIGERS. The news media often refer to an Auburn team as the WAR EAGLES or an Auburn player as a WAR EAGLE. In fact, when the TIGERS play a game on the road, there is often an article written in the local paper wondering why Auburn has three nicknames — the Auburn TIGERS, the Auburn WAR EAGLES, and the Auburn PLAINS-MEN. Officially, Auburn has one nickname, the TIGERS. WAR EAGLE is a battle cry, used by Auburn fans in the same manner Alabama fans yell "Roll TIDE!" and Arkansas fans yell "Sooie Pig!" According to legend, a spectator at the first Auburn-Georgia game in 1892 had with him a golden eagle which had been his pet for 20 years. The eagle broke free and began circling the field. As the eagle soared, the Auburn team began a steady march down the field, and the fans took on its presence as an omen for success. At the game's end, the eagle fell to the field and died! The nickname TIGERS comes from a line in Oliver Goldsmith's poem "The Deserted Village," published in May 1770, "where crouching TIGERS wait their hapless prey . . ." The term PLAINSMEN comes from a line in the same Goldsmith poem, "Sweet Auburn, loveliest (sic) village of the plain . . ." Since Auburn athletes were, in the early days, men from the

PLAINS, it was only natural for newspaper headline writers to shorten that to PLAINSMEN. Confused? Add this — WAR EAGLE VI, Auburn's golden eagle mascot, is named TIGER. As a side note we're told that (if he could read) standing at one end of a football field, an eagle can read the date on a penny at the other end of the field.

BALL STATE CARDINALS

In November of 1927 discontent emerged among the Ball Teachers College HOOSIEROONS about their nickname. Quickly, BTC's weekly newspaper sponsored a contest to decide a new name with the award of a $5 prize in gold (in 1927!) going to the winner. Some of the names considered included INDIANS, BALL PLAYERS, FLYING CRIMSON, THE EASTERNERS, BTC BRAVES, SCRAPPIN' TEACHERS, and BALL BULLETS. It was Professor Billy Williams, a loyal fan of the St. Louis CARDINALS baseball team, who commented that the "cardinal" on Rogers Hornsby's sweatshirt was "distinctive." The name was submitted, and in a student election, CARDINALS became the new nickname for Ball Teachers College athletics over other finalists INDIANS, DELA-WARES, and HOOSIEROONS. Since 1927, the name CARDINALS has remained synonymous with teams from Ball Teachers College, Ball State Teachers College, and finally Ball State University.

NICKNAME: "CARDS"

BAYLOR BEARS

It was almost San Jacinto University, and then Milam University, but Baylor University finally won out. When the Texas Baptist Education Society petitioned the Congress of the Republic of Texas for a charter to start a university, the first name suggested was San Jacinto, to recognize the victory that enabled the Texans to become an independent nation. Then it was changed to honor revolutionary hero Ben Milam. Just before the final vote of the Congress, the petitioners requested the university be named in honor of Judge R. E. B. Baylor. Republic of Texas president Anson Jones signed the Act of Congress on February 1, 1845, officially chartering it as Baylor University. The nickname could have been the BUF-FALO, ANTELOPE, FROG, FERRET, or BOOKWORM, but after 70 years without an official mascot, students in 1914 voted to name the BEAR the official "Patron Saint of all Baylordom," two-to-one over the BUF-FALO. School colors of green and gold were selected in 1897 when a student riding a train admired the passing wild spring dandelions. *Pro Ecclesia, pro Texana* (For Church, for Texas) became the school motto in 1851.

BOISE STATE BRONCOS

At the time, it didn't seem like a momentous decision — just a handful of athletes choosing the school colors and mascot for their tiny 80-student junior college. Little did they know that decades later, 20,000 football fans would be wearing all forms of blue and orange, and that the BRONCO symbol could have been seen everywhere from corporate offices to neighborhood bars. In 1932 the junior college was preparing to play more established teams like Gooding College and the College of Idaho, and students such as Preston Hale decided Boise needed a mascot and colors. Hale says he and his fellow students picked blue and orange because they wanted to come up with something different than their rivals' colors. "Boise Junior College was pretty small then. We didn't realize the impact it [the decision] would have," he says. "We were just eager to get a team together and start playing somebody." BRONCO was selected because in those days, ranches and cattle country surrounded Boise, and many of the students rode horses. Hale owns one priceless piece of memorabilia — the college's first BRONCO jacket. He'd bought a suede jacket, and art teacher Frances Westfall drew a Bronco on it. "It's about the same symbol you [Boise] use now," Hale says. French Canadian explorers named the city of Boise in the 1800s — "Les Bois" means trees. It is now known as the city of trees.

BOSTON COLLEGE EAGLES

One Rev. Edward McLaughlin, incensed at a Boston newspaper cartoon depicting the champion Boston College track team as a cat licking clean a plate of its rivals, penned a passionate letter to the student newspaper, the *Heights*, in 1920. "It is important that we adopt a mascot to preside at our pow-wows and triumphant feats. And why not the Eagle, symbolic of majesty, power and freedom? Its natural habitat is high places. Surely the *Heights* is made to order for such a selection." And so it was. The EAGLE was adopted as mascot and nickname that same year. The national attention that followed brought gifts of two live mascots, but one escaped and the other was injured attempting to. After a 40-year hiatus, another live bird named Marge — a combination of the first letters of the school colors maroon and gold — began attending home games. When she died in 1966, the status of the eagle as an endangered species made it undesirable for BC to replace Marge, and a costumed human has been cavorting along the sidelines ever since.

BOSTON TERRIERS

Not to be outdone by the Yale BULLDOG and the Princeton TIGER, Boston University students selected the Boston TERRIER as their football nickname and mascot shortly after the sport received official University recognition in 1917. The terrier is one of the few dogs originally bred in the United States. Interestingly enough, it was in 1869, the year the University was incorporated, that a Boston dog breeder crossed the English terrier with a bulldog and came up with this American favorite.

BOWDOIN POLAR BEARS

The POLAR BEAR moniker symbolizes the spirit of exploration, and refers specifically to the active role Bowdoin College played for well over 100 years in exploring the Arctic. Scores of Bowdoin faculty members, students, and alumni made trips to the Arctic on missions of exploration and of scientific research. The most famous of these explorers were Rear Admiral Robert E. Peary and Rear Admiral Donald B. MacMillan. Peary, class of 1877, became the first man to reach the North Pole on April 6, 1909. MacMillan, class of 1898, was Peary's chief assistant on that historic expedition, and he later made 26 voyages of his own to the Arctic. The move toward making the POLAR BEAR the mascot of Bowdoin was made by MacMillan, who, in 1915, presented a mounted polar bear to the college as a mascot. That polar bear is preserved in a large glass case in the lobby of Bowdoin's Morrell Gymnasium. A life-size statue of a polar bear stands in the Hyde Plaza on the Bowdoin campus. The statue, erected in 1937, was a gift from the class of 1912 as a memorial to its deceased members on the occasion of their 25th reunion. Sculptor Frederick George Richard Roth carved the base and statue. Incidentally, the nose of the polar bear on the statue points to the north.

BOWLING GREEN FALCONS

The 2001-02 athletic year marked the 75th anniversary of Bowling Green State University's nickname, the FALCONS. Before 1927, BG teams were called the NORMALS or TEACHERS. Ivan Lake, class of 1923, suggested the nickname after reading an article on falconry. Lake, at the time the managing editor and sports editor of the *Sentinel Tribune* in Bowling Green, proposed the name change because it fit headline space and because falcons were "the most powerful bird for their size and often attacked birds two or three times their size." Burnt orange and seal brown have been the school colors since the first year of classes — 1914. Former Cleveland BROWNS head coach Paul Brown liked the combination as well. Following a trip to Bowling Green in the 1940s, Brown used the same colors for his All-American Conference team. "Ay Ziggy Zoomba" is BG's unofficial fight song. Gil Fox, an Air Force bombardier stationed in Italy in World War II, brought a loose translation of a Zulu war chant back with him, and it has been in campus spirit history since its introduction in 1946.

BRIGHAM YOUNG COUGARS

Brigham Young University, founded in 1875, is part of the Church of Jesus Christ of Latter-Day Saints Educational System, serving more than a million people worldwide in education. The university traces its roots to Utah's rich pioneer heritage. The original school, Brigham Young Academy, was established on October 16, 1875, on a little over one acre of land in what is today downtown Provo. At that time, Brigham Young, the second president of the LDS Church, charged that all secular learning at the institution should be fused with teachings from the scriptures. The academy's high school and college curriculum improved and strengthened, and on October 23, 1903, the name was officially changed to Brigham Young University. In the search for a school mascot in 1923, the native Utah cougar was looked on favorably, primarily for its grace, agility, and great strength. It was felt that the mountain lion combined the qualities of its symbolic relatives, embodying the strength and majesty of the lion, the symbol of kings; the speed of a cheetah, the symbol of Pharaoh; the beauty of the leopard; and the cunningness of a panther. In 1923, David Rust, an alumnus of BYU and guide on the Colorado River, captured a mother cougar and her three kittens. Two of these kittens were brought to Provo and kept as University mascots, fixing the COUGARS nickname for athletic teams forever. The COUGARS won the national football championship in 1984, going 13-0.

CALIFORNIA GOLDEN BEARS

It was Charles Mills Gayley, a professor of English at the University of California at Berkley, who suggested the school's nickname. Originally called the BLUE AND GOLD in the 1860s, after the school colors, Gayley saw an opportunity for a name change when the track team travelled back east for an event with a blue banner (made of silk). On the banner was a gold-colored bear. Shortly thereafter, Gayley wrote a song entitled "Our Sturdy Golden Bear," based on the banner. The name stuck. That was in 1895, and they have been called the GOLDEN BEARS ever since. The team was also known as the BRUINS, sort of a subnickname, until UCLA's adoption of that moniker in the 1920s.

NICKNAME: "GO-BEARS"

CALIFORNIA STATE MARITIME KEELHAULERS

Playing in the California Coastal Conference, the California State University Maritime Academy's sports teams are proud to be the only athletic team in the world named after a form of punishment. On merchant ships, keelhauling was considered second only to hanging in terms of severity. Hands were tied to one end of a spar (the mast, yard, boom, or gaff), while feet were tied to the other end. The unfortunate captive was then dragged under the keel of the ship, and if he didn't drown, he was usually cut so badly by the barnacles that he bled to death, or died from infection. Founded by a special act of legislature in 1929, the California Nautical School was known informally as the SEA HORSES, and MARINERS. In 1973-74, the student council held a name-the-team contest, and considered names such as SEA HAWKS and SEA SNAKES. Then known as the California Maritime Academy, nicknamed "Keema" by students, they also considered CRABS for the alliteration. But the name KEELHAULERS, and all the notoriety that came with it, was the winning entry. The mascot is a pirate.

CALIFORNIA STATE NORTHRIDGE MATADORS

Dr. James Sefton, professor of History at Cal State-Northridge, said this about the nickname: "In January 1958, as a tiny branch campus among the orange groves looked ahead to its separate identity as San Fernando Valley State College, it also sought those ultimate hallmarks of collegiate distinction, a nickname and school colors of its own." Dr. Sefton writes that the student body was invited to suggest nominations with simple criteria: universal adaptability to teams, mascots, and yells, good taste, and being easily pronounceable. Among the nominees were ATOM SPLITTERS, CHMULTAPULTAPECS, DESERT RATS, HELIANS,

HUSTLERS, LLAMAS, MINOTAURS, OUTCASTS, SUNWORSHIP-PERS, VALKYRIES, and YOGIS. The five finalists were APOLLOS, FALCONS, MATADORS, RANCHEROS, and TITANS. On March 14, 1958, as announced at a semiformal dance called the "Blarney Ball," they became the MATADORS, who would wear red and white. In the spring elections of 1994, following the January 17 Northridge earthquake, a referendum was placed on the ballot to determine if the student body was interested in changing the nickname to QUAKES, or any other nickname. The final vote? MATADORS 1,334; QUAKES 392; and anything else, a paltry 172.

CENTRAL FLORIDA KNIGHTS OF PEGASUS

In 1970 at the University of Central Florida, "Operation Mascot" yielded the name KNIGHTS OF PEGASUS, a link to the university seal, which features the winged horse of Greek mythology. Other schools in the Trans America Athletic Conference include Southeastern Louisiana University and its LIONS, a name provided by a center on the football team in the 1930s, and the Mercer University BEARS, borrowed from a bemused spectator who asked "Whence cometh that bear?" while watching a brawny Mercer lineman, with long hair and a handlebar moustache, charge onto the field. The Jacksonville State football team chose the new nickname GAMECOCKS in the early 1970s, in honor of the bird's fighting spirit, replacing EAGLE OWLS; formerly known as the SUNBLAZERS, the Florida International University GOLDEN PANTHER nickname was adopted in 1987, with its golden color distinguishing it from other similar mascots; and the College of Charleston adopted the alliterative COUGARS nickname in 1970.

CENTRAL MICHIGAN CHIPPEWAS

The nickname CHIPPEWAS reflects the rich heritage of the Mid-Michigan region, but has not always been applied to Central Michigan University athletes. The first official nickname was the DRAGONS, which appeared in 1925. The student newspaper began calling the Central athletes BEARCATS three years later, which lasted until 1942 when student and faculty dissent led to CHIPPEWAS. The nickname actually has changed fewer times than the school name. Central opened its doors in 1892 as Central Michigan Normal and Business Institute. Central Michigan Normal School was initiated in 1896 along with the first football team and the unofficial nickname NORMALITES for all the students. The school offered its first four-year degree program in 1919. Subsequent name changes include Central State Teachers College (1927), Central Michigan College of Education (1941), Central Michigan College (1955), and the present CMU (1959).

CHAMINADE SILVERSWORDS

Chaminade University of Honolulu athletic teams are called the SILVERSWORDS. This is the name of a rare plant found on Haleakala, a dormant volcano on the neighboring island of Maui. The flowers of this exotic plant are said to resemble the Cross, the symbol of the Christian faith. The silversword grows from 4 to 20 years before it produces a single one- to nine-foot flower! The basketball team is also synonymous with the nickname the GIANT KILLERS. The name comes from Chaminade's series of great basketball upsets, including what is possibly the greatest college hoops upset in history, the 1982 defeat of Ralph Sampson and the No. 1 nationally ranked University of Virginia CAVALIERS.

CINCINNATI BEARCATS

There are at least three stories as to how University of Cincinnati teams earned their nickname of BEARCATS. One version has the moniker a result of a 1913 cartoon of UC lineman Leonard K. "Teddy" Baehr standing on the field next to a Stutz Bearcat automobile. Another theory traces the nickname's origin to another sports cartoon that followed the 1914 UC-Kentucky game which showed a bearlike, catlike animal harassing a wildcat. A third story holds that in a 1912 newspaper account of a UC game, *Cincinnati Enquirer* sports editor Jack Ryder stated that "the team played like bearcats." Beyond that speculation it is known that the bearcat is a native animal of Southeast Asia, a carnivorous mammal known to be ferocious if provoked. The bearcat, also known as a binturong, is a relative to the mongoose. UC's athletic teams sport a logo in which the letter "C" has been converted into a paw.

CLEMSON TIGERS

In Thomas Green Clemson's will, he bequeathed the Fort Hill plantation and a considerable sum from his personal assets for the establishment of the Clemson Agricultural College of South Carolina. Opened in 1893, after Clemson's death, the college was an all-male military school until 1955 when the change was made to "civilian" status. In 1964 the college was renamed Clemson University. William J. Latimer, a 1904 Clemson grad, suggested that Professor Walter Merritt Riggs, who coached Clemson's first football team in 1895, planted the TIGER nickname seed, saying this about his players: "Due to the lack of helmets and head protection they wore long hair. These long manes might have gained them the name of LIONS had it not been for the orange and purple striped jerseys and stockings that resembled TIGERS. The latter nickname seemed to stick." Latimer's findings are substantiated by the fact Coach Riggs had played football at Auburn (nicknamed TIGERS) whose colors were orange and blue.

COASTAL CAROLINA CHANTICLEERS

In Chaucer's *Canterbury Tales*, more specifically, the "Nun's Priest's Tale," we become acquainted with the Chanticleer. It was a proud and fierce rooster who dominated the barnyard. "For crowing there was not his equal in all the land. His voice was merrier than the merry organ that plays in church, and his crowing from his resting place was more trustworthy than a clock. His comb was redder than fine coral and turreted like a castle wall, his bill was black and shone like a jet, and his legs and toes were like azure. His nails were whiter than the lily and his feathers were like burnished gold." Additionally, he was greatly feared and mightily respected by all. CHANTICLEER was chosen to be Coastal Carolina's mascot after a group of Coastal students and their English professor brought up the idea of a new mascot in the late 1960s. At the time, Coastal athletic teams were known as the TROJANS. CHANTICLEER gave Coastal a mascot which resembled big brother South Carolina's GAMECOCK, but still gave the college its own identity.

COLBY WHITE MULES

Colby College historian Ernest Cummings Marriner wrote: "The POLAR BEAR of Bowdoin and the BLACK BEAR of the University of Maine antedated the Colby WHITE MULE by several years. In his senior year, Joseph Coburn Smith was editor of the Colby *Echo*, just as Frank Johnson had been 33 years earlier. Like Johnson, Joe was interested in the honest promotion of athletics. On November 7, 1923, Joe published an editorial suggesting that, because Colby football teams so often upset predictions of the newspaper dopesters, Colby no longer appeared as a 'dark horse,' but ought to be symbolized by a WHITE MULE! A group of students got busy, located a white mule on Kennebec farm, borrowed the animal for the Bates game on Armistice Day in 1923, and placed the animal, properly caparisoned in blue and gray, at the head of the band and student body as they marched onto the field." From dark horse to WHITE MULES — Colby won.

COLORADO BUFFALOES

Prior to 1934, Colorado University athletic teams usually were referred to as the SILVER AND GOLD, but other nicknames sometimes used included SILVER HELMETS, YELLOW JACKETS, HORNETS, ARAPAHOS, BIG HORNS, GRIZZLIES, and FRONTIERSMEN. The campus newspaper announced a contest in the fall of 1934, with a $5 prize going to the author of the winning selection. Claude Bates of New Madrid, Missouri, and James Proffitt of Cincinnati, Ohio, were co-winners for the prize as both submitted BUFFALOES as their entry. Athletics Director Harry Carlson, graduate manager Walter Franklin, and Kenneth Bundy of the SILVER AND GOLD were the judges. Through the years, synonyms which quickly came into use included BISONS, BUFFS, THUNDERING HERD, STAMPEDING HERD, GOLDEN AVALANCHE, and GOLDEN BUFFALOES. The University of Colorado possesses perhaps the most unique mascot in all of intercollegiate athletics — an actual buffalo named "Ralphie." The buffalo first appeared in 1943, three weeks after the contest to select an official nickname was completed. It is truly one of the special sights that exists anywhere in college or professional sports, especially for opposing teams, who often stop in their tracks watching the massive buffalo round the end zone and head directly at their sideline.

NICKNAME: "THE BUFFS"

COLORADO STATE RAMS

Unknown even to many Colorado State University fans is that CAM, the live ram mascot's nickname since 1946, is an abbreviated acronym for Colorado State College of Agricultural and Mechanical Arts, the school's original name. At that time, the University athletic teams were called the AGGIES, an agricultural reference. While the AGGIES, team mascots included "Peanuts," a homely little English bulldog. The unfortunate animal was poisoned in 1917, and was replaced by a second mascot in 1919. This black bear marched proudly in parades and was a regular attendant at football games. His job was finished in the late 1920s, and it wasn't until "Buck" arrived in 1946 that CSU had another mascot. This ram provoked a slight nickname change to AGGIE RAMS, eventually shortened to simply RAMS. Historical records do not indicate exactly how many rams have preceded the present mascot, but all save the first have been named CAM.

CONNECTICUT HUSKIES

The HUSKIES nickname was chosen in 1934 after the editor of the student newspaper questioned why the University of Rhode Island had a mascot (a ram) and UConn did not. Soon it was suggested that the HUSKY would be the perfect mascot because of the "frigid hills" of the Storrs campus. The actual dog which symbolizes the mascot is named Jonathan after Connecticut's Revolutionary War-era governor, Jonathan Trumbull. The first dog, which was brown and white, boasted a great-grandfather who journeyed to the North Pole with Admiral Robert E. Peary in 1909. It is buried on the campus next to the steps of old Whitney Hall across from the Storrs Congregational Church.

DELAWARE FIGHTING BLUE HENS

The University of Delaware's FIGHTING BLUE HENS is a name that stretches back over 200 years of Delaware history. On December 9, 1775, the Continental Congress resolved that a military battalion was to be raised from the lower three counties along the Delaware River. The second company of the Delaware Regiment was composed of men from Kent County and was under the command of Captain John Caldwell, who was an avid fan and owner of gamecocks. The militia often amused themselves by staging cockfights with these birds, which were of a breed known as the Kent County BLUE HEN, having some BLUE plumage. These BLUE HEN chickens quickly developed a reputation for ferocity and fighting success, as did Captain Caldwell's men, nicknamed the Blue Hen Chicken company. In 1939 the Blue Hen Chicken was named Delaware's official state bird. The University of Delaware's College of Agriculture maintains a breeding group of the Blue Hen Chickens on its campus farm. The mascot's name is "YoUDee."

NICKNAME: "HENS"

DICKINSON RED DEVILS

The nickname RED DEVILS was first applied to a Dickinson College — playing in the Eastern College Athletic Conference — football team in the 1930 season. Despite losing by a 27-6 score to a heavily favored George Washington University squad, Dickinson impressed a sportswriter from the Washington, D.C. area with its fighting spirit and he gave it the name that it still bears today. In 1936, the Dickinson Board of Athletic Control changed the name to COLONIALS, but a student petition sent to college president Fred Corson convinced him to sanction the name RED DEVILS as the official college moniker. The colors red and white were Dickinson's colors from the beginning. The colors had been adopted soon after the Revolutionary War. In 1903, Dickinson switched from red and white uniforms to black uniforms with white and red stripes because the color on the red uniforms would run when wet! They switched back 25 years later.

DUKE BLUE DEVILS

What would have been different about Princeton had the University accepted an endowment from the tobacco baron James Buchanan Duke? Its name! All Princeton needed to do to get the tobacco dough was change its name to Duke. Not surprisingly, the regents turned down the offer and Duke took his business to Durham, North Carolina, where a small institution called Trinity College was transformed into Duke University. Only then did the issue of a team nickname come up BLUE DEVILS. First used by the *Chronicle* newspaper in 1922-23, the nickname BLUE DEVILS was derived from the French BLUE DEVILS. This originated with the nickname given the French Infantry in World War I. Then the name was applied to a French crack alpine team which wore a striking blue uniform with a blue beret. Fight songs include "Fight BLUE DEVIL," "Dear Old Duke," and "Blue and White" — a song in honor of the school colors.

NICKNAME: "DEVILS"

EAST CAROLINA PIRATES

The PIRATE, a symbol of East Carolina University and its athletic teams, was adopted from the legend and lore of coastal North Carolina and was a natural choice for the nickname when intercollegiate athletics began at the school more than 57 years ago. Pirates, fearful and colorful, were prominent in North Carolina's colonial period. The state's Outer Banks, which jut far out into the Atlantic Ocean, were ideal hideouts for these legendary gangsters of the high seas. Many had homes and families in small villages along the Carolina coast. East Carolina University's interest in pirates and sea lore began in 1934. That year, the Tecoan, the yearbook for what was then East Carolina Teachers College, carried PIRATES as its theme. The pages were filled with paintings and sketches of patched-eye figures, tall ships, and buried treasure. The book referred to the tales of the infamous "Teachy the Pirate" often told by natives in the nearby historic town of Bath. The bigger-than-life PIRATE cartoon figure enjoyed by East Carolina University fans today is a 1983 creation. At first, this swaggering, tough-guy creation was called "Pee Dee," named after a river that extends through parts of North and South Carolina. In the mid-1970s, the defensive players on the PIRATES' football team were called the WILD DOGS because the players performed like a vicious pack of them. By the way, a live wildcat was the mascot in 1930-31!

EASTERN MICHIGAN EAGLES

The EAGLES name was officially adopted on May 22, 1991, when the Eastern Michigan University Board of Regents voted to replace the existing HURONS nickname and logo with the new one. EMU originally went by the nicknames NORMALITES and MEN FROM YPSI and various other titles down through the years before HURONS was adopted in 1929. The HURONS first came into being as the result of a contest sponsored by the Men's Union. Two students, Gretchen Borst and George Hanner, submitted the name. Hanner was working at the Huron Hotel at the time and was no doubt as much influenced by his place of employment as by the Huron Indian tribe. The runner-up in that contest was PIONEERS. EMU began investigating the appropriateness of its HURON Indian logo after the Michigan Department of Civil Rights issued a report in 1988 suggesting that all schools using such logos drop them, indicating that the use of Native American names, logos, and mascots for athletic teams promoted racial stereotypes. At that time, four colleges, 62 high schools, and 33 junior high/middle schools in Michigan used Indian names. The EMU Board of Regents voted to replace the HURONS name with EAGLES, taken from three recommendations from a committee charged with supplying a new name. The other two finalists were GREEN HORNETS and EXPRESS.

ENDICOTT POWER GULLS

The campus of Endicott College, a senior college in Beverly, Mass-achusetts, with its enrollment of 800 students, is located on the Atlantic

Ocean. This geographical reality was the primary reason a student vote in the early 1980s turned to the sea for the school's first official nickname, and the unique POWER GULLS was the end result. Other considered and rejected names included RIP TIDE and the CLIPPERS. School colors are also water-related: royal blue, kelly green, and white.

NICKNAME: "GULLS"

FLORIDA GATORS

Austin Miller, a native of Gainesville, Florida, was enrolled in the University of Virginia in the fall of 1907, and was visited by his father, Phillip. The elder Miller owned a combination drug and stationery store in Gainesville, a popular rendezvous for university students. While in Charlottesville, Virginia, visiting his son, the father decided to order some college pennants and banners for his Florida shop from the Mitchie Company, which was engaged in the manufacturing of such items — but found the University of Florida had no emblem! The name ALLIGATORS occurred to young Austin as a suitable nickname, both because the Mitchie manager said no other school had adopted it and because the alligator was native to Florida. Problem was, the Mitchie manager had never seen an alligator so he didn't believe he could design one. Austin volunteered to find a suitable picture of a GATOR, and located one in the library of the University of Virginia. The first appearance of the alligator emblem for UF was in Miller's store in 1908. In 1965 researchers at the University of Florida used the school's football team as guinea pigs to test a special beverage they had developed to combat dehydration and enhance athletic performance. The players liked the stuff, which was christened Gatorade, named after the university's mascot.

FLORIDA STATE SEMINOLES

The SEMINOLES nickname was chosen by students in 1947, when Florida State College for Women became Florida State University. The brand new football team played its first game without benefit of a symbol. So, a contest was held on campus, and numerous nicknames poured in, including the FLEAS, TALLYWHACKERS, GOLD DIGGERS, and PINHEADS. According to FSU history professor James P. Jones, the name SEMINOLES was selected from a final list of six that included the GOLDEN FALCONS, STATESMEN, SENATORS, CRACKERS, and INDIANS. But writer Bill McGrotha's account states that the other finalists were

CRACKERS, FIGHTING WARRIORS, REBELS, STATESMEN, and TARPONS. The Seminoles are a tribe of North American Indians who left their traditional homeland in Georgia after separating from the Creek during the 18th century to live independently in Florida. Many escaped black slaves took refuge with the Seminoles. When the Seminoles obstructed the advance of white landseekers and refused to return slaves, Andrew Jackson pushed them farther south in the First Seminole War (1817-18). In 1819 the United States purchased Florida from Spain, and pressure from whites increased. The treaty of Payne's Landing (1832) called for the removal of the Seminoles, but the tribe resisted in the Second Seminole War (1835-42) under the leadership of Osceola, Wildcat, and Halek. At last, beaten and destitute, 4,000 of the 4,300 Seminoles moved west to Indian Territory. They became one of the so-called Five Civilized Tribes, and many tribespeople gradually lost their Indian identity. Those who stayed in Florida, however, living on three reservations near Lake Okeechobee, retained many of their traditional ways. In the late 1980s, about 1,500 SEMINOLES lived in Florida and about 4,000 in Oklahoma. Florida State, founded in 1857, wears the SEMINOLES nickname with pride, as well as its garnet and gold colors, and the symbols of Chief Osceola and Renegade.

NICKNAME: "NOLES"

FRESNO STATE BULLDOGS

Late in the 1921 season, student body president Warren Moody and friends were continually greeted outside the main Fresno State campus building by a white bulldog. The dog adopted the group and they decided to make him the mascot. Arids Walker made the motion to adopt BULLDOGS as the official nickname in a student body meeting. It was November 21, 1921, that the *Morning Republican* first referred to Fresno State as the BULLDOGS. The colors evolved out of an argument by women from Fresno Normal School and men from Fresno Junior College. The women were seeking blue and white versus the men's red and white. A compromise was struck with the school adopting red and blue with the red later changed to Cardinal. Fresno State's fan following is commonly referred to as the RED WAVE, which was coined by *Fresno Bee* sportswriter Ron Orozco in the early 1980s.

GEORGETOWN HOYAS

Georgetown was founded in 1789, the same year that President George Washington took office. Its colors are blue and gray, adopted at the end of the Civil War to signify the union of the North and South. In the days when all Georgetown students were required to study Greek and Latin, the University's teams were nicknamed the STONEWALLS. A student, using Greek and Latin terms, started the cheer "HOYA Saxa." HOYA is from the Greek word "hojos," meaning "such a" or "what a." The neuter plural of this word is "hoia," which agrees with the neuter plural of the Latin word "saxa," meaning rocks; thus we have "hoya," substituting the "y" for an "i," which translates into "What Rocks!" The name proved popular and the term HOYAS was eventually adopted for all Georgetown teams. The team's mascot is Jack the Bulldog, which is a Georgetown student in a bulldog suit. One of Jack's predecessors, an actual terrier named Stubby, was a decorated war hero. You see, Stubby served 18 months on the front during World War I. His efforts included saving his regiment from surprise mustard attacks, finding wounded soldiers, and literally capturing a German spy by the seat of his pants. Among many famous Georgetown alumni are former President Bill Clinton and John J. Sirica, the judge who presided over the Watergate trials.

NICKNAME: "G'TOWN"

GEORGIA BULLDOGS

The University of Georgia's first mascot for its first football game against Auburn, on February 22, 1892, in Atlanta, was a goat. Old newspaper clippings say the goat wore a black coat with red UG letters on each side. He also had a hat with ribbons all down his high horns, and the Auburn fans yelled throughout the game, "Shoot the billy-goat!" Two years later, in 1894, the BULLDOGS mascot was a solid white female bull terrier owned by a student, the late Charles Black of Atlanta. Then came the BULLDOG mascots, beginning with a couple of brindled English bulldogs. Butch served from 1947 till 1951, and was succeeded from 1951 till 1956 by Mike. Then came the famous "Uga" lineage. The solid white English bulldogs have served as faithful mascots since 1955, and have now reached "Uga V." The BULLDOG moniker was adopted for its reputation and characteristics of "stubbornness and strong-jawed, unrelenting commitment."

NICKNAME: "THE DOGS"

GEORGIA TECH YELLOWJACKETS

The YELLOW JACKET nickname and mascot are two of the most beloved trademarks of Georgia Tech athletic teams, but many conflicting accounts exist as to the origins and beginnings of the YELLOWJACKET. One thing that is clear, however, is that the nickname did not grow out of the familiar six-legged insect. Rather, the insect mascot, known as "Buzz," grew out of the nickname. As far as can be determined, the first reference to Tech students as YELLOWJACKETS appeared in the *Atlanta Constitution* newspaper in 1905, and came into common usage at the time Historians say the name, spelled as one word, was first used to describe supporters who attended Tech athletic events, dressed in yellow coats and jackets. The actual mascot was conceived at a later date, still undetermined. Other common nicknames which have applied to Georgia Tech teams include ENGINEERS, which is still used by some writers; the TECHS, the first known nickname, which was phased out sometime around 1910; and the BLACKSMITH, which was common between 1902 and 1904, and is thought to be an invention of sportswriters at the time. The GOLDEN TORNADO is another former nickname, thought to be created by sportswriters when coach John Heisman led Tech to its first national championship in football in 1917. Tech was the first team from the South to earn the honor bestowed by the International News Service, and any team thereafter which approached the same level of excellence was referred to as the GOLDEN TORNADO. The nickname was used as late as 1929, when Tech defeated California in the Rose Bowl. And it was in 1891, two years before Georgia Tech fielded its first football team, that the colors white and gold were voted on at a mass student meeting.

NICKNAME: "RAMBLING WRECK"

HARVARD CRIMSON

Founded in 1636, Harvard University is the oldest institution of higher learning in the United States. This storied house of academia is a member of the Ivy League, along with Brown, Cornell, Columbia, Dartmouth, Princeton, Yale, and the University of Pennsylvania — a clique of northeastern universities identified with academic achievement and social prestige. Their only official association is on the football field, where they have played mostly each other since 1900. The Ivy League once implied gridiron valor as well as the right academic stuff; now their teams are relatively weak, though in some cases ardently supported. Perhaps the most important date in Harvard football history occurred on May 6, 1875. That was the day Harvard undergraduates held a plebiscite on the University's color and chose CRIMSON. As was often the case in the last century, the team color became also the team name. Had the vote gone the other way, Harvard athletic teams would be known as the MAGENTA, the student newspaper still would be named — as it was then — the MAGENTA, and the fight song might be "The MAGENTA in triumph flashing." Instead, CRIMSON was supported by a large majority and became the name not only of the newspaper but of Harvard's representatives on the athletic field.

HAWAII RAINBOW WARRIORS

Before 1923, University of Hawaii teams were nicknamed the DEANS. Then, in the final game of the 1923 season, UH head coach "Otto" Klum's squad upset Oregon State 7-0 at Moiliili Field. During the game, a rainbow appeared over the field. Reporters started calling UH teams the RAINBOWS, and the tradition began that Hawaii would not lose a game if a rainbow appeared. Rainbows, however, had magical powers long before football came to the islands. Hawaiian chiefs considered them sacred and used them as signs of a chief's presence. A rainbow hovering over a newborn child indicated that he was of a godlike rank. The WARRIOR holds an honored place in Hawaiian history for it was Kamehameha I, the great warrior, and his armies that united the Hawaiian Islands. The Hawaiians expected the warrior to display great strength, courage, skill, and a fighting spirit. Although it wasn't until 1974 that UH football adopted the nickname RAINBOW WARRIORS, the University's use of the name goes back a number of years. Only the football team is dubbed the RAINBOW WARRIORS. All other men's teams are the RAINBOWS.

HOUSTON COUGARS

Athletic teams at the University of Houston have been called the COUGARS since 1927, the year the school was founded as a junior college. One of the original faculty members, John R. Bender, tutored a volunteer football squad and named them the COUGARS. Bender came to Houston after serving as the head football coach at Washington State University, which also had the nickname of COUGARS. The name must've been contagious, because he brought it to Houston, saying he liked the mountain lion as a symbol of courage and tenacity. The school became a four-year university in 1932. The student newspaper adopted the name in 1935 and when the University of Houston began sponsoring intercollegiate athletics in 1946, COUGARS was adopted as the name for athletic teams. Houston has not used a live mascot since 1988, when the mountain lion Shasta V (shortened form of she-has-to) reigned over COUGAR athletic events. The cougar's name beat out finalists SPIRITANA and RAGUOC — cougar spelled backwards. Scarlet and white, the colors on General Sam Houston's family shield, were adopted in 1938.

IDAHO VANDALS

The silver and gold VANDALS first took to the court around 1918 when the University of Idaho basketball team had the reputation of destroying their opponents. The press in the Northwest took up the cause, initially referring to the team as the WRECKING CREW. Vandals was the name of an East Germanic tribe that ravaged Gaul, Spain, and North Africa, and sacked Rome in 455 A.D. So effective were these Vandals, their name became a word in the dictionary describing a person who destroys with malice! It was in 1921, with the encouragement of College of Liberal Arts Dean Edward M. Hulme and school sports editor Lloyd McCarty, that VANDALS became the official nickname of all University athletic teams. The mascot is nicknamed "Joe Vandal." A large silver and gold VANDAL head graces the front of Student Union in glowing neon lights and the burly, bewhiskered individual can be seen throughout the campus. Members of the Idaho rodeo team are called the VANDAL RIDERS. In 1996, the VANDALS fielded their first football team in Division I-A.

ILLINOIS COLLEGE BLUEBOYS

Tom Rowland, former football star for the Illinois College BLUE-BOYS, was drafted by the Green Bay PACKERS in 1968. There's a story that when he stood on his chair in the training room one night and prepared to make the traditional rookie speech, he panicked. "I stood up and shouted, 'I am Tom Rowland of the Illinois College TIGERS,'" Rowland recalled. "Hall of Fame player Ray Nitschke was sitting there looking at me with no teeth. There was no way I was saying BLUEBOYS." Reflecting on the incident in 1993, Rowland was the track and wrestling coach back at the college, and was trying to change the nickname to the FIGHTING BLUE. But since the moniker comes from the days when Illinois students fought in the Civil War and were known as Blue Boys, the traditionalists at this oldest school in the state, established in 1829, will not bend.

ILLINOIS FIGHTING ILLINI

The symbol of Chief Illiniwek, originally dressed in an authentic outfit made by a Sioux woman, has stirred pride and respect at the University of Illinois since 1926. Illiniwek (pronounced "ill-EYE-nih-wek") was the name of the loose confederation of Algonquin tribes that once lived in the region. The French changed the ending to "ois" in naming what became the state of Illinois. Illiniwek means "they are men" and former Illinois football coach Robert Zappke is believed to have suggested calling the UI symbol "Chief Illiniwek." According to sports information at Illinois, the term ILLINI is simply a shorter form of Illiniwek, and FIGHTING ILLI-NI implies an aggressive behavior on the field. In 1930, an Indian trader helped the school make contact with an old Sioux woman, who created an authentic Chief Illiniwek outfit to be worn by the mascot.

INDIANA HOOSIERS

Ask a HOOSIER what one looks like or from where the name sprung and you're likely to draw a blank stare. Historians have unearthed many theories but find agreement in few of them. One that seems to have more validity than most, cites a Samuel HOOSIER, who, in 1825, was a contractor on the Louisville & Portland (Ohio Falls) Canal. He appreciated the "better workers" from the Indiana side of the river, and these men later brought home a proud new moniker, the HOOSIERS, named after their boss. Another, less authentic version was that of Col. Jacob Lehmanoski. This Polish officer, who had served with Napoleon before settling in Indiana, delivered a series of stirring lectures in which he extolled the courage and endurance of the Hussars, which he pronounced as HOOSIER. According to the story, the natives adopted it for themselves. There are others who say it originated from the habit of travellers hailing a cabin for a night's lodging as they approached. The cautious pioneer would, before unlatching the door, call out, "Who's there?" It's only a step through frontier enunciation from there to HOOSIER. And there's that light-hearted explanation stemming from the rowdy, brawling nature of the early settlers. It is credited to Indiana's James Whitcomb Riley and no doubt was Riley's whimsy. He claimed they were vicious fighters who not only gouged and scratched but also frequently bit off noses and ears. "Whose ear?" was a common remark when sweeping up afterward. Others? Indiana Governor Joseph Wright claimed the term derived from HOOSA, an Indian word for corn. The dictionary tells us that HOOJEE means tramp, but no HOOSIER would buy that. HOOZER was an English dialect word meaning "anything unusually great." Historian Jacob P. Dunn wrote that the word was a term common in the South, applied to uncouth persons. Regardless, HOOSIERS can take comfort in the fact that it carries a very positive and inspirational connotation these days — thanks to the storied teams from Indiana University.

IOWA HAWKEYES

The University of Iowa borrowed its athletic nickname from the state of Iowa many years ago. The name HAWKEYE was originally applied to a hero in a fictional novel, *The Last of the Mohicans*, written by James Fenimore Cooper. In the book Cooper had the Delaware Indians bestow the name on a white scout who lived and hunted with them. In 1838, 12 years after the book was published, people in the territory of Iowa acquired the nickname, chiefly through the efforts of Judge David Rorer of Burlington and James G. Edwards of Fort Madison. Edwards, editor of the *Fort Madison Patriot*, moved his paper to Burlington in 1843 and renamed it the *Burlington HAWK-EYE*. The two men continued their campaign to popularize the name and were rewarded when territorial officials gave it their formal approval. The HAWKEYE nickname gained a tangible symbol in 1948 when a cartoon character, later to be named "Herky the Hawk," was hatched. The creator was Richard Spencer III, instructor of journalism. The impish hawk was an immediate hit and he acquired a name through a statewide contest staged by the athletic department. John Franklin, a Belle Plain alumnus, was the man who suggested Herky. Since his birth more than 30 years ago, Herky has symbolized Iowa athletics and epitomized University life. He even donned a military uniform during the Korean War, and became the insignia of the 124th Fighter Squadron. During the mid-1950s, Herky came to life at a football game as the Iowa mascot with a black, leather head and gold felt feathers. Since then, Herky has become a familiar figure at HAWKEYE athletic events.

IOWA STATE CYCLONES

On September 28 of 1895, the Iowa State Agricultural College swept into Illinois to play a tough Northwestern football squad. The next day a *Chicago Tribune* headline proclaimed, "Iowa Cyclone Devastates Northwestern, 36-0." According to Iowa State historian Earle D. Ross in his 1943 book, *History of Iowa State College*, a *Chicago Tribune* sportswriter reported: "Northwestern might as well have tried to play football with an Iowa cyclone as with the Iowa team it met yesterday. At the end of fifty minutes of play the big husky farmers from Iowa's Agricultural College had rolled up 36 points, while the 15 yard line was the nearest Northwestern got to Iowa's goal." The analogy used by the Chicago sportswriter stuck and eventually became the official nickname for all Iowa State sports teams.

IRVINE ANTEATERS

Playing in the Big West, the advent of the ANTEATER at the University of California at Irvine was in 1965, the year that the University opened. As a fledgling intercollegate athletics program was initiated, the search for an official nickname began. Pat Glasgow and Bob Ernst, two water polo players, are regarded as the main instigators for the campaign to select the ANTEATER as mascot, with some inspiration from the Johnny Hart comic strip "B.C." The two student-athletes, along with the marketing creativity of fellow student Schuyler Hadley Bassett III, organized an intense promotional effort. By student election time only the ANTEATERS, EAGLES, UNICORNS, GOLDEN BEARS, and SEAHAWKS had obtained the required 100 signatures to be included on the ballot. The ANTEATERS emerged victorious in the final tally with 55.9 percent of the vote. Bassett borrowed the war cry "Zot!" from the Anteater in the "B.C." comic strip and established his own fraternity, Zeta Omega Ta. The successful campaign led to an article on the nickname in an issue of *Sports Illustrated* and into the news-commentary segment of the wel-known Huntley-Brinkley newscast. To this day, the ANTEATERS remain popular, being listed as one of the top five nicknames in national polls conducted by ESPN and Collegiate Directories, Inc.

KANSAS JAYHAWKS

The word JAYHAWK was first used in present-day Kansas around 1858. The name combines two birds: the bluejay, a noisy, quarrelsome thing known to rob nests; and the sparrow hawk, a stealthy hunter. The message here: Do not turn your back on this bird. JAYHAWK was originally associated with robbing, looting, and general lawlessness in the Kansas Territory. During the Civil War it took on new meaning. In 1861 surgeon Dr. Charles R. Jennison used it when he was commissioned as a colonel by Kansas governor Charles Robinson, and charged with raising a regiment of cavalry. Jennison called his regiment the Independent Mounted Kansas JAYHAWKERS, although it was officially the First Kansas Cavalry and later the Seventh Kansas Regiment. During the Civil War the word JAYHAWK became associated with the spirit of comrade-ship associated with efforts to keep Kansas a free state. Following the war, most Kansans were proud to be called JAYHAWKERS. By 1886, the University of Kansas had adopted the mythical bird as part of the KU yell.

KANSAS STATE WILDCATS

Prior to 1915, Kansas State Agricultural College teams had been known as the AGGIES. But the nickname WILDCATS was given to the football team in 1915 by head coach John "Chief" Bender because of what he called the squad's "fighting spirit." The moniker was changed to FARMERS in 1916, but head coach Charles Bachman switched back to the WILDCAT nickname in 1920. Kansas State itself is referred to in many different shortened versions. The most popular is K-STATE, which is used by alums, friends, and journalists from coast to coast. Fans are called CATBACKERS, or PURPLE PRIDE, in reference to the team's only official color. The tradition of "Touchdown," the bobcat mascot, began in 1922, but the creature no longer attends the games. Touchdown XII resides at Manhattan's Sunset Zoo.

NICKNAME: "CATS"

KENT GOLDEN FLASHES

Originally Kent Normal School, the origin of the Kent State University nickname GOLDEN FLASHES has been a topic of debate. According to documentation in Phillip Shriver's book, *The Years of Youth*, widely regarded as historically correct, it is noted that in a letter to Linda Baugeman, dated August 6, 1959, Merle Wagoner recalled that the change in the name of Kent athletic teams from SILVER FOXES to GOLDEN FLASHES occurred in 1926 after the dismissal of President John E. McGilvrey, for whose silver fox farm east of the campus the teams had first been named. With acting President T. Howard Winters providing the impetus, a contest was held to select the new name. GOLDEN FLASHES, a subtle nod in the direction of the school color, was used first in 1927 by the basketball team. Also laying partial claim to the origin was Oliver Wolcott, onetime Kent grid great who played center on the 1921 and 1922 teams. As former sports editor of the *Kent Courier Tribune*, the local newspaper, the name SILVER FOXES seemed pretty frail to him. So, during the 1927 football season, he began referring to the team as GOLDEN FLASHES. By the way, Kent's school colors are blue and gold purely by accident. In the 1910 State Charter, Kent's school colors were orange and purple. However, a local laundry changed the colors. The orange and purple basketball uniforms went into the hot water, and came back gold and blue-black. Word has it that the team and the student body liked the colors so well, they adopted them as the new school colors!

KENTUCKY WILDCATS

The official nickname for the University of Kentucky's athletics teams is WILDCATS. The nickname became synonymous with UK shortly after a 6-2 football victory over Illinois on October 9, 1909, on the road. Commandant Carbusier, then head of the military department at old State University, told a group of students in a chapel service following the game that the Kentucky football team had "fought like WILDCATS." Later the name WILDCATS became more and more popular among UK followers as well as with members of the media. As a result, the University adopted the nickname. Blue was added to white to make the official colors in 1892 when a student pulled off his blue necktie and tossed it into the selection process. In April 1994, WILDCAT Brent Claiborne finished eighth nationally in the mascot division of the Universal Cheerleaders Association competition.

NICKNAME: "BIG BLUE"

LOUISIANA STATE FIGHTING TIGERS

In the fall of 1896, Coach A.W. Jeardeau's Louisiana State University football team posted a perfect (6-0-0) record, and it was in that pigskin campaign that LSU first adopted the TIGER nickname. TIGERS seemed a logical choice as most collegiate teams were adopting the names of ferocious animals that year, but the underlying reason for the nickname dates back to the Civil War. During the "War Between the States," a battalion of Confederate soldiers, comprised of New Orleans Zouaves and Donaldson Cannoneers, distinguished themselves at the Battle of Shenandoah. Contemporaries had known these Louisianans as the fighting band of Louisiana Tigers. Thus when LSU football teams entered the gridiron battlefields in their fourth year of intercollegate competition, they tagged themselves the TIGERS. It was the 1955 LSU "fourth-quarter ball club" that helped the TIGER moniker grow into the nickname FIGHTING TIGERS. Just to the north of TIGER Stadium is the home of "Mike V," LSU's Bengal TIGER mascot. The Tiger Cage, constructed for the first Mike in 1937, was renovated in 1981 to include a grassy area, a tiger-sized wooden scratching post, a pool, a climbing platform, and an indoor area for use in inclement weather.

NICKNAME: "BAYOU BENGALS"

LOUISIANA TECH BULLDOGS

In 1899, five Louisiana Tech students were returning home from school and came upon an old, hungry bulldog sitting under a tree. The boys fed it, and upon arriving home found the dog had followed. They sought permission for it to stay the night, and the landlord agreed — but the dog had to stay in the kitchen. That night the house caught fire. The dog awakened first, and ran from room to room until all occupants were alerted to the danger. The homeless dog re-entered the burning house when it was discovered that one boy remained inside. When the fire was extinguished and the smoke cleared, the lifeless bulldog was found in an unburned corner of one room — dead from the smoke and heat. The shaken students buried the dog where they'd found him, wrapped in two jackets; one red, the other blue, now the school's colors. The whole campus mourned the death of the dog with no name. Two years later, when Tech organized a football team, the choice of mascot was unanimous. BULLDOGS, named after the first hero of Louisiana Tech, was given the honor.

NICKNAME: "TECH"

LOUISVILLE CARDINALS

The University of Louisville's athletic symbol, chosen sometime after 1913, is a CARDINAL. The Cardinal bird was chosen to give Louisville statewide identification, since the CARDINAL is the state bird of Kentucky. The school colors — red, black, and white — were adopted at the suggestion of Mrs. John L. Patterson. The bright-red, crested American songbird is the nickname of a number of college and pro teams, but not Stanford, whose CARDINAL moniker actually refers to the color — to which, of course, there is no plural ("Don't call us the Cardinals!"). The CARDINAL'S namesake, *Richmondena cardinalis*, is related to the finch.

NICKNAME: "THE CARDS"

MARYLAND TERRAPINS

Dr. H. C. Bird, a football coach who later became University president, recommended the diamondback TERRAPIN as the Maryland school nickname and mascot in 1932, in response to the student newspaper's search for an "official" leader. Byrd's childhood in Crisfield, Maryland, apparently included skirmishes with this brand of snapping turtle, indigenous to

Chesapeake Bay, and with a reputation for intimidation and unpredictability. The mascot is nicknamed Testudo — derived from a Latin word meaning a shelter held over the head of Roman soldiers, like a tortoise shell. Earlier, Maryland had been referring to itself as OLD LINERS. Historians are in a scrimmage over whether that nickname is a reference to a Revolutionary War Troop of Maryland soldiers who distinguished themselves on the field of battle, or if it refers to a squabble with Pennsylvanians over just where the border between the two states should be. Further turtleization came when the student yearbook, the *Reveille*, became the TERRAPIN in 1935. Then local newspapers took to shortening TERRAPIN to TERP for headline writing ease.

NICKNAME: "TERPS"

MEMPHIS TIGERS

Nineteen-twelve references to the college football team in Memphis, Tennessee, had them tabbed as the BLUE AND GRAY WARRIORS of West Tennessee Normal School. It became West Tennessee State Teachers College in 1925, Memphis State College in 1941, Memphis State University in 1957, and finally the University of Memphis in 1994. After the final game of the 1914 season, there was a student parade where several Normal students shouted, "We fight like TIGERS!" Campus publications loved the new nickname, but the newspapers downtown stuck with NORMALS and BLUE AND GRAY. Under Coach Laster Barnard in 1922, the team adopted the motto "Every man a TIGER!" In the late 1920s, student publications and downtown newspapers began referring to the football team as the TEACHERS or TUTORS. But the TIGER moniker would return, and in 1939 was finally adopted as the school's official nickname. For nearly a quarter century the mascot has been a Bengal Tiger. This naming contest attracted 2,500 entries, including SPOOK, SAMPSON, GOLIATH, BENGO, SULTAN, SAHIB, BIG CAT, PTAH, TOUCHDOWN, SONNY, SHILOH, and BENGIE, WOUGIE, BENGAL BOY FROM TENNESSEE. The winner was "TOM," for Tigers Of Memphis.

METROPOLITAN STATE COLLEGE OF DENVER ROADRUNNERS

These ROADRUNNERS were students, named for the necessity of dodging the traffic as they made their way between campus buildings!

Playing in the Colorado Athletic Conference, the Metropolitan State College of Denver nickname of ROADRUNNERS did not originate with the desert bird, and was not chosen to refer to the athletic prowess of any of the school's sports teams. In the old "rent-a-campus" days, Denver residents watched students dodge traffic to get to and from classes, and "roadrunning" became the term used to describe the process. Horror stories still abound of close calls with traffic, and it was a rare day that students did not hear horns blaring at people dodging cars. While the first mascot was actually a Mustang, the swift Roadrunner was soon adopted as a more fitting mascot. With the building of North Classroom to replace the East Bank facilities, and the closure of Lawrence and Larimer streets, "roadrunning" is no longer an integral part of life here. Students will have to think up a different excuse for being late to class.

NICKNAME: "METRO"

MIAMI HURRICANES

Why HURRICANES? Because on opening day of the University of Miami's 1926 football season, a real-life HURRICANE hit the field! The event was postponed. Even the birth of the nickname began in stormlike conditions. Some reports say the 1927 football club held a team meeting to select HURRICANES, hoping they would sweep away opponents just as the devastating storm did on September 16, 1926. Another version holds that *Miami News* columnist Jack Bell asked end Porter Norris of the 1926 squad what the team should be called. Told that the local dignitaries and University officials wanted to name the team for one of the local flora or fauna, Norris said the players wouldn't stand for it and suggested HURRI-CANES as a nod to that opening game. From time to time, opposition has arisen to the name that would "reinforce Miami's negative reputation as a weather-beaten community living constantly under the threat of destruction." But as one University of Miami official rationalized in the 1960s, "Does anyone think Chicago is overrun by BEARS just because the town has a football team by that name?" The school colors address the local flora and fauna, however. Ruth Bryan Owens, daughter of famed attorney William Jennings Bryan, while a member of the board of regents suggested the colors of the Florida orange tree. Orange symbolizes the fruit of the tree, green represents the leaves, and white is the blossom. Folklore maintains that the ibis, a symbol of knowledge found in the Everglades and Egypt, is the last sign of wildlife to take shelter before a HURRICANE, and the first to reappear after a storm. The local marsh bird was first considered the school's mascot in 1926, and through the years has become one of the most recognizable in the United States.

NICKNAME: "CANES"

MIAMI (OHIO) REDSKINS

Use of the nickname REDSKINS for Miami, Ohio, athletic teams dates back to the 1930-31 school year when the Miami alumni magazine, then edited by the school's lone publicity man, Ralph McGinnis, announced the new nickname as successor to BIG RED, which had caused confusion with Denison University teams. A similar tag had popped up in a 1928 story in the *Miami Student* that referred to BIG RED-SKINNED WARRIORS, but the transition wasn't made for another three years. For a time in 1931, REDSKIN and BIG RED were used inter-changeably in the *Student*. Throughout the sports world, Miami University has the unique reputation as the "Cradle of the Coaches." At last count, more than 100 Miami graduates were active in coaching or administrative work at the pro and collegiate levels.

NICKNAME: "THE 'SKINS"

MICHIGAN STATE SPARTANS

Starting life as the Michigan Agricultural College and nicknamed the AGGIES, the exact origin of the SPARTANS nickname came from a *Lansing State Journal* sportswriter who detested another former nickname, Michigan STATERS. He commented that the old nickname was too long to write in articles. So he searched through old entries from a contest that had been held to pick the nickname and found SPARTANS as one of the entries. The person who made the SPARTAN suggestion is unfortunately unknown. However, the writer liked the name and began using it in his articles on April 5, 1926. No administrators or alumni protested, and the name stuck. The SPARTAN nickname is shared with about a dozen other college teams, including the University of Tampa, Manchester College, and the University of Dubuque. When World War II ended, a new campus fixture greeted the returning GIs — the SPARTAN statue. The statue, fondly known as "Sparty," is the largest free-standing ceramic sculpture in the world. Designed by faculty member Leonard D. Jungvirth, it is symbolic of the spirited warriors of ancient Sparta, designed in the ideal classical form reinterpreted in the Art Deco style popular in the 1940s. It features incised figures on the base of the statue representing various campus sports. The SPARTAN helmet shows the image of Gruff, created in 1955.

MICHIGAN WOLVERINES

Since the earliest recorded moment of Michigan sports history in 1861, students of the University of Michigan have been calling themselves WOLVERINES. The reason for this nickname probably comes from the fact that Michigan has been called the Wolverine State, but the creation of that moniker is an interesting story. Wolverines are the largest members of the weasel family, measuring about three feet long and weighing about 26 pounds. Other members of this family include the otter, skunk, mink, weasel, and the wolverine's closest relative, the badger. Wolverines are crafty and destructive, and enjoy killing just for the sake of killing even members of its own kind. Even though wolverines have very poor eyesight, they were despised by the Indians and early pioneers because of their ability to find and consume vast amounts of stored food. Wolverines also were hated because of their fondness for eating the catch out of traps before the trapper himself had the opportunity to retrieve it. Early reports indicated that hunters would rather stumble into the den of a mother bear than come in contact with a mother wolverine, because "she is a tigress of ferocity, absolutely fearless, and so strong and quick that a man, even armed with a gun, is taking risks if he gets too near." The nickname of WOLVERINES probably arose during the Michigan-Ohio border dispute of 1803, but it is unclear whether Ohioans pinned this name on Michigan natives or Michiganders chose it as a symbol of tenacity. However, it is a certainty that Wolverines have never been abundant in the state of Michigan and would not be the reason for the nickname. The University of Michigan originally started in Detroit but was transferred to Ann Arbor after local citizens there donated a 40-acre plot of land in 1837 to entice the University to move. A very loose nickname for Michigan's team is the MAIZE AND BLUE. In 1879, the new football team was automatically called the WOLVERINES.

MINNESOTA GOLDEN GOPHERS

Over the years there has been a good deal of banter regarding the University of Minnesota's nickname, but history shows that the name goes way back to 1857. First it must be realized that Minnesota was tabbed the "Gopher State" as the result of a cartoon satirizing the "Five Million Loan Bill," which appeared in the legislature on February 24, 1858. That bill, providing a loan for the building of railroads in Minnesota, was bitterly opposed, and in order to bring the subject into perspective, a cartoon was circulated showing the "Gopher Train" drawn by nine striped Gophers with human heads. It permanently fastened upon Minnesota the nickname "Gopher State." In the early 1930s, the Minnesota football teams, under the direction of Coach Bernie Bierman, were establishing themselves as national champions. During those championships, the local press described the GOPHER teams as the "golden-shirted horde" and the "golden swarm." These descriptions were simultaneous with the team's change to golden-colored jerseys, bringing the name GOLDEN GOPHERS.

MISSISSIPPI REBELS

The University of Mississippi, informally known as Ole Miss (suggested by Elma Meek in 1896), was chartered on February 24, 1844. For a while referred to as the FLOOD, and the RED AND BLUE, in 1936 Coach Ed Walker decided that Ole Miss needed a new nickname. The school newspaper received 600 entries from its name-the-team contest, but it took until the following year to select one from the final five: RAIDERS, CONFEDERATES, STONEWALLS, OLE MISS, and REBELS. Ole Miss alumnus Ben Guider suggested REBELS with these comments: "The name is short, musical, inspiring, simple for publication purposes, and should catch the eye of the sports public. In addition, the name recalls to mind the glories of the Old South and that historic struggle of the Civil War in which the State of Mississippi took so noble and outstanding a part, and for which every Mississippian should feel proud. Inasmuch as so many sections of our state are rich in tradition and memory of classic battles of that famous war, this name seems to me to be closely and peculiarly identified with the State of Mississippi, just as much so as the CAVALIERS of Virginia, GATORS of Florida, or the GAMECOCKS of South Carolina."

NICKNAME: "REBS"

MISSISSIPPI STATE BULLDOGS

As with many universities, Mississippi State teams answered to different nicknames through the years. The first squads representing Mississippi A&M College were proud to be called AGGIES, and when the school officially became Mississippi State College in 1932 the nickname MAROONS, for State's uniform color, gained prominence.

BULLDOGS became the official title for State teams in 1961, not long after State College was granted university status. Yet references to school teams as BULLDOGS go back to early in the century. This name was used almost interchangeably with both AGGIES and MAROONS since at least 1905, when, after a victory, the cadets held a mock funeral parade for the losers. The *Reflector*, the campus newspaper, reported, "A coffin was secured, decorated with University colors and a bulldog pup placed on top." Other reports of the victory commented on the "bulldog" style of play, and the BULLDOG was soon publicly accepted as a school athletic symbol. The official mascot is an American Kennel Club-registered English Bulldog given the inherited title of "Bully."

MISSOURI-KANSAS CITY KANGAROOS

The KANGAROO issue was first brought up in 1936 when the editors of the University (then named Kansas City University) newspaper decided it was time for a mascot for, of all things, the debate team. There were no organized athletic teams at that time, and the fire was lit later that year when an article appeared in the *Kansas City Star* titled "Kangaroo May Go to KCU . . . Student Editors Believe University Should Have a Symbol." Even the Kansas City Zoo contributed to the groundswell when it purchased two baby kangaroos. In 1937, the University yearbook, the *Crataegus*, decided the kangaroo was not an appropriate school symbol. Just as the criticism began to mount and support for the kangaroo was beginning to wane, a famed cartoonist came to the rescue. A University humor magazine had been established, and on its second cover was a cartoon of one Kasey (K.C.) the Kangaroo alongside none other than Mickey Mouse! Only one other college in the nation uses KANGAROOS as its nickname, Austin College in Sherman, Texas, and one other uses the creature as its mascot — the Akron ZIPS. The University of Missouri-Kansas City is annually listed among the top 10 most unusual mascot names in NCAA Division I.

NICKNAME: "THE ROOS"

MISSOURI TIGERS

The nickname TIGERS, given to the University of Missouri's athletic teams, traces its origin to the Civil War period. At that time, plundering guerilla bands habitually raided small towns, and Columbia people constantly feared an attack. Such organizations as temporary "home guards" and vigilance companies banded together to fight off any possible forays. The town's preparedness discouraged any guerilla activity and the protecting organization began to disband in 1854. However, it was rumored that a guerilla band, led by notorious Bill Anderson, intended to sack the town. Quickly organized was an armed guard of Columbia citizens, who built a blockhouse and fortified the old courthouse in the center of town. This company was called "The Missouri Tigers." The marauders never came. The reputation of the intrepid TIGERS presumably traveled abroad, and Anderson's gang detoured around Columbia. Soon after Missouri's first football team was organized in 1890, the athletic committee adopted the nickname TIGERS in official recognition of those Civil War defenders. The MU mascot, "Truman the Tiger," is named for the Missouri-bred President of the United States, Harry S Truman.

NAVY MIDSHIPMEN

The United States Naval Academy athletic teams from Annapolis, Maryland, use the nickname MIDSHIPMEN. The name is derived from the Navy term "midship man." The word first appeared in English in the 17th century in the form of the word "midshipsman" (note the extra "s") to designate those men who were stationed "amidships" — i.e., in the waist or middle portion of the vessel — while on duty. By 1687, however, the second "s" had been dropped to give the current form of the word. MID-SHIPMEN were originally boys, sometimes as young as seven or eight, who were apprenticed to sea captains to learn the sailor's trade. In the early days of the U.S. Navy, MIDSHIPMEN trained aboard ship until they were eventually commissioned as ensigns. With the founding of the Naval Academy in 1845, it became possible, as it still does today, for a Midshipman to enter the Navy directly from civilian life. The name of students at the Naval Academy changed several times between 1870 and 1902, when Congress restored the original title of Midshipman, and it has remained unchanged since. Since the term Midshipman is considered a rank, both the men's and women's athletic teams at the Naval Academy are known as the MIDSHIPMEN. The term MIDDIES is considered inappropriate.

NICKNAME: "MIDS"

NEBRASKA CORNHUSKERS

A newspaper account reported that Nebraska fans celebrated victories by waving banners of old gold. The date was November 27, 1890, and the state university of Nebraska had just won its first game. In the early years,

Nebraska's football team had several nicknames, including the BLACK KNIGHTS (probably the most common), RATTLESNAKE BOYS, ANTELOPES, OLD GOLD, and BUGEATERS. The team was first called CORNHUSKERS in 1900. Cy Sherman, a sportswriter for the *Lincoln Daily Star* newspaper, assigned the name in reference to the expansive cornfields of the team's home state. When Edward O. "Junto" Stiehm was hired as coach in 1911, the team's unofficial moniker became the STIEHM ROLLERS. A similar assignment occurred in 1915 when a tough Nebraska team was referred to as the MANKILLING MASTODONS in an Eastern newspaper. Nebraska is the only state to bear a nickname based on a college football team. Football at the university is so popular with the Nebraskans that on Saturdays when there is a home game, the stadium in Lincoln becomes "the third largest city in the state" after Omaha and Lincoln.

NICKNAME: "THE HUSKERS"

NEVADA-LAS VEGAS RUNNIN' REBELS

Men's basketball was the first sport organized at the University of Nevada-Las Vegas, opening play in 1958 under head coach and athletic director Michael "Chub" Drakulich. Baseball, also coached by Drakulich, started in 1960 and football came to campus nearly a decade later when head coach Bill Ireland's squad went 8-1 in 1968. Women's sports such as tennis emerged in 1960 under administrator Alice Mason, but basketball became the first women's varsity sport in 1974. The nickname REBELS was given to UNLV athletic teams because the school, emerging from the shadow of the University of Nevada-Reno, in effect REBELLED against its bigger and older brother to the north. The name RUNNIN' REBELS, always spelled without a "g," was coined in 1974 by then-Sports Information Director Dominic Clark, but refers only to the UNLV men's basketball team. The school colors of scarlet and gray can be traced to the late 1950s when UNLV adopted as mascot a wolf wearing a Confederate uniform. Scarlet and gray were traditional colors of the Confederacy with its gray uniforms and red-based flag. Initially, a Colonial-like REBEL soldier was the official logo and there was talk at one time of changing UNLV's nickname to MINUTEMEN. When a group of black athletes voiced displeasure with having a mascot associated with the "wrong side" of the Civil War, authorities agreed. Former school president Don Baepler explained that "UNLV was rebelling against the status quo," and the nickname actually has nothing to do with the Civil War. So, in the early 1970s, the human REBEL logo was born.

NEVADA WOLF PACK

The Nevada WOLF PACK, one of only two teams nationally to use the designation — NC State uses one word, WOLFPACK — has been using the moniker since at least the early 1920s. Nevada's first athletic teams in the late 1890s and early 1900s were referred to as the SAGE-BRUSHERS or even SAGE HENS after Nevada's state flowering plant, the sagebrush. There are references in print to the SAGE WARRIORS, although none of these names became the official mascot. In the 1921 or 1922 athletic season, a local writer described the spirited play of a Nevada team as a "pack of wolves." The name stuck, and soon almost every reference to the athletic teams was the Nevada WOLVES. In 1923, students "officially" designated WOLVES as the school's mascot. Since all teams are a group of players, the word PACK followed quickly. In the 1928-29 Nevada student handbook under athletics, the teams are referred to as the WOLF PACK. The two "wolf packs" have met only once in athletic competition, when defending national champion North Carolina State and Nevada were paired up in the first round of the 1985 NCAA Basketball Tournament, with NC State winning 65-56.

NICKNAME: "THE PACK"

NEW MEXICO LOBOS

When the University of New Mexico began playing football in 1892, the team was simply referred to as THE UNIVERSITY BOYS or VARSITIES, to distinguish themselves from the prep school kids. The student body, at least as early as 1917, began to seriously explore the possibilities for both a nickname and new name for the UNM weekly student newspaper. Several names were suggested, including the RATTLERS, the SAND DEVILS, the KI-YO-TE, and the CHERRY AND SILVER. But it wasn't until September 22 of 1920, that sophomore George S. Bryan suggested that the University teams be given a mascot name, which many universities at that time were doing. Bryan suggested LOBO, the Spanish word for wolf, and the nickname was enthusiastically received at a student council meeting. The October issue of the student newspaper said, "The LOBO is respected for his cunning, feared for his prowess, and is the leader of the pack. It is the ideal name for the Varsity boys who go forth to battle for the glory of the school." A captured wolf pup became the mascot, but in the late 1920s it bit a child at one of the games, and a live wolf was never used again. School colors are silver for the winding Rio Grande, and cherry, the color of the majestic Sandia Mountains' sunset.

NEW MEXICO STATE AGGIES

Here's a school with two official nicknames, one for the men, and another for the women. The New Mexico State University AGGIES nickname depicts the major area of study (agricultural) at the school. It was New Mexico A&M prior to becoming NMSU as it is a land grant college under the Morrill Act. After first being named Las Cruces College in 1888, the next change was New Mexico College of Agriculture and Mechanic Arts. Thus, the school has been AGGIES a long time. The women officials decided upon something indigenous to the area and the ROADRUNNER bird, also called chaparral or paisano, seemed to be a natural. It is a common sight in the southern portion of New Mexico.

NEW ORLEANS PRIVATEERS

Cruising over the blue waters of Lake Pontchartrain, a silver and blue privateer patrols its boundaries from the old barracks of Camp Leroy Johnson on the East Campus to Hangman's Tree, not far from Bienville Hall on the University of New Orleans' main campus. The "armed" vessel, originally created to attack and capture enemy ships, was the Louisiana State University in New Orleans' way of drifting apart from the mother institution, Louisiana State University in Baton Rouge — and its TIGERS. One student complained, "We not only did not have an identity that was distinct from Baton Rouge, we really had no identity at all." In the fall of 1964, students' entries in the mascot suggestions varied from spiky reptiles to hairy mammals. The final vote reduced all entries to these finalists: PANTHERS, DOLPHINS, PRIVATEERS, MARLINS, and MARINERS. But there was a lot of thought about PANTHER and the Black Panther movement of that time in the U.S., and the student body changed its mind, wanting something that was new. In a final runoff election, the PRIVATEER emerged victorious, receiving 583 votes to 423 for the DOLPHINS. Freshman nicknames were changed from BABY BEN GALS, the final reference to the Baton Rouge TIGERS, to PRIVATEER PLEBES.

NICKNAME: "BUCS"

NORTH CAROLINA STATE WOLFPACK

In the early days of intercollegiate competition, North Carolina Agricultural & Mechanical College teams were called the FARMERS &

MECHANICS, AGGIES, TECHS, and most often, RED TERRORS. Then, in 1922, the football team received a new name from a disgruntled fan. He was unhappy with the team's 3-3-3 season, and complained to athletics officials that State would never have a winning season as long as players behaved "like a WOLFPACK." Students laughed at the comparison, and then adopted the name WOLFPACK for the football team. Originally, the other sports kept the RED TERROR moniker. The label stuck for more than 20 years before Chancellor J. W. Harrelson called for a new nickname in 1946, reasoning that the WOLFPACK label put the school in an unfavorable light. "The only thing lower than a wolf is a snake in the grass," he said, even reminding students that the Nazi submarines had been called the wolfpack. Suggestions poured in to the contest, including NORTH STATERS, CARDINALS (the State bird), HORNETS, CULTIVATORS, COTTON PICKERS, and PINEROOT-ERS — the tag given to pigs in parts of North Carolina. WOLFPACK won, with one student saying, "The wolf is a scrappy, tough animal, the spittin' image of our team." So it was decided in 1947 that all NCSU varsity teams would be called WOLFPACK. In 1987, the NCSU men's and women's basketball teams were Atlantic Coast Conference champions, the only time in the conference's history that a school won both titles in one year.

NICKNAMES: "THE PACK"
           "CARDIAC PACK" (Basketball 1983)

NORTH CAROLINA TAR HEELS

North Carolina's principal industry for many years was the production of tar, pitch, and turpentine, and, thus, it is known as the TAR HEEL state. One legend has the nickname being applied to the state's residents as long ago as the Revolutionary War. The troops of British general Charles Cornwallis were fording what is now known as the Tar River between Rocky Mount and Battleboro, when they discovered that tar had been dumped into the stream to impede their crossing. Their observation that anyone who waded North Carolina rivers would acquire tar heels led to the nickname first being used. Others credit the nickname to Civil War general Robert E. Lee, who commented of those soldiers who didn't run in battle, but stuck steadfastly to their positions, with "God bless the Tar Heel boys." The TAR HEELS mascot is a ram, named in honor of a bruising fullback named Jack Merritt, the star of the 1922, 9-1 football team. Merritt's nickname? "The battering ram."

NORTH FLORIDA OSPREYS

OSPREYS was adopted officially as the University of North Florida nickname and mascot in November 1979 by an election conducted by the Student Government Association. OSPREYS received 47 percent of the votes, winning over other suggestions ARMADILLO, SEA GULL, MANATEE, and SHARK. It's not unusual to see an osprey gliding majestically over the campus. Described as "trendy birds" in National Geographic magazine for their success in adapting to suburban neighborhoods, the osprey is also into recycling. Children's toys, styrofoam containers, cork buoys, and doormats are many of the items they use to construct their gigantic nests. Ospreys, like UNF alumni, reside on all the world's continents — except Antarctica.

NORTH TEXAS EAGLES

The school itself has experienced six name changes since it was founded in 1890 as Texas Normal College. In 1899 it were North Texas State Normal College, North Texas State Teachers College in 1923, North Texas State College in 1949, North Texas State University in 1961, and finally the University of North Texas in 1988. In the spring of 1922, a campus-wide election was held to choose an official nickname. Other names had been unofficially used at the time, but the ones considered were the BOYS FROM NORMAL and TEACHER'S TEAM. Neither of these projected the image the students felt they needed. So the EAGLE was chosen because of its status as both noble and majestic.

NICKNAME: "MEAN GREEN"

NORTHEAST LOUISIANA INDIANS

Northeast Louisiana University's athletic teams have been known as INDIANS since the school began as Ouachita Parish Junior College in 1931. It is believed the nickname was taken because of the legend of the Ouachita Indians, a subtribe of the Caddo Indians who supposedly roamed and raided along the Ouachita River basin. In 1974, Northeast recreated the Ouachita Indian on canvas, a profile portrait true to the legend. It is believed the Ouachita eschewed bright war paints, instead adorning themselves with jewelry and strings of animal teeth. When Northeast became a full university in 1970, the school adopted the abbreviation of NLU for second reference, giving the university's unique identity among state schools. Other schools under the state Board of Trust with directional names use "ern" in their names, like Southwestern and Southeastern.

NICKNAMES: "NORTHEAST LA."
                "NORTHEAST"

NORTHERN ILLINOIS HUSKIES

In almost a century of intercollegiate competition, old NIU has been identified with several nicknames. PROFS was a moniker used in the early days, an obvious expression of the institution's mission as a teacher's college. CARDINALS stuck in the 1920s, probably due to the school's jersey colors. The EVANSMEN tag became a cognomen in the 1930s, a reverent recognition of athletic pioneer George G. "Chick" Evans. Other more direct provincial terms included NORTHERNERS and TEACHERS. In 1940, a four-man committee, all members of the Varsity Club, was appointed to search for a "term with a trifle more dash." After much debate and research, a final accord was reached as reported in the January 25, 1940 *Northern Illinois*, the student newspaper and forerunner of the *Northern Star*: "Not only does the term have color and meaning, but it is particularly apt as in regard to NI's varsity teams. From now on the word HUSKIES will be used constantly in this paper and in other papers to indicate our athletic squads." Why? The dog is "Bold. Aggressive. On the move." The HUSKIE literally represents the entire burgeoning Northern Illinois program. According to Athletics Director Gerald O'Dell, "When I look at it, the Huskie plays on the direction in which the athletic progam is moving. It's coming at you. It's not static. It's always moving."

NORTHERN KENTUCKY NORSE

Norse warriors took their shields and swords into battle on large warships with dragon figureheads, used to intimidate their opposition. The name Norse is given to the men and women of the Scandinavian countries of Norway, Sweden, and Denmark, situated in the northernmost region of Europe. NORSE has been the nickname of Northern Kentucky University student-athletes and athletic teams since the NKU intercollegiate athletics program was started in 1971. The name NORSE, selected in a campus-wide contest that year, is a fitting nickname for NKU's students and athletic teams since the University is the northernmost university in Kentucky and is located at the highest spot in northern Kentucky. "Heyu" is the school's mascot, unveiled in 1992.

NORTHWESTERN WILDCATS

These lines were written by Wallace Abbey in the *Chicago Tribune* following the memorable Northwestern-Chicago game in 1924 that heralded a new era in Northwestern football: ". . . football players had not come down from Evanston; WILDCATS would be a name better suited to Coach Thistlethwaite's boys. Once Chicago had the ball on the nine yard line and had been stopped dead by a Purple wall of wildcats." From that day on, all the Northwestern athletic teams have borne the nickname of WILDCATS. A special committee selected the color purple (with white) in 1894 as the official school color, not only for the athletic teams, but for the entire university. Nine years after the birth of the nickname, in 1933, the Northwestern athletic department teamed up with an advertising firm to create the first caricature of "Willie the WILDCAT."

NICKNAMES: "PURPLE CATS"
                "PURPLE FOLKS"

NOTRE DAME FIGHTING IRISH

One story suggests the FIGHTING IRISH moniker was born in 1899 with Notre Dame leading Northwestern 5-0 at halftime of a game in Evanston, Illinois. The Wildcat fans supposedly began to chant, "Kill the Fighting Irish, kill the Fighting Irish," as the second half opened. Another tale has the nickname originating at halftime of the Notre Dame-Michigan game in 1909. With his team trailing, one Notre Dame player yelled to his teammates — who happened to have names like Dolan, Kelly, Glynn, Duffy, and Ryan — "What's the matter with you guys? You're all Irish and you're not fighting worth a lick." Notre Dame came back to win the game and the press, after overhearing the remark, reported the game as a victory for the "Fighting Irish." The most generally accepted explanation is that the press coined the nickname as a characterization of Notre Dame athletic teams, their never-say-die fighting spirit and their Irish qualities of grit, determination, and tenacity. The term likely began as an abusive expression tauntingly directed toward the athletes from the small, private, Catholic institution. The *Notre Dame Scholastic*, in a 1929 edition, printed, "The unkind appellation became symbolic of the struggle for supremacy on the field . . . The term, while given in irony, has become our heritage . . . So truly does it represent us that we are unwilling to part with it . . ." Notre Dame competed under the nickname CATHOLICS during the 1800s and became more widely known as the RAMBLERS during the early

1920s, in the days of the Four Horsemen. University president Matthew Walsh officially adopted FIGHTING IRISH as the Notre Dame nickname in 1927. Other names throughout the years included PAPISTS, HORRIBLE HIBERNIANS, DUMB MICKS, DIRTY IRISH, GOLD AND BLUE, WARRIORS, NOMADS, HOOSIER HARPS, WANDERING IRISH, ROCKNE'S ROVERS, and BLUE COMETS.

NICKNAMES: "IRISH"
             "GOLDEN DOMERS"
             "THE WONDER TEAM" (Knute Rockne's squad)
             "UNIVERSITY OF NOTRE GAME"

OHIO BOBCATS

Until 1925, all teams representing Ohio University had been known as OHIO or the GREEN AND WHITE — named after the school colors adopted in 1896. The school's athletic board decided the team should have a nickname, so the members sponsored a contest, offering a prize of $10 for the nickname that best exemplified their fighting spirit. Hundreds of names were suggested. Many animals common in the United States were mentioned. After much debate, the BOBCAT, "a sly, wily and scrappy animal," won. Hal. H. Rowland, a former student and a resident of Athens, entered the BOBCAT name. The new nickname was passed by the board on December 7, 1925, and officially adopted by President E. B. Bryan. In addition to the "Bobcat" and "Bobkitten" costumes which symbolize Ohio University's mascot, a live bobcat was introduced to OU's fans in 1983, nicknamed "Sir Winsalot." A new bobcat, nicknamed "Paws," has since joined "Sir Winsalot." Both cats may be seen at the Columbus Zoo.

OHIO STATE BUCKEYES

The Ohio State University BUCKEYES nickname arrives by way of the state of Ohio itself. The BUCKEYE State nickname comes from the tree that grew so abundantly in the territory before European settlers used it for building. Native Americans supposedly gave the tree this name because the light spot in its brown seed resembled the iris in the dark eye of a buck deer. During the presidential election campaign of 1840, the name was also applied to the people of Ohio. Today, more than one-fourth of Ohio's land area is still wooded. A large part of the tree stand is made up of red oak, white oak, and hard maple. Although the buckeye gave Ohio its nickname, and is the state tree, it is no longer significant in the region.

OKLAHOMA SOONERS

The University of Oklahoma fielded its first football team in 1895, 25 years after the game was started in the United States, 5 years after the opening of the University, and 12 years before Oklahoma became a state! University of Oklahoma athletic teams were called either ROUGH RIDERS or BOOMERS for 10 years before the current SOONER nickname emerged in 1908. Historically, a SOONER was a settler who came into Oklahoma Territory before the land run officially began (having arrived SOONER), but the University of Oklahoma SOONERS actually derived their name from a pep club called "The SOONER Rooters." But one of the old monikers lives on in the school mascot. The SOONER Schooner is a Conestoga wagon, or covered wagon, reminiscent of the mode of travel for the pioneers who settled Oklahoma. The Schooner is powered by matching white ponies named BOOMER and SOONER. The Schooner circles the goalposts after each Oklahoma score. Crimson and Cream, a group of volunteers especially schooled on details about their football team (as well as the team's colors), will tell you that the SOONERS hold the NCAA record for the longest winning streak in the history of collegiate football. They won 47 consecutive games between 1953 and 1957.

NICKNAME: "BIG RED"

OKLAHOMA STATE COWBOYS

The power of the press! When Oklahoma A&M College fielded its first athletic teams in 1901, two faculty members, who were graduates of Princeton, suggested TIGERS with orange and black colors. The colors remain to this day, but the nickname evolved. In 1925 there was sentiment to drop TIGERS and adopt AGGIES because it was an agricultural school. Sports editor Chades Saulsberry of the *Oklahoma City Times* began referring to the AGGIES as the A&M COWBOYS, and other papers soon took up the name. COWBOYS was firmly adopted, although AGGIES was used interchangeably until the school became Oklahoma State University in 1957. The school mascot, "Pistol Pete," was patterned after an authentic Oklahoma cowboy. He fires his pistol at every OSU athletic event. A women's team mascot, "Cowgirl Cale," was adopted in 1978.

OREGON DUCKS

Mistaken identity? Many think it was natural for the University of Oregon's original nickname, the WEBFOOTS, to evolve into DUCKS, but the meaning of the original term has been totally misinterpreted. The term WEBFOOTS was first used to describe fishermen off the coast of Massachusetts in the 1700s. In fact, it was the WEBFOOTS of 1776, under the command of General George Washington, that helped evacuate 10,000 troops across the East River to New York City. The WEBFOOTS helped the colonists avoid a sure defeat and saved the war for the colonies. When Oregon's Willamette Valley was being settled in the 1840s, the name WEBFOOTS was given to new residents — partly because of the nonstop rain and partly because so many settlers hailed from the New England area. When the University first opened in 1876, it did not take long for its athletic teams to be dubbed WEBFOOTS. In the 1890s, students voted the name in as their nickname. But as athletics got more news coverage, headline writers constantly searched for shorter names: DUCKS, thought by writers to be the same thing as WEBFOOTS, was installed by 1930 and was soon a popular name among fans. In the late 1940s, Athletics Director Leo Harris capitalized on his friendship with Walt Disney and received permission to use Donald Duck as the official Oregon mascot. That gave Oregon the distinction of being the only college in the United States to have a Disney cartoon character as its official mascot.

OREGON STATE BEAVERS

Oregon State University, like many universities in the United States, is named after its home state's official animal — the BEAVER. In the early days, when the school in Corvallis had a coyote named Jimmie as a mascot and was known as Oregon Agricultural College, the athletic teams were known as the AGGIES. When orange uniforms replaced the drab sweatshirt-gray and tan jerseys, the teams were referred to as the ORANGE-MEN. But in 1916, when the school yearbook was renamed the *Beaver*, the name BEAVERS became associated with the school. It is believed the press also had some influence in changing the name, particularly L. H. Gregory of the *Oregonian* newspaper. At any rate, the name gained instant popularity among alumni and students. Oregon State played its first football game in 1893. Reference to "Benny the Beaver" dates back to 1946, but the costumed beaver's first appearance was in 1952.

PACIFIC TIGERS

Nicknames for college athletic teams in the United States began as early as the 1860s. When the University of Pacific played Santa Clara College in baseball in 1866, the *San Jose Mercury* called the team the UNIVERSITIES, since UOP was California's first chartered university (1851) among several state colleges. Occasionally other names would surface, such as DIRIGO (?) in 1885, but they were short-lived. TIGER was first used in the fall of 1908, when football replaced rugby at Pacific. The nickname evolved because the uniform jerseys and socks were black with orange stripes, making the team look like tigers. The *Pacific Pharos* reported: "New suits have been ordered and when the team appears in action they will wear the TIGER stripes, which will be of great assistance to the players because they can locate their own men without any difficulty." The students expressed hope that the TIGER moniker would inspire the team to play with the same intensity and fierceness as the jungle cat. Not only was TIGER used to describe the team, but the student body embraced this animal persona as its own identity. The main campus location spreads over 170 acres along the Calaveras River in a peaceful setting in a residential area of Stockton, approximately 80 miles east of San Francisco in the San Joaquin Valley.

PENN STATE NITTANY LIONS

Penn State's athletic symbol, chosen by the student body in 1906, is the mountain lion, which once roamed central Pennsylvania. H. D. "Joe" Mason, a member of the Class of 1907, conducted a one-man campaign to choose a school mascot after seeing the Princeton tiger on a trip with the Penn State baseball team to that New Jersey campus. A student publication sponsored the campaign to select a mascot and Penn State is believed to be the first college to adopt the lion as a mascot. Since Penn State is located in the Nittany Valley at the foot of Mount Nittany, the lion was designated as a NITTANY LION. In regional folklore, Nittany was a valorous Indian princess in whose honor the Great Spirit caused Mount Nittany to be formed. A later namesake, daughter of Chief O-Ko-Cho, who lived near the mouth of Penn's Creek, fell in love with Malachi Boyer, a trader. The tearful maiden and her lost lover became legend and her name was given to the stately mountain. Penn State's student-athletes are instantly identified by their blue and white uniforms — but those weren't the original school colors. The Class of 1887 was asked to select their colors from a number of options, and they chose the combination of dark pink and black.

Soon, many students and the baseball team were sporting pink- and black-striped blazers and caps. However, problems arose when the pink faded to white after several weeks of exposure to the sun. The students then opted for blue, rather than black, and white. The official announcement of the new choice was made on March 18, 1890. The NITTANY LIONS and the LADY LIONS have worn the colors ever since.

PEPPERDINE WAVES

Playing in the West Coast Conference, Pepperdine University was founded in 1937. Even though its present address is on the Pacific Coast Highway in Malibu, California, the school adopted WAVES as the nickname for its athletic teams while it was located in South Los Angeles at Vermont Avenue and 79th Street. One school history says the moniker was proposed by a group of students who were from Tennessee and became captivated by the beach, which was eight miles away. The WAVES compete in team colors of blue and orange.

PITTSBURGH PANTHERS

The PANTHER (*Felis concolor*) was adopted as the University of Pittsburgh's nickname and mascot at a meeting of students and alumni in the autumn of 1909. According to George M. P. Baird, 1909, who made the suggestion, it was chosen for the following reasons: (1) the PANTHER was the most formidable creature once indigenous to the Pittsburgh region; (2) it had ancient, heraldic standing as a noble animal; (3) the happy accident of alliteration; (4) the close approximation of its hue to the old gold of the University's colors (old gold and blue), hence its easy adaptability in decoration; and (5) the fact that no other college or university then employed it as a symbol.

NICKNAME: "GOLDEN PANTHERS"

POMONA SAGEHENS

The tradition of athletics at Pomona is nearly as old as the college itself. Pomona was one of the founders of intercollegiate competition in Southern California, and the first issue of the student newspaper, printed in 1889, refers to the college's tennis team and courts as the BASEBALL NINE. The sagehen, a bird native to desert regions of the Southwest, was selected as the college nickname and mascot in 1917. In 1923, Pomona played against the University of Southern California in the first football game held at the Los Angeles Memorial Coliseum, which Pomona lost 23-7. Today, the Pomona College SAGEHENS remain true to one of the original assumptions of intercollegiate athletics: that college athletes must be students first. Interestingly, Pomona combines its forces with Pitzer College to field varsity athletic teams in 19 NCAA Division III sports, including men's football and women's basketball.

PURDUE BOILERMAKERS

Contrary to popular belief, Purdue's athletic teams are not named for a shot and a beer. The Purdue Football Media Guide tells us that BOIL-ERMAKERS was originally meant as a term of derision and was among several terms applied to Purdue by Wabash College supporters following a lopsided (18-4) victory by Purdue in 1889. Located just 30 miles from Lafayette, Indiana, and bitter athletic rivals of the day, students of the liberal arts school were inclined to shun the cultural background of Purdue players who represented a school devoted to the practical arts of engineering and agriculture. BOILERMAKERS struck the fancy of the Purdue players, who were also being called the PUMPKIN SHUCKERS, BLACKSMITHS, FARMERS, CORNFIELD SAILORS, HAYSEEDS, and the RAIL SPLITTERS. There is also an unsubstantiated story that Purdue, in the late 1880s, once enrolled eight boilermakers from the shops of the Monon Railroad during the football season.

RICE OWLS

Until 1962, Rice University was known formally as the William Marsh Rice Institute of Literature, Science and Art. William Rice, a Massachusetts-born businessman who made the bulk of his fortune in Houston following the Civil War, had willed the original endowment for the Institute in 1891. Death under mysterious circumstances in 1900 at age 83 provoked a legal battle over the will. Rice's valet and an attorney were later charged with Rice's death and a sensational murder trial followed. It was not until 1912 that the Rice Institute, Houston's first university, could be realized. The OWL nickname is derived from the University's heraldic shield. The designer of the crest noted that the arms of several families named Houston and Rice had both chevrons and three avian charges, and he adapted those for the Institute. In the official shield, a double chevron divides the field and the charges are the OWLS of Athena as they appear on a small ancient Greek coin. When athletic activities began at the Institute in 1912, the teams were named for the bird on the Institute's seal.

RICHMOND SPIDERS

From 1876 until 1893, the University of Richmond teams carried the nickname COLTS into their athletic contests, so dubbed for their play as an "energetic group of young colts." In the summer of 1894, a new nickname was born. A baseball team comprised of UR athletes and city residents adopted the name SPIDERS. Star pitcher Puss Ellyson's lanky arms and stretching kick confused batters to such an extent that *Richmond Times-Dispatch* writer Ragland Chesterman used the name of that clever creeping insect, the spider, to fittingly describe the erudite members of the team. So was created one of the nation's more unique nicknames. To this day, the University of Richmond is the only school in the country to sport the SPIDERS nickname.

RUTGERS SCARLET KNIGHTS

When Rutgers was still known as Queen's College, the athletic teams were referred to as the QUEENSMEN. The mascot was a Chanticleer; and though it was a fighting bird, to some it bore the connotation of "chicken." In fact, broadcast station WCTC in New Jersey had its call letters derived from the word ChanTiCleer. In the early 1950s, in the hope of spurring both the all-around good athletic promise and Rutgers University fighting spirit, a campuswide selection process changed the mascot to that of a Knight. Meanwhile, Rutgers was a pioneer in establishing a college color, scarlet being first proposed in the campus newsletter in 1869. Scarlet was chosen because it was a striking color and because a good scarlet ribbon could be easily obtained! By 1955, the SCARLET KNIGHTS had been established, and a new mascot, riding a spirited white charger, came to represent a new era. Sports lore at Rutgers has also known terms such as "Scarlet Scourge" and the lasting "Upstream Rutgers."

NICKNAMES: "SCARLET"
                   "RED TEAM"

ST. JOHN'S RED STORM

In June of 1994, St. John's University joined the movement away from nicknames found potentially offensive to Native Americans — they'd been called the REDMEN from the time the school was located in Brooklyn, New York. Polled by a committee composed of students, alumni, and administrators, RED STORM was selected because it was very original, and no other school in the country had a name close to it. Another reason the name was selected was that it lent itself to a very sharp and marketable logo. Other considered names included RED RAIDERS, rejected because Colgate University and Texas Tech were already using it; and RED DRAGONS, rejected because the school was not very receptive to it.

NICKNAME: "JOHNNIES"

ST. LOUIS BILLIKENS

The BILLIKEN is a design based on an ancient Oriental symbol of good luck. Back in the 1900s, a St. Louis company had the word BIL-LIKEN in its name, and it decided to adopt and trademark the symbol. Designed and manufactured at that time as a bank and statuette, the BIL-LIKEN became the national rage for about six months. By 1912, the BIL-LIKEN and its value as a good luck charm were just memories for all except the loyal fans of St. Louis University. How the BILLIKEN became attached to the University remains a matter of debate. It seems to have happened between 1910 and 1911 — at the height of Billikenmania! St. Louis sportswriter William O'Connor decided that SLU football coach John Bender resembled the BILLIKEN. Later, Charles McNamara drew a cartoon of Bender in the form of a BILLIKEN and posted it in the window of a drugstore. The team soon became known as Bender's BILLIKENS. One last point on luck ... to buy a BILLIKEN gives the purchaser luck but to have one given to you is better luck!

SAN DIEGO STATE AZTECS

Founded in 1897, the school was located initially above a downtown drugstore! It now has an enrollment of more than 32,000 students and occupies a sprawling 300-acre campus nicknamed Montezuma Mesa — home of the AZTECS. The school adopted this unique, Southwestern nickname in 1926. Until then, there had been no official name, although San Diego State teams had been referred to as STATERS and PROFESSORS in the sports pages of their day. The nickname AZTECS was approved without dissent when proposed by Fred Oserberg and Lewis Schellbach, editors of the school newspaper and yearbook. This was announced on January 14, 1925, when the two scribes flipped a coin to decide on

AZTECS. The losing name? The INCAS. At that time the AZTEC colors were purple and gold, considered too similar to other local clubs. Today the AZTECS are made easily distinguishable by their all-black uniforms. On May 15, 2001, SDSU president Stephen Weber announced that long-time mascot "Monty Montezuma," a red-faced, loincloth-wearing character, would be retired for one that is more politically correct and respectful to the Aztec Indians.

SAN JOSE STATE SPARTANS

In 1924, students at San Jose State University were called upon to submit names for their athletic teams. Before this time the school had no official name and had been called various things, including the DANIELS, TEACHERS, PEDAGOGUES, NORMALS, and NORMAL-ITIES. In 1925 the SPARTANS took to the field, the new nickname just beating out the GOLDS. Historically, SPARTANS were inhabitants of the city of Sparta — a power among the states of Greece, due to her warlike nature, and the innovation of a strict system of physical training. The system developed the youth of the country, both boys and girls. This was done by a severe system of body training and instruction in the fundamentals of physical education by which the race was improved so greatly that its warriors were feared by all other people. On December 8, 1941, San Jose State was scheduled to play the University of Hawaii, but the game was cancelled due to the Pearl Harbor bombing the previous day.

SANTA BARBARA GAUCHOS

It was in 1921 that the then-called Santa Barbara State introduced its first football team. Called the ROADRUNNERS in honor of the bird that frequented the Riviera campus, the team was forced to play its home games on the all-dirt field of the original, clapboard Pershing Park — a facility normally used for horse shows. Coach Spud Harder complained at the time, "We'd have to play with horse dung all over the place. I wouldn't let my players on the field without having inoculations for tetanus." Since the growing roadrunner population was also defecating all over the school's campus, it wasn't too surprising that the university changed its nickname. A student election was held to pick the new moniker, and the campus coeds — enamored with Douglas Fairbanks Sr. in the movie "El Gaucho" — stuffed the ballet box in his honor. Beginning with the 1934-35 school year, Santa Barbara State's sports teams were known as LOS

GAUCHOS. GAUCHO describes a cowboy of mixed Indian and Spanish ancestry.

SANTA CRUZ BANANA SLUGS

Did you notice? In the award-winning film *Pulp Fiction*, 1970s demigod John Travolta immortalized the BANANA SLUGS by wearing a school T-shirt throughout the last few scenes of the film. For many years, the BANANA SLUG served as the unofficial mascot and nickname for the University of California at Santa Cruz. The students felt the SLUG mollusk (once under consideration as the official state mollusk of California) represented many of the strongest elements of the campus: contemplation, flexbility, nonaggressiveness, and an iconoclastic challenge toward the status quo. The SLUG is also indigenous to the region and shares a symbiotic relationship with the California Redwood that populates the campus. In 1981 the school chancellor made SEA LION the official nickname in order to make the campus more mainstream, sparking a student revolt five years later when reinstating the BANANA SLUGS moniker bested the SEA LIONS at a 12-1 ratio in a student referendum. Leaders of the pro-SLUG movement even appealed to late-night czar David Letterman in their case (SLUGS being nocturnal creatures, of course). In 1992, *Sports Illustrated* magazine named the BANANA SLUGS the nation's best college nickname. The students of Santa Cruz are proud to tell you that BANANA SLUGS are hermaphroditic, and can actually mate with themselves if necessary.

NICKNAME: "SLUGS"

SCOTTSDALE ARTICHOKES

What was intended as a protest has become a college sports legend. Students and the government elected to represent them felt athletics should be low on the Scottsdale Community College budget list, putting them in conflict with the administration who saw the future written on the white chalked grid of a football field. The year was 1970, a new decade born of the protests and campus turmoil of the '60s, and the SCC students felt they were being sold out by yet another "establishment" false promise. The administration, while hearing the vague footsteps of dissension, went ahead with plans for making SCC a national junior college athletic power. It asked an infuriated student government to run an election to find a nickname, so they reacted by giving the students three selfparodying choices: the ARTICHOKE, the RUTABAGA, or the SCOUNDRELS. The shocked administration tried to declare the election null and void when ARTICHOKE won. They held another election, pitting DROVERS against the vegetable. ARTICHOKE won big. For the majority of students entering SCC tody, the nickname is no more than a quirky reminder of a time when students chose academic reputation over athletics.

SOUTH CAROLINA FIGHTING GAMECOCKS

The University of South Carolina is the only major college athletic program in the U.S. that uses FIGHTING GAMECOCKS as its official nickname and mascot. At the turn of the century, after struggling for more than a decade under numerous nicknames, the school's feisty and spirited football team was first referred to unofficially as the GAME COCKS. In 1903, Columbia's morning newspaper, the *Stale*, shortened the name to one word, and the school's teams have been GAMECOCKS ever since. A GAMECOCK is a fighting rooster known for its spirit and courage. A cockfight, which was a popular sport throughout the U.S. in the 19th century, would last until the death of one of the combatants. Cockfighting has been outlawed by most states for humanitarian reasons, but it's still held surreptitiously in many areas. The state of South Carolina has long been closely connected with the breeding and training of fighting gamecocks. General Thomas Sumter, famed guerilla fighter of the Revolutionary War, was known as "The Fighting Gamecock." Introduced in 1980 as "Big Spur's" replacement, "Cocky," the garnet and black plumed GAME-COCK, captured national championship titles as the number one mascot in 1986 and 1994.

SOUTH DAKOTA TECH HARDROCKERS

South Dakota is a name from the Sioux Indians. Lakota or Dakota is a word mearing "friends" or "allies." The HARDROCKER nickname was derived from the gold miners who came to the area in the mid-1870s. The Black Hills is the home of the largest gold mine in North America, operated by Homestake Mining. The miners mined hard rock in attempting to find gold, thus the name HARDROCKERS was adopted by the school in the early 1920s to recognize them. "Grubby" is the official mascot of the South Dakota School of Mines and Technology HARDROCKERS. He is a miner, and symbolizes those mining engineers that were the first graduates of South Dakota Tech.

NICKNAMES: "ROCKERS"
                "MINERS"

SOUTHERN CALIFORNIA TROJANS

Up until 1912, the University of Southern California teams were called the METHODISTS or WESLEYANS, nicknames that were not looked upon with favor by University officials. So Warren Bovard, director of athletics and son of university president Dr. George Bovard, asked *Los Angeles Times* sports editor Owen Bird to select an appropriate nickname. Bird came out with an article prior to a showdown between USC and Stanford in which he called attention to the fighting spirit of the USC athletes, calling them TROJANS. "The term TROJAN as applied to USC means to me that no matter what the situation, what the odds or what the conditions, the competition must be carried on to the end and those who strive must give all they have and never be weary in doing so," wrote Bird. In the center of the USC campus stands one of the most famous collegiate landmarks in the country: Tommy Trojan. Unveiled in 1930 for USC's 50th jubilee, the statue of the bronzed TROJAN warrior has served as a symbol of the University's fighting spirit. It has served as the focal point in the crosstown rivalry between USC and UCLA. The pregame tradition of the statue being painted blue and gold by UCLA pranksters was first recorded in 1941. It seems as though the TROJANS are also in proud possession of college ball's most rabid fan. Giles Pellerin, a 90-year-old retired phone company executive, viewed, in person, more than 750 consecutive TROJAN games, home AND away! Pellerin's still-unbroken streak began in the 1926 season and ended in 1999, when he passed away. By the way, another name change in USC TROJAN history was that of footballer Marion Morrison. He later became known to the world as movie star John Wayne. USC also has one of the most recognizable mascots in sports — "Traveller," the white stallion, racing up the sidelines with its TROJAN rider.

NICKNAMES: "THUNDERING HERD"
                "SOUTHERN CAL"

SOUTHERN COLORADO THUNDERWOLVES

The previous nickname, INDIANS, was selected by the student population in 1933 at the old Pueblo Junior College, which became the University of Southern Colorado. When a change was sought, a campuswide committee received recommendations from students and the community. The USC New Look Committee forwarded three finalists — THUNDER, THUNDERWOLVES, TRAILBLAZERS — to the University president, who selected THUNDERWOLVES because "the name reflected the university as a modern, forward-looking institution which strives to be an excellent regional university; name sent a message out of state that the university is located in the beautiful state of Colorado; name served as an effective image for publications, stationary and banners, as well as for tee shirts, jackets, mugs, bookstore supplies and other marketable items." The university moved to its new location in 1964, adopted its new nickname in 1995, and adopted its motto at the same time, "shake, rattle and howl!"

NICKNAMES: "THE PACK"
                 "T-WOLVES"

SOUTHERN ILLINOIS SALUKIS

In 1967, Southern Illinois University at Carbondale basketball coach Jack Hartman wrote, "Old Duke has its DEVILS, St. Louis plays its BILLS, Texas Western digs the MINERS like there's gold in them thar hills. But from Loo'ville on the bluegrass to St. Peter's on the bogs, the scene was bad last winter, they all went to the DOGS." The SALUKI is an ancient breed of Arabian dog, a choice consistent with a bit of local lore — the southern one-third of Illinois is often referred to as Egypt! This was the result of a drought that dried streams and fields of wheat in the early 1800s all over Illinois — but not the southern part of the state! A similar "miracle" had once occurred in Egypt, and appears in the Bible. In Egypt at that time, Salukis were the finest animals a family could own. Known for their speed and hunting skills, Salukis are the oldest purebred dogs, dating back to 3600 B.C. Other nicknames considered in 1951 were REBELS, KNIGHTS, FLYERS, MARAUDERS, and MAROONS.

SOUTHERN METHODIST MUSTANGS

Originally, the football team was unofficially known as the PARSONS because of the number of theology students that were on the squad. Then Dorothy Amann, secretary to Southern Methodist University's first president, Robert H. Hyer, submitted MUSTANGS to a school contest in 1917. She said the football players looked like a bunch of wild Texas MUSTANGS when they ran onto the field. The students agreed, selecting MUSTANGS from among the other entries and making it official on October 25, 1917. Peruna, the name of a well-known elixir manufactured up until a few years ago, was the nickname given to SMU's miniature pony mascot. Of further interest, Lee Iacocca named the Ford MUSTANG after seeing the school's football team play Michigan. In the SMU locker room, Iacocca announced, "Gentlemen, Ford is coming out with a new sports car and we have been considering four animal nicknames. It will be light, like your team. It will be quick, like your team. It will be sporty, like your team. Today, watching Southern Methodist's MUSTANGS play with such flair, we reached a decision. We will call our new car the MUSTANG." SMU adopted the Ford Mustang logo, and it was agreed that the school's logo would always run facing the right, while the Ford logo would always run facing the left. Check it out.

NICKNAMES: "THE PONIES"
            "THE HILLTOP" (campus nickname)

SOUTHERN MISSISSIPPI GOLDEN EAGLES

After having seen great masses of black-eyed Susans in a pine forest, Mississippi Normal College committee member Mrs. Moran Pope suggested the colors of black and gold for the school. After being known as the SOUTHERNERS for over 60 years, the University of Southern Mississippi athletic teams underwent an identity change on November 11, 1972. More than 400 different suggestions were made during a five-month campaign to determine a new name. Suggestions were turned in to an ad hoc committee by alumni, students, and friends of the University. The committee narrowed the suggestions down to five possible nicknames — the WAR LORDS, GOLDEN RAIDERS, TIMBER WOLVES, SOUTHERNERS, and GOLDEN EAGLES. It took two votes to get the 60 percent majority needed, but GOLDEN EAGLES eventually beat out the other finalist, SOUTHERNERS.

SOUTHWESTERN LOUISIANA RAGIN' CAJUNS

The University of Southwestern Louisiana has one of the most unique nicknames in college sports with RAGIN' CAJUNS. Formerly called the BULLDOGS, the school's football teams were coined the RAGIN' CAJUNS in 1963 by the USL athletics director, Bob Henderson, shortly after Russ Faulkinberry was named head football coach. It resulted from the fact that at the time, more than 90 percent of Faulkinberry's teams were composed of Louisiana high school players, many with French-speaking, Acadian backgrounds. The nickname stuck, and now all USL athletic teams are called the RAGIN' CAJUNS. Women's teams are called LADY

CAJUNS. The mascot remained an English Bulldog, and his name is RAGIN'. A recent development, including the renaming of USL as the University of Louisiana, is the possible introduction of a new "partner" mascot and nickname — the PELICANS.

NICKNAME: "CAJUNS"

STANFORD CARDINAL

What we know as Stanford is properly called Leland Stanford Junior University. Rail magnate Leland Stanford founded the distinguished institution in Palo Alto, California, in 1885 as a memorial to his only son. When the school first accepted students in 1891, the student body actually voted for gold as the school's official color. However, another student assembly chose CARDINAL. A few days after this vote, local sportswriters picked up the CARDINAL theme after Stanford defeated Cal in the first "big game" — March 19, 1891 — i.e., "CARDINAL Triumphs O'er Blue and Gold." As for the nickname history, Stanford officially adopted the INDIAN on November 25, 1930. For years prior to the resolution, the INDIAN had been part of the Stanford athletic tradition. Perhaps it grew out of the fact that Cal's symbol was a bear or it may have come from the large INDIAN population of the area, or from INDIAN paraphernalia in abundance in the late 1800s. Whatever the origin, it was accepted by sportswriters and gained wide recognition. The INDIAN symbol was dropped in 1972 when meetings between Stanford Native American students and University president Richard Lyman concluded that the mascot and moniker were an insult to their culture and heritage. The latest incident concerning the Stanford nickname came on November 17, 1981, when University president Donald Kennedy declared that all Stanford athletic teams "will be represented and symbolized exclusively by the color CARDINAL." That's right, not the bird, but the color. "While various other mascots have been suggested and then allowed to wither, the color has continued to serve us well, as it has for 90 years. It is a rich and vivid metaphor for the very pulse of life," Kennedy said.

STETSON HATTERS

Originally named DeLand Academy, Stetson University was renamed after the famous Philadelphia hatmaker John B. Stetson in 1889. The nickname HATTERS, stemming from Stetson's business, started at the turn of the century. Another school in the Atlantic Sun

Conference is the Campbell University FIGHTING CAMELS. Formerly the HORNETS, the new name was derived from a misheard comment which included school founder Dr. James Archibald Campbell's surname; a student poll in the early 1960s resulted in Georgia State PANTHERS being selected, replacing the old OWLS nickname — a reference to the Night Owl image of the former Georgia Tech Night School. The PANTHER choice made good local sense as the teams already played many of their contests in the area still known as Panthersville. The Florida Atlantic University campus was designated a Burrowing OWL sanctuary in 1971 by the Audubon Society because of the birds of prey that live there. The feisty bird, traditionally associated with wisdom and determination, serves as that university's mascot and nickname. And the Samford University BULLDOG is a name newswriters' earliest recollections place somewhere around 1930.

SYRACUSE ORANGEMEN

Things got off to a rather humbling start in 1889 when, on November 23, the Syracuse PINK-and-BLUEMEN suffered a rather embarrassing 36-0 defeat at the hands of the University of Rochester, in Syracuse's only game of the year. PINK-and-BLUEMEN? That's right. SU played the game attired in white canvas uniforms trimmed with SU's school colors of pink and blue. Not only was the team much improved in 1880, finishing at 8-3, but so were the school colors. As the 1890 season began, Syracuse adopted orange as its new school color and the ORANGEMEN, and sartorial splendor, were officially born. For nearly half a century the painted and befeathered Saltine Warrior, presumably named because the area was known as Salt City, tomahawked the air and whooped along the sidelines of Archbold Stadium. But when the Native American campus organization, Onkwehonweneha, protested the mascot as racist and degrading, the Warrior went the way of the Indian mascots at Dartmouth and Stanford. He was supplanted by a gladiator of indeterminate origin, who lasted about as long as a Christian among the lions. Since then Syracuse hasn't had an official mascot. But when the ORANGE began playing both football and basketball in the Carrier Dome in 1980, a clan of dome gnomes sprang up. These included Dome Ranger in an orange cowboy outfit; Dome Eddie, a gnatlike figure in orange tights; the Beast from the East, a splash of electric green; and the Orange, a juiced-up, bumbling citrus fruit from which two legs encased in furry brown booties protrude. It's known on campus as "the official embarrassment." If ever a mascot is chosen, a member of the Lambda Chi Alpha fraternity will portray it, as they have since the 1950s.

NICKNAME: "THE ORANGE"

TARLETON STATE TEXANS

Back in 1925, when the college was known as John Tarleton Agricultural College, the athletic teams were called the PLOWBOYS, a name selected by then-Athletics Director W. J. Wisdom. Now playing in the Lone Star Conference, in 1961, college officials decided to have a contest to come up with a new athletic nickname to reflect Tarleton's new status as a four-year college. The top three vote-getters were TEXANS, ROCKETS, and PACKRATS. Although cognizant of current events — in 1961 the space race was about to take full bloom in Texas — ROCKETS finished second! The Tarleton TEXANS women's athletic teams have traditionally been known as the TEXANNS. This nickname was adopted in the late 1960s and borrowed, actually, from Ranger Junior College, which had taken to calling its female athletic teams the RANGE-ANNS.

TEMPLE OWLS

The OWL is the symbol and mascot for Temple University and has been since the school's founding in the 1800s. Temple was the first school in the United States to adopt the owl as its symbol. (Not as popular as the eagle or hawk, the owl nevertheless has special meaning for students at a dozen other four-year colleges and seven two-year colleges as well.) Story has it that the owl, a nocturnal hunter, was initially adopted as a symbol because Temple University began as a night school for ambitious young people of limited means. Russell Conwell, Temple's founder, encouraged these students with the remark, "The owl of the night makes the eagle of the day." Since those modest beginnings more than a hundred years ago, the owl's role and significance have expanded along with those of the university. The owl, in its splendid variety, inhabits all parts of the world. The owl is accepted as a universal symbol for wisdom and knowledge, and as such makes an excellent symbol and emblem for a center of learning. It must be remembered that the owl was the symbol of Athena, who was not only the goddess of wisdom, but was also the goddess of arts, skills, and even warfare. Because of its other attributes, the owl also makes an appropriate mascot for the athletic teams. Besides being perceptive and resourceful, quick, and courageous, the owl is a truly fierce fighter.

TENNESSEE VOLUNTEERS

The University of Tennessee was founded as Blount College in 1794 in a lone two-story house. As the state's land grant university, it draws the nickname of its athletic teams from the name most associated with the state — VOLUNTEERS. Tennessee acquired its name, the Volunteer State, in the early days of the 19th century when General Andrew Jackson mustered large armies from his home state to fight the Indians and later the British at the Battle of New Orleans. The name became even more prominent in the Mexican War when Governor Aaron V. Brown issued a call for 2,800 men to battle Santa Anna, and some 30,000 volunteered. The dragoon uniform worn by Tennessee regulars during that conflict is still seen adorning the color guard at UT athletic events. Charles Moore, a member of UT's first football team in 1891, selected the colors orange and white. They were the colors of the common American daisy that grew in profusion on "The Hill." Tennessee players did not appear in the now-famous orange jerseys until the season opening game in 1922. Good choice? The VOLUNTEERS defeated the team from Emory and Henry by a score of 50-0.

NICKNAME: "VOLS"

TEXAS A&M AGGIES

From its founding in 1876 until 1963, Texas Agricultural and Military was an all-male military school — a fact that has impacted many of its traditions. The Corps of Cadets is among the largest uniformed student groups outside the three U.S. service academies, and members are required to be in uniform at all official University functions, including athletic events. The nickname AGGIES was common for agricultural schools at the turn of the century, and Texas A&M was no exception. Though many schools adopted new monikers as the century unfolded (i.e., NC State became the WOLFPACK, and Colorado State became the RAMS), Texas A&M did not. "Reveille" is the name of the AGGIES' mascot. Now an American Collie, the original "Reveille" was a stray brought to campus after being hit by a car filled with AGGIES returning from a football game. She earned her name the next morning when, apparently feeling better, she howled through the morning. Reveille, indeed!

NICKNAME: "THE WRECKING CREW" (football's defense)

TEXAS CHRISTIAN HORNED FROGS

A *New York Sun* article dated December 1, 1911, referred to the team from Texas Christian University as the PURPLE HORNED FROGS, followed by the comment "Gosh, what a name!" and an upcoming confrontation against the Southern Methodist RED-and-BLUE MUSTANGS. The university adopted the HORNED FROG in 1897 for the school annual. Gradually, the plural HORNED FROGS, now minus the PURPLE, also became the recognized nickname for TCU's varsity athletic teams. The final considerations were the CACTUS and the HORNED FROG, commonly known throughout the Southwest as the horned toad or horny toad. Both were the most typically Texas subjects they could think of but the name CACTUS had already been adopted by State University in Austin — now the University of Texas. For a while, after TCU moved to Fort Worth when its main building in Waco burned down, the school was referred to as the CHRISTIANS. In 1980, the ESPN Sports Network selected the Texas Christian University's HORNED FROGS as the best sports nickname in the United States. The colors were selected in 1896 . . . purple to stand for royalty, and white for a clean game.

NICKNAME: "THE FROGS"

TEXAS-EL PASO MINERS

The University of Texas at El Paso was founded in 1914 as the School of Mines and Metallurgy. The first campus was destroyed by fire, and the school was moved to just a stone's throw from the Rio Grande. In 1919 the institution became a branch of the University of Texas System, and in 1949 was renamed Texas Western College. When the school changed its name once again in 1967 to the University of Texas at El Paso, it looked back to its own history for a nickname — the MINERS. School colors are white with blue accent and the mascot's name is "Paydirt Pete." Today, UTEP is the largest Hispanic-majority university in the continental United States.

TEXAS LONGHORNS

Christopher Columbus brought the first LONGHORN cattle to the New World on his second voyage; Santa Domingo reportedly brought them to Texas, which is where they are predominantly found. In the fall of 1903, Alex Weisberg, who later became one of the more prominent lawyers in Dallas, was editor-in-chief of the *Texan*, where D. A. Frank was a sports reporter. One day Weisberg told Frank, "D. A., hereafter in every sports article, call the team the LONGHORNS and we'll so have it named." Frank obeyed that instruction, and passed it on to his reporters after he became editor-in-chief. In 1907 the name became official, and the team has been called the LONGHORNS ever since. For over a hundred years of football, the school colors have been burnt orange and white. Today, the very impressive LONGHORN steer named "Bevo" is the University of Texas mascot.

NICKNAME: "HORNS"

TEXAS TECH RED RAIDERS

Prior to 1930, the athletic teams from Texas Tech University were called the MATADORS, a cultural nod in the direction of the local Mexican influence — a matador being a bullfighter whose specialty is killing the bull with a sword thrust. It was the wife of then-gridiron head coach Pete Cawthon who suggested a name change. Considering the red uniforms the football team wore, and the fact that the team was now travelling from coast to coast to challenge other university teams, she offered up the new moniker, RED RAIDERS. School authorities went for it immediately, and the teams have been called the RED RAIDERS ever since.

NICKNAME: "RAIDERS"

TOLEDO ROCKETS

Referred to as the BLUE AND GOLD, MUNIES (for municipal university), and DWYER'S BOYS (after coach James Dwyer), when the University of Toledo played then-powerful Carnegie Tech in football in 1923, Pittsburgh sportswriters were surprised to learn that UT did not have an official nickname. As the game unfolded, writers pressed James Neal, a UT student working in the press box, to come up with something. The student labeled the team SKYROCKETS, obviously impressed by his school's flashy performance against a superior team. The sportswriters shortened the name to ROCKETS, which has been used since. Many suggestions for UT's nickname have been considered through the years, including a Spanish theme of TOREADORS or BULLS, in honor of Toledo's sister city in Spain. Others suggestions have included COMMODORES, TURTLES, BANCROFT HIGHWAYMEN, and JEEPS. In 1961, UT procured a genuine rocket from the U.S. Army missile program. The one-ton rocket, which sits outside the Glass Bowl, carries two sets of fins and a propellant booster capable of guiding the missile to supersonic velocity. It was donated, in part, because of the University's affiliation with the Ordinance Corps of the U.S. Department of Army. Midnight blue and gold have been the school's colors since 1919.

TRINITY CHRISTIAN TROLLS

Trinity Christian College is the only college or university from among 3,200 in the U.S. to have the TROLLS nickname. In 1966, Dr. Peter Steen, Trinity's professor of theology and basketball coach, made a request of the college's first president: "We're starting a basketball team, and we need a name!" President De Jong's family, which included three sons and wife Joanne, began to ponder the problem. Joanne suggested using the dictionary. "We'll work for a name with alliteration, using the TR in 'Trinity'and find some noun from the tr's to use with it," she said. Soon they came upon TROLL: in Scandinavian folklore, any of a race of supernatural beings, variously conceived of as giants or dwarfs, living underground or in caves. They loved it! The Trinity TROLLS would need supernatural powers to develop into a viable team, and there was hope that they would soon emerge from their cave of anonymity to become a team which would cheer and enliven student life at this fledgling college in Palos Heights, Illinois.

TULANE GREEN WAVE

From 1893 to 1919, the athletic teams of Tulane were known as the OLIVE AND BLUE. In 1919, the *Tulane Weekly* began calling the football team the GREENBACKS. On October 20, 1920, Earl Sparling, editor of the *Tulane Hullabaloo*, wrote a football song that was printed in the newspaper. The song was titled "The Rolling Green Wave." Although the name wasn't immediately adopted, it began to receive acceptance. On November 19, 1920, a report of the Tulane-Mississippi A&M game in the *Hullabaloo* referred to the team as the GREEN WAVE. By the end of the season, the *Hullabaloo* was using the term GREEN WAVE to refer to all Tulane athletic teams, as were many daily newspapers, although as late as 1923, the name GREENBACKS was still in use. In its infancy, Tulane's mascot was a pelican riding a surfboard, becoming an angry-looking wave in 1964. The block "T" with waves arrived in 1986, and a mascot resembling the character "Gumby" is now the GREEN WAVE mascot.

TULSA GOLDEN HURRICANE

Did a HURRICANE really make it all the way to Tulsa, Oklahoma? Sort of. Back in 1922, a new football coach named Howard Archer came to Tulsa all the way from Pennsylvania. Before Archer's arrival, local sportswriters referred to the school team as the KENDALLITES, the PRESBYTERIANS, TIGERS, the ORANGE AND BLACK, and the TULSANS. In the fall of 1922 they were being hailed as the YELLOW JACKETS, apparently due to the fact that they were wearing new yellow and black uniforms instead of the traditional orange and black. Archer was on the bandwagon immediately to give his team a more distinctive name. After hearing a remark in practice one day about how his team was "roaring through opponents," and because of their new jersey colors, he thought of the GOLDEN TORNADOES. He quickly found out, however, that Georgia Tech took the name in 1917. Archer quickly evolved the name from a tornado to a hurricane, a team vote turned yellow into gold, and the team officially became the Tulsa GOLDEN HURRICANE.

UCLA BRUINS

In 1919 the University of California in Los Angeles was known as the "Southern Branch" of the University of California. The UCLA football team, then known as the CUBS because of their younger relationship to the California BEARS in Berkeley, were playing their first season against such powerhouses as the Occidental College freshmen and Manual Arts High School. (Manual Arts defeated the CUBS 74-0!) In 1922 the team won its first game and celebrated by changing its name to the more aggressive GRIZZLIES. But in 1925, when the University joined the Pacific Coast Conference, a problem arose. The University of Montana, also in the PCC, had prior rights to the nickname GRIZZLIES. So UCLA, which had changed its name from the Southern Branch in 1927, became the BRUINS in 1928 and have been recognized as such with increasing importance and success over the years. The difficulty in obtaining and caring for live bears eventually led to the appearance of costumed student mascots. Joe and Josephine BRUIN make UCLA one of the few select universities that has both male and female mascots. While the nickname BRUINS seemed to be attached to the football team in the early years, the success of UCLA in as many as 18 different sports — most notably, men's basketball in the 1960s and '70s under legendary coach John Wooden — has made BRUINS recognized the world over.

UTAH STATE AGGIES

Utah State University was originally founded on March 8, 1888, as the Agricultural College of Utah. According to John Lewandowski of the Utah State Sports Information Department, the nickname AGGIES is a natural extension of the school's founding as the state's land grant institution. The Utah State Legislature changed the school's name to Utah State University on March 8, 1957. Athletic teams continued to be officially called the AGGIES, but fans and supporters of all types also refer fondly to their teams as BIG BLUE, a reference to the school colors of navy blue and white. Lewandowski says, "Our research does not indicate that any other nickname has ever been used, nor have we been able to find any history of the choosing of the nickname." Many agricultural schools have used the nickname AGGIES, and it seems it was simply a natural selection for Utah State.

UTAH UTES

The state of Utah was named for the Ute Indians who lived in Utah prior to the arrival of white settlers. On April 9, 1865, tensions transformed into violence when a handful of Utes and Mormon frontiersmen met in Manti, Sanpete County, to settle a dispute over some killed cattle. The Indian delegation, which included a dynamic young Ute named Black Hawk, left, promising retaliation for a considered slight. The ensuing Black Hawk Indian War was the longest and most destructive conflict between pioneer immigrants and Native Americans in Utah history. The word "eutaw" means "dwellers in the tops of the mountains." The Beehive State has a beautiful state insect, the midnight butterfly. In deciding to pick a nickname with a nod to the state, however, the University of Utah selected UTES over all else. Playing in the Western Athletic Conference, the University of Utah campus is located in the capital city of Salt Lake City. School colors are crimson and white.

VANDERBILT COMMODORES

Beginning with the efforts of Cornelius Vanderbilt in the early 19th century, the Vanderbilt family amassed a fortune in the shipping and railroad industries. It became one of the wealthiest and most prominent families in the United States. Cornelius was born in 1794, and when he died in New York City on January 4, 1877, he left behind a fortune of about 100 million dollars! He contributed a large sum of money to Central

University, renamed Vanderbilt University, in Nashville, Tennessee. The school's athletic teams are also named in honor of Vanderbilt, who was a commodore — an officer ranking above a captain and below a rear admiral — in the U.S. Navy. The mascot, "Mr. Commodore," wears white hair, a white beard, a coat with tails, and a big hat.

NICKNAME: "VANDY"
           "THE 'DORES"

VIRGINIA CAVALIERS

Since being founded by Thomas Jefferson in 1819, the most prominent and widely accepted nicknames at the University of Virginia include CAVALIERS, WAHOOS, and HOOS, although V-MEN, VIRGINIANS, and OLD DOMINION have also been used. CAVALIERS, WAHOOS, and HOOS are used almost interchangeably to refer to teams and players. CAVALIERS is more often used by the media, while WAHOOS and HOOS are frequently used by Virginia students and fans. Legend has it that Washington and Lee baseball fans dubbed the Virginia players WAHOOS during the fiercely contested rivalry that existed between the two in-state schools in the 1890s. By 1940, WAHOOS was in general use around school grounds to denote University students or events relating to them. The abbreviated HOOS sprang up later in student papers and has gained popularity in recent years. In 1923, the college newspaper, *College Topics*, held a contest to choose an official alma mater fight song. "The Cavalier Song," written by Lawrence Haywood Lee, Jr., Class of 1924, with music by Fulton Lewis, Jr., Class of '25, won. Although this song failed to become part of University tradition, "The Cavalier Song" inspired the nickname CAVALIERS.

NICKNAME: "CAVS"

VIRGINIA TECH HOKIES

This story leads back to 1896 when Virginia Agricultural and Mechanical College changed its name to Virginia Polytechnic Institute. With the name change came the necessity for a new cheer, for which the student body held a contest. Senior O. M. Stull won first prize for his "HOKIE!" yell, which was first used that fall and is still heard today. Later, when asked if HOKIE had any special meaning, Stull explained that the word was solely the product of his imagination! He put it in his cheer because he thought it sounded good. It soon became a nickname for all Tech students. Virginia Tech has the distinction of two nicknames. The teams came to be known as the FIGHTING GOBBLERS, thanks to the efforts of Floyd Meade, who appeared at Tech football games in the 1900s dressed as a clown for the entertainment of fans. The clown act grew tiring and Meade began training a large turkey to pull him around in a small cart. Meade and his turkey first appeared on opening day 1912, and over the next few years, made the GOBBLER a part of Virginia Tech history. In 1962 the live turkey evolved into a costumed mascot, and the HOKIE BIRD'S antics at all Virginia Tech sporting events have long been loved by children and alumni alike. The official colors of Chicago maroon and burnt orange were selected in 1896 because they made a "unique combination" not worn elsewhere at the time.

WAKE FOREST DEMON DEACONS

Reports indicate that by the early 1920s, Wake Forest College nicknames were the BAPTISTS and THE OLD GOLD & BLACK. Most historians believe that the old-gold-and-black color scheme of the athletic uniforms came from the connection with the tiger mascot, created by 19-year-old John Heck, and not, as some have proposed, from any association with the Bible. In 1923 Wake Forest had a major reversal of athletic fortunes, and it was felt that the nicknames of the time were not descriptive enough of the new-found spirit. After Wake Forest defeated rival Trinity (now Duke), school newspaper editor Mayon Parker first referred to his team as DEMON DEACONS, in recognition of what he termed their "devilish" play and fighting spirit. Wake Forest's news director, Henry Belk, liked the title and began using it extensively. In his deacon top hat, tails, and a black umbrella, the DEMON DEACON mascot has drawn praise from national media, such as sportscaster Bob Costas, who said, "I love the Deacon. He's the mascot of protocol. I've never known him to be rude. He represents the gentility of the Old South, a very dapper guy. I think one day a year all Wake Forest men should dress as the Demon Deacon and walk — no, promenade — that way to class."

WASHINGTON BEARS

The earliest nickname for this St. Louis school's athletic teams was PIKERS, a name whose roots lie in the 1904 World's Fair! The PIKE, which ran along Lindell Blvd. between DeBaliviere and Skinker, was the World's Fair's amusement section. After the Fair, when the University moved to the Hiltop campus, the new campus' proximity to the PIKE led to the tradition of using the nickname PIKERS to refer to both athletic teams and Washington University students in general. The teams were known as the PIKERS until 1926, when Chancellor Herbert S. Hadley called a meeting of the students, suggesting the name to be changed to the BEARS, and the name has been used ever since. While no longer used in connection with sports, the name PIKERS lives on as the name of the male a cappella ensemble. There are 31 four-year colleges and universities using the BEAR nickname, ranking it in the top 10 for most common names, with EAGLES topping the collegiate list.

WASHINGTON HUSKIES

The University of Washington's teams were called SUN DODGERS before the 1920s, originating when a college magazine of the same name was banned from campus and, in protest, students adopted the name for their teams. But the SUN DODGERS didn't do much for the Northwest's image, so a committee set out in 1921 to pick a new nickname. The decision came down to MALAMUTES and HUSKIES. The committee felt those were appropriate because of Seattle's close proximity to the Alaskan frontier. The HUSKY was voted the most appropriate. Remnants of the SUN DODGER name remain, however. Before the 1920s, Washington's football mascot was a three-and-a-half-foot-tall wooden statue named Sunny Boy, a sculptured replica of the happy-faced character, Sunny, who appeared in the University's humor magazine, *Sun Dodger*. When Washington changed its mascot in 1923, Sunny Boy disappeared and was not discovered until 1948 in South Bend, Indiana! Twenty-three years later, Notre Dame promptly returned it. The HUSKIES have one football record that may never be beaten. From the last game of the 1907 season until the 1917 campaign, Washington did not lose one of its 63 games, winning 59 and tying 4. Another HUSKY first occurred on October 31, 1981, when cheerleader Rob Weller (yes, the same Rob Weller who hosted television's *Entertainment Tonight*) instructed the Washington crowd to start in one section and make a human wave. That's right, despite claims by others, the Wave can trace its origin to HUSKY Stadium.

WASHINGTON STATE COUGARS

Following the first football game between Washington State and California in 1919, an Oakland cartoonist portrayed the Washington State team as fierce Northwest COUGARS chasing the defeated GOLDEN BEARS. A few days later, on October 28, 1927, Washington students officially designated COUGARS as their nickname. During homecoming, Governor Roland Hartley presented Washington State students with a live COUGAR cub. The first COUGAR mascot was named BUTCH, to honor Herbert "Butch" Meeker of Spokane. He was Washington State University's gridiron star at the time — a diminutive halfback who played like a COUGAR. Governors have continued to present COUGARS to WSU over the years.

WEST POINT BLACK KNIGHTS

Perhaps better known as the Army CADETS — with colors black, gold, and grey, and the motto, "Duty, Honor, Country"—the United States Military Academy at West Point was founded in New York on March 16, 1802. Football had its birth in 1890, the result of a challenge from the U.S. Naval Academy. The Army CADETS lost that first game to the MID-SHIPMEN from Annapolis, but revenged that loss a year later. Since 1972 the Commander in Chief's Trophy has been awarded annually to the winner of the round-robin football competition among the Army CADETS, Navy MIDS, and the Air Force FALCONS. The CADETS nickname, a clear reference to military ranking, is not the only one Army has used. The first reference to the boys from the Point as the BLACK KNIGHTS was in a *New York Sun* article, in December of 1944. It was in a poem written in support of the CADETS in their Army-Navy classic: "The Gold Crests gleam as the BLACK KNIGHTS ride,/ Out to uphold the Corps, and its pride." Four mules, heirs of a tradition that dates back to 1899, serve as the team mascots for the Corps of CADETS.

NICKNAMES: "ARMY"
                "CADETS"
                "THE POINT"
                "DRAGOONS"
                "THE CORPS"

WEST VIRGINIA MOUNTAINEERS

The origin of the state's name is from the English-named neighboring state of Virginia. Nicknamed the Mountain State, the motto is "MOUNTAINEERS are Always Free." When West Virginia University was founded in 1867, the University adopted the MOUNTAINEERS moniker from the state, as the term had already been identified with the area for more than a century. After that, no other nickname was ever considered. Early WVU teams used the nickname SNAKES, although it is not now known why. The MOUNTAINEER mascot first roamed the sidelines in the late 1920s. Mascots wore the familiar coonskin cap and carried a rifle, but they dressed in coveralls and flannel shirts until the late 1940s. It was then that the genuine buckskin outfit made its debut. The rifle is a true flintlock that requires the user to become schooled in the amount of powder required to fire the charge.

WESTERN KENTUCKY HILLTOPPERS

The evolution of the nickname HILLTOPPERS is obvious to those who have seen the Western Kentucky University campus. The operations of the Western Kentucky State Normal School were moved from the site of its forerunner, Southern Normal School, to a commanding hill in the southwestern portion of Bowling Green, Kentucky, on February 4, 1911. The move was completed as the entire student body marched to the new site, carrying various articles of school equipment! Since the summit of "the Hill" rises 232 feet above nearby Barren River and a comparatively level plain surrounds the Hill, it was only natural that the young athletes who represented the institution centered on the crest should come to be known as HILLTOPPERS. Still, the name did not come into use until the 1925-26 school year. Prior to that time, Western's athletic teams were commonly referred to as PEDAGOGUES and TEACHERS.

WESTERN MARYLAND GREEN TERRORS

The female basketball team from Western Maryland College named itself after a fish found in the Amazon — *Aequidens rivulatus*, or GREEN TERROR. Immediately, the rest of the Western Maryland teams followed suit. From the genus *Aequidens*, the creature is found in South America, in the Amazon Basin. Western Maryland joins colleges like the Santa Cruz BANANA SLUGS and the California State University Maritime KEEL-HAULERS for an appreciation of the aquatic side of life.

WESTERN MICHIGAN BRONCOS

In 1939, the Athletic Board of the then-Western State Teachers College adopted the nickname of BRONCOS because the former name of

HILLTOPPERS was often confused with similar monikers used by other colleges. Many suggested names were turned in for consideration at the time. John Gill, who was the assistant football coach under M. J. "Mike" Gary, submitted the nickname BRONCO. (Gill later served as the BRONCO head gridiron coach and as Western Michigan University's associate athletic director until his retirement in 1969.) The most popular BRONCO ever is "Buster Bronco," the school's mascot, who works diligently to spread "Gold Pride" throughout the area.

NICKNAME: "BRONCS"

WICHITA STATE SHOCKERS

Two viable-sounding stories have reached us about the nickname from Wichita State University in Kansas. In 1904 football manager R. J. Kirk was helping post signs the week before Fairmont College (as Wichita State was then known) played Chilicco. Kirk tagged Chilicco with the nickname INDIANS on the posters, and a press agent from the Wichita Fall Festival, who was helping promote the event, demanded that Kirk come up with an appropriate moniker for Fairmount to balance the poster design. On the spot, Kirk wrote WHEATSHOCKERS on the poster. As a result, the football manager made his way into the athletic history books. The other story concerns the players on the football team earning money SHOCKING wheat, which is gathering wheat into bundles, tying it, and standing it on end to dry out — a process that technology has made obsolete. Other schools found out, and used the terms WHEAT SHOCKER, or simply SHOCKER, as an insult. As with many names that began as insults, SHOCKERS eventually became a badge of honor. "WuShock," the mascot, became a reality in 1948, but only became flesh and blood in 1954 when Dave Johnson and members of the art department made a costume. WuShock has since been in the movies, been thrown out of a basketball game, and been kidnapped, and has entertained thousands of SHOCKER fans.

WISCONSIN BADGERS

The University of Wisconsin's nickname, BADGERS, was borrowed from the state. The territory was dubbed the "BADGER State," not because of the animals in the region, but rather from an association with lead miners in the 1820s. Prospectors came to the state looking for minerals. Without shelter in the winter, the miners had to "live like badgers" in tunnels burrowed into hillsides. The badger, a strong and belligerent animal, had been attending Wisconsin home games in a cage on the sidelines for a long time. On more than one occasion, the live badger stopped a football game for up to five minutes before a sideline hero recaptured the animal with a flying tackle. It was finally decided in the interest of fan safety that Wisconsin's beloved mascot be retired to the Madison Zoo. In 1946, William C. Shafer, Jr., drew a badger on his feet, wearing a sweater and carrying a football. This mascot was alternatively named Benny, Buddy, Bernie, Bobby, Bouncey, Regdab (BADGER backward) and finally Bucky — short for Buckingham U. Badger.

NICKNAME: "THE BIG RED"

WYOMING COWBOYS

The nickname COWBOYS was applied to Wyoming athletic teams as early as 1891, two years before the first official football game. The story is that the Wyoming pickup football team appealed to a 220-pound cowpuncher, Fred Bush, for help in a game against the Cheyenne SOLDIERS. Bush signed up for a course or two and came out for the team. When he trotted onto the field decked out in a checkered shirt and COWBOY hat, someone yelled, "Hey, look at the COWBOY!" Since many of the members of the team were also ex-COWBOYS, the name stuck. In the Spring of 1895, the first ever University of Wyoming Alumni Banquet was held. Decorations for the event included brown-eyed Susans, a flower native to southeastern Wyoming. The Alumni were so impressed with the brown-and-yellow beauties that they decided to select them as the official school colors at UW. And that familiar fight song sung by the fans after every Wyoming victory? Ragtime COWBOY Joe.

Part 6

The Best of the Rest

ABILENE PRAIRIE DOGS

In 1993, when independent baseball's Texas-Louisiana League co-founders Pierce and John Bryant were scouting the state for potential host cities for their fledgling league, Pierce came to Abilene. The old Abilene BLUE SOX played their final game in the Big State League in 1957 before packing it in. The team had played 11 seasons in the Key City at the old Blue Sox Stadium, but America's fascination with air conditioning and television put pro baseball on hold in Abilene for the next 38 years. When $850,000 in improvements were made to Abilene Christian University's Crutcher Scott Field, the PRAIRIE DOGS came to town. While PRAIRIE DOGS may not have been the first choice if a survey had been taken of the fans, Abilene businessman K. O. Long's suggestion in the name-the-team contest seemed to capture their imaginations (especially the young ones!). The quest for a friendly, approachable mascot ended when "Grounder" was introduced. Three local schoolchildren were winners in a name-the-mascot competition.

ACADIA AXEMEN

Acadia was the name of the French colony on the northeast coast of North America from 1604 until 1713, and is the native name of Nova Scotia. Acadia University, founded in 1838 in Wolfville, Nova Scotia, was built initially by hand. The land was cleared and the trees felled by that pre-chainsaw tool — the ax. This action forms the heritage of the name of the university's men's athletic teams, the AXEMEN. The women's teams are known as the AXETTES, and they were national soccer champions in 1989. The AXEMEN of Acadia have won national athletic titles in swimming, basketball, hockey, and football.

ALTOONA CURVE

Ballpark groundbreaking ceremonies for the CURVE took place in March of 1998, when Double-A baseball came to a very enthusiastic Altoona in central Pennsylvania. In June of that year, Altoona's minor-league entry selected CURVE as its nickname. The clever combination railroad/baseball moniker beat out several other finalists including LAKE MONSTERS, RIDGE RUNNERS, and, believe it or not, FISH. Local dreams came true in 1998 when the team became affiliated with long-time local fan favorites — the Pittsburgh PIRATES.

ARSENAL GUNNERS

Initially known as DIAL SQUARE after a workshop at the Royal ARSENAL — where most of the original team worked — this British Premier League soccer club began life in 1886 under founder Daniel Danskin, a Scotsman from Kirkcaldy. From the earliest days until 1891, it played under the name Royal ARSENAL, an obvious nod in the direction of the gunnery. The leading light at the time was former Nottingham Forest player Fred Beardsley, who got his old club to help out by giving him some spare red shirts and a football. Apart from a brief trial with red and light blue stripes in 1895, the team played in an all-red strip until 1933. A pig farm was among the local venues used until the club moved to the Invicta Ground at Plumstead in 1890. Becoming professional as Woolwich ARSENAL in 1891, the club was elected to the Football League's Second Division two years later. Promoted to the First Division in 1904, increasing debts forced the club into liquidation in 1910 only to be rescued by property developer Henry Norris, who initially suggested a merger with Fulham. Relegated in 1913 after winning only one home game, a new start was made, despite vociferous local opposition, at Highbury in North London. In 1914, the club was re-christened "THE" ARSENAL before, in 1927, it adopted the simple ARSENAL name which has become famous throughout the world. A favorite nickname, again in reference to the club's origins in gunnery, is THE GUNNERS.

ASHEVILLE TOURISTS

The Asheville Professional Baseball Club was first called the TOURISTS around 1924. Prior to that time, the team was known as the SKYLANDERS. The SKYLANDERS name was taken from the phrase "Land of the Sky," which is used to describe the Western North Carolina Mountains where Asheville is situated. The name TOURISTS developed because of Asheville's reputation as a TOURIST mecca. The city is located at the conjunction of the Blue Ridge and Great Smoky Mountains. Asheville is about 2,200 feet above sea level and the home of the famed Biltmore Estate (George Vanderbilt's 250-room mansion). The region boasts outstanding hunting, trout fishing, hiking, golf, and water sports. Grandfather Mountain and Chimney Rock Park are other nearby attractions. Downtown Asheville has many great examples of Art Deco architecture of the early 20th century. In 1972, the TOURISTS switched their working agreement to the Baltimore ORIOLES, who insisted they change their name to the Asheville ORIOLES. This affiliation lasted through the 1975 season, when the renamed TOURISTS became a part of the Texas

RANGERS organization. Asheville, playing in the South Atlantic League, has since seen its parent club affiliation go from the Houston ASTROS to the Colorado ROCKIES, but the traditional TOURISTS name has endured!

ASTON VILLA VILLANS

Legend has it that Aston Villa began life on a foggy winter night with a meeting of cricket fans under a gaslight on an anonymous street corner in Birmingham, England, in 1874. Members of Villa Cross Wesleyan Chapel were keen to find a way of keeping fit during the close season. The British Premier League club's first proper ground was reportedly at Aston Lower Grounds amusement park where rival attractions included a variety of performers such as trick cyclists. Moving to a field in Perry Barr in 1876, the team rapidly captured the local imagination and decided to build Villa Park as its permanent home. In 1888, Villa joined the newly formed Football League instigated by a Villa committee member, Scotsman William McGregor, a wealthy draper who had moved to Birmingham in 1870. The VILLANS — the nickname, which is a wordplay on their location—soon made their mark with four First Division championships in less than a decade: 1894, 1896, 1897, and 1899. The VILLANS were proud of their collection of star names, including the unforgettable Charlie Athersmith — who, so the story goes, played one rain-hit game carrying an umbrella.

ATLANTA KNIGHTS

Atlanta's former International Hockey League franchise president Richard Adler and wife Judi decided on KNIGHTS after looking through the dictionary for names which appealed to them, and could be adapted appealingly to a logo. Remaining a family affair, Judi's father designed the team logo, featuring a skating suit of armour. Established in 1992-93, the KNIGHTS made IHL history when they became the first pro team to employ a female goaltender in a regular season game when Manon Rheaume of Quebec played against Salt Lake on December 13, 1993. In 1996 the Atlanta franchise moved north to Quebec City, replacing the National Hockey League's NORDIQUES who had become the Colorado AVALANCHE.

BISHOP GAITERS

No, this GAITER has nothing to do with the cousin of the crocodile. In fact, the Bishop's University GAITERS nickname does not refer to a beast of any description. Instead, in simplest form, a gaiter is a legging! To explain requires a brief examination of history for this Canadian university. The Anglican Church—the Church of England — founded Bishop's. In earlier days, a School of Divinity prepared some graduates for holy orders and many of the faculty were referred to as CHURCHMEN. Part of the traditional garb worn by such individuals was the gaiter. According to Funk and Wagnalls, "gaiter" is defined as a "covering, as of leather or canvas, worn over the leg." As the first of Bishop's intercollegiate teams entered competition, one naturally looked to some unique attribute of the University as a nickname. By 1949, the use of GAITER became so prominent that the University officially changed its nickname from PURPLE AND WHITE, which was in reference to the school colors. On a side note, even though the school is Bishop's University, the sports teams are known to be from Bishop University, without the apostrophe and "s." The school mascot, not surprisingly, is an alligator.

BOLTON WANDERERS

Under schoolmaster and captain Thomas Ogden, this British Premier League club dates from 1874 — when its president was local vicar Reverend J. F. Wright. To become a member, men had to pay two-and-a-half pence. When the vicar of Christ Church attempted to put too many restrictions on how church premises could be used, the club broke away and, in 1877, formed the Bolton WANDERERS. For the next 18 years, they had no permanent home — consistent with their nickname. Initially called the REDS, because of their original red-and-white quartered shirts, they experimented with several strips. For a time in the early 1880s, they even played in white shirts with red spots because they thought it made players look larger and more intimidating. One of the original 12 members of the Premier Football League in 1888, they remained in one of the top two Divisions until the 1970s. After a period of decline, accompanied by the 1946 Burnden Park disaster in which 33 fans died, success returned in the 1950s. Promotion to the British Premier League marks the return to former glory days after a 30-year downward drift, culminating in 1987 when — for the first time — the TROTTERS descended to the lowest division in the League.

NICKNAME: "TROTTERS"

BRITISH COLUMBIA LIONS

The remarkable Annis Stukus was the coach, general manager, and publicity manager of the British Columbia LIONS from the team's inception in the Canadian Football League ("Started something from nothing") in 1953 until 1955. When he retired after his three-year contract, the team had to hire five men to take his place. Stukus graciously offered wonderful anecdotes for this book. The LIONS nickname was the product of a fan contest held in all media. Twin mountain peaks can be seen just north of the city of Vancouver, and legend has it they look like LIONS guarding over British property. They are actually called the LION Peaks. Stukus rejected the Vancouver LIONS because he wanted the team to embrace all of B.C. The only other name he remembered from that time was the Vancouver ELECTRICS, after the B.C. Electric Company, because, as a fan suggested, "They're big and strong and powerful and never get beaten." Stukus was responsible for financing and came up with a novel approach for getting funds. He sold memberships to the club for 20 dollars apiece. He announced that it was his intention to sell only 3,000 memberships, and after that it didn't matter if you knew the King of England, you couldn't get one. He sold 5,000, including memberships to Bob Hope and Bing Crosby! Stukus' contribution to the second-year ad campaign was the line "The Lions will roar in '54." They only roared at the box office, winning just one game on the field. The fans went crazy after that lone win, tearing down the wooden goalposts. They sold pieces of this "authentic" wood door to door for 2 dollars apiece. Stukus laughed, "If we got all that sold wood back we could've built goalposts from here to the clouds."

NICKNAME: "LEO"

BROOKLYN CYCLONES

Baseball returned to the Brooklyn, New York, area in a fury in 2001 with the CYCLONES, an affiliate of the New York METS. The CYCLONES were named through a name-the-team contest. About 7,000 entries were submitted, with "The CYCLONES" being submitted about 1,000 times. The Cyclone is a national icon at Coney Island. It is one of the country's oldest roller coasters, and a wooden one at that! It is the one thing most commonly associated with Coney Island. Some other names submitted were THE BUMS, METS, DODGERS, THE HOT DOGS, THE SWEATHOGS, and many more. They were all considered, but in the end, the CYCLONES was by far the most popular and appropriate nickname. The team's mascot is "Sandy the Seagull." Sandy's name has a dual significance. The stadium is located right on the beach (thus, the sand), and it is also a nod to a former Brooklyn DODGER, Sandy Koufax. The team colors are blue, red, and yellow — colors predominant in Coney Island history. They are seen on the Parachute Jump and throughout

Astroland. The CYCLONES mark the return of baseball to Brooklyn after a 44-year absence!

CALGARY DINOSAURS

Long before *Jurassic Park* made nicknames like RAPTORS contemporary, the University of Calgary's teams were called DINOSAURS. Originally the University of Alberta at Calgary, the campus became autonomous in 1966. Students were looking for a name unique to the vicinity. Legend has it that while excavating the ground for the new campus in 1966, a huge skeleton was dug up. It belonged to a *Tyrannosaurus rex*, the "terrible lizard" that ruled North America 65 million years ago. A nickname was born. The Calgary area is rich with dinosaur bones, and 90 miles from campus is the world-famous Tyrell Museum and its impressive collection of prehistoric skeletons found in and around Alberta. Remembering that this was in the early 1980s, long before the dinosaur fad, there was a student uprising against the less than friendly moniker and T-Rex mascot, but that blew over — as did the female athletes referring to themselves as DINIES. In fact, Calgary DINOSAUR pins are more popular than ever at Canadian college athletic events.

NICKNAME: "DINOS"

CHARLESTON RIVERDOGS

This Class-A affiliate of the Tampa Bay DEVIL RAYS moved their team into Joseph P. Riley Park in Charleston, South Carolina, and two things happened. First, they changed their name with the help of the local media, selecting RIVERDOGS over RIVERRATS because of Charleston's location right on the river. Second, they received a wonderful accolade from *USA Today* when the national newspaper in 2000 selected Joseph P. Riley Park one of the top 10 best ballparks to visit in Minor League Baseball. The team from Charleston has two mascots, Charlie the RIVERDOG and Chelsea the RIVERDOG, both of whom are used for community relations and to entertain the crowds.

CHATTANOOGA LOOKOUTS

In 1888, and still with amateur status, the Chattanooga baseball club was called the SULLIVANS. Then in 1909, O. B. Andrews obtained a

South Atlantic professional franchise for Chattanooga and the games were played at Chamberlain Field. Johnny Dobbs was manager and the team was given their new nickname, the LOOKOUTS, at this time. It was as a result of a fan contest, won by W. O. Powell. They were named at that time after LOOKOUT Mountain, right there in Chattanooga. The LOOKOUTS went on to win the South Atlantic (Sally) League pennant, walking off with the first half of the season. The team from Augusta won the second half. In the playoff, the story goes that when the LOOKOUTS went to Augusta, the hometown fans kidnapped Chattanooga's pitcher! Now more than a hundred years old, the Chattanooga LOOKOUTS are a Double-A affiliate of the Cincinnati REDS and play in the Southern League.

CHICAGO WOLVES

Established in 1994-95, Chicago's team president and general manager Grant Mulvey of the International Hockey League chose the WOLVES moniker. Mulvey said he "wanted to make sure that this team had a name that would last forever; a name that would weather all trends and obstacles ... we went through lists and lists of possible names and then one day the name WOLVES came up, and it stuck for good." The Chicago WOLVES sold out their first-ever home game on October 14, 1994, which at the time was the 10th-largest crowd in league history.

CHILLICOTHE PAINTS

The PAINTS nickname and team logo were chosen to stay within the theme set by the Frontier Professional Baseball league. The moniker originated as the result of a name-the-team contest, along with help from the owner and friends. The Paint Horse is documented as being the preferred horse by the American Indians, considered by many authorities to be the greatest horsemen who ever lived. The Paint Horse and Chillicothe are part of the tradition of the Old Frontier. The Paint Horse is known to be a combination of versatility, strength, and aggressiveness, with an extra dash of color and individuality, which is displayed in the logo — a horse with "painted" markings and colorful war feathers flowing from the horse's mane. The feathers have accents of red and gold tones. The PAINT Horse is to symbolize the team spirit and is known as the "Sport Model of the Horse World."

CINCINNATI CYCLONES

The dictionary definition of the word CYCLONES loosely suggests a windstorm with a violent, whirling movement; tornado or hurricane; a storm with strong winds rotating clockwise in the Southern Hemisphere, counter-clockwise in the Northern Hemisphere, about a moving center. CYCLONES was actually carried over from the Cincinnati team's days in the East Coast Hockey League. Moving to the International Hockey League, owner Doug Kirchoffer recognized that the name would sound good alongside Cincinnati, and it would certainly lend itself to an active logo. Established in 1992-93, Cincinnati had already been home to the MOHAWKS from 1952 to 1958.

CLEVELAND LUMBERJACKS

Lumberjacking might not be the first thing a fan would think of when Cleveland is mentioned, but this 35-year-old hockey franchise actually started in Muskegon, Michigan. The lumberjacking industry was prevalent when the city of Muskegon was formed, so it was no surprise that more than 600 people submitted it as their entry in a name-the-team contest, conducted in 1984 when owner Larry Gordon bought the franchise. LUMBER-JACKS remained in place when the franchise moved to Cleveland in 1992. It played under the name ZEPHYRS from 1960 to 1965, the MOHAWKS from 1965 to 1984, and finally the LUMBERJACKS from 1985 to 2001, when this International Hockey League team ceased operation.

DALLAS BURN

Major athletic shoe companies originally sponsored most of the franchises in Major League Soccer, and the BURN franchise was no exception, supported by Nike. The team submitted this: "The Dallas BURN logo system starts with the cowboy of the asphalt West; the loners, outsiders, and rebels found on cycle jackets and gas tanks. With a street-inspired, aggressive typeface and a fire-breathing mustang, the BURN logos reflect the raw horsepower of the team and the speed of the game all mixed together in the combustion chamber of a hot Texas field." Brings new meaning to the phrase "getting BURNED on the pitch."

DURHAM BULLS

Not just a great movie! Unlike so many "Johnny-come-lately" minor league teams that have chosen unique names, the name Durham BULLS dates back to the 19th century! The first use of the word BULL in conjunction with Durham came as the name for a brand of locally produced tobacco. It was called "Bull Durham" tobacco, and research indicates that as the Duke family searched for a name for their product, someone showed them a jar of English mustard, which had a bull on the label. The mustard was manufactured in Durham, England. Thus, "Bull Durham" tobacco was born. When Durham fielded its first professional baseball team in 1902, it was only natural that the team be called the Durham BULLS. The BULLS they have remained, with the exception of two years (1970-71) when a co-op team called the Raleigh-Durham TRIANGLES split its home dates between Durham and Raleigh. When that team folded, there was no professional baseball in the area until 1980, when the Durham BULLS were reborn in the Carolina League as an affiliate of the Atlanta BRAVES. In 1998, the BULLS became an affiliate for the Tampa Bay DEVIL RAYS.

EVERTON TOFFEEMEN

Nicknamed after the city of Everton, England's world-famous toffee, the origins of Everton FC (Football Club) go back to an English Methodist congregation called New Connexion, founded in 1797. They decided in a meeting in 1868 to renew their social activities in the Liverpool area by building a new chapel there. The following year, they bought some land on Breckfield Road North, between St. Domingo Vale and St. Domingo Grove. This was located near the district of Everton (originally OFER TUN), which had become part of the City of Liverpool in 1835. So, like many other British Premier League teams, Everton began life as a church team. They were founded in 1878, and were called St. Domingo's. The team first played using homemade goalposts in Stanley Park. Expanding and changing to their current name a year later, the team earned an early nickname as the BLACK WATCH because of their black shirts with white sash. The world-famous royal blue strip was adopted, after several experiments, in 1901. Quick to take advantage of employing professional players, the TOFFEEMEN were among the 12 clubs that were original members of the newly formed Football League in 1888. Since then, the club has been in the top flight for all but four seasons. In 1892, the TOFFEEMEN moved from Anfeld to their permanent Goodison Park home. In August of 1936, the British Broadcasting Company chose Everton's away game against Arsenal to be the first football match to be broadcast in Britain.

FORT WAYNE KOMETS

The dictionary definition of the word "comet" suggests a heavenly body in the solar system, having a starlike nucleus with a luminous mass around it, and, usually, a long luminous tail that points away from the sun. One of the original owners of the Fort Wayne International Hockey League franchise, Ernie Berg, had a wife named Katherine. When the results of a local contest produced the name COMETS, Berg, in keeping with his wife's name, converted the team nickname to be spelled with a "K." The KOMETS are the IHL's most established franchise, joining in 1952-53, the league's eighth year of operation.

FORT WAYNE WIZARDS

After almost two months without a name, the Fort Wayne (Indiana) professional baseball affiliate of the San Diego PADRES, found its iden-tity on October 22, 1992. In early September, the name-the-team contest was announced to have fans of Fort Wayne submit suggestions for the nickname of a baseball team, which started as an affiliate for the Minnesota TWINS. With the promotional help of a local restaurant, radio station, television station, and Delta Airlines, more than 20,000 entries were reviewed during the five-week promotion. With more than 1,500 dif-ferent names entered, the screening committee had a difficult time making a short list of finalists: CAVALRY, KEKIONGAS, SANDBAGGERS, and SUMMIT CITY PIONEERS. Paula King's submission of WIZARDS was randomly drawn from all of the other contestants who entered WIZARDS. She received two WIZARDS season tickets and two round-trip airline tick-ets. "Amazing Baseball" was the theme of the inaugural season for this Midwest League entry.

FREDERICK KEYS

Prior to the 1989 season, the Maryland Baseball Limited Partnership ran a name-the-team contest in the local paper. Some of the entries included the Frederick FLINTSTONES, FALCONS, FLYERS, and FLAMES. The orga-nization picked the Frederick KEYS from an entry by Bob Reed. The name is in honor of Francis Scott Key, the author of the "Star-Spangled Banner," who is from the area and is buried across from the team's current stadium. For having the winning entry, the Frederick KEYS, a Class-A affiliate of the Baltimore ORIOLES, gave Bob two season box seats for life. The Frederick KEYS play in the Carolina Baseball League.

GRAND RAPIDS MACKERS

Minor league basketball found a home in west Michigan when Grand Rapids was awarded an expansion franchise in the Continental Basketball Association for the 1989-90 season, and the team was nicknamed the HOOPS. After the 1993-94 season, the HOOPS were sold to the inventors of the nationally known Gus Macker 3-on-3 outdoor street basketball tournaments. Accordingly, the team's nickname and colors were changed to reflect the owner's business ... hence, MACKERS. Team colors for the HOOPS were purple, green, and orange. The MACKERS adopted Macker Maroon and Gus Gold with a Navy accent as their team colors.

HAMILTON TIGER-CATS

On Wednesday, November 3, 1869, in a room above George Lee's Fruit Store, the Hamilton (Canada) Football Club was formed. Hamilton clubs captured the Canadian Football League's Grey Cup in every decade of the 20th century, a feat matched in pro sport by only one other franchise, the National Hockey League's Montreal CANADIENS. Prior to World War II, the football team of the City of Hamilton was known as the TIGERS. The colors of yellow and black were well represented and the present philosophy of tough football was established in those early days. The only time that football was interrupted in Hamilton as a spectator sport was during the First and Second World Wars. After World War II, the TIGER Football Team started competition once again. At the same time, a new group in the City was formed and they became known as the Hamilton WILDCATS. The TIGER and WILDCAT competition for fan participation was so great that both teams were unable to operate on a sound financial basis. It was decided that the two clubs should amalgamate and form one representative team for Hamilton. The present name, TIGER-CATS, and what is known as the modern era of football, started in 1950. And contrary to popular belief the move toward U.S. expansion dates back before World War I when the *New York Herald* published an invitation for two Canadian teams to strut their stuff at an exhibition game. And so it was on December 11, 1909, that 15,000 curious Americans at Van Cortlandt Park watched the Hamilton TIGERS beat the Ottawa ROUGH RIDERS 11-6.

NICKNAMES: "TI-CATS"
                "THE TABBYS"
                "STEEL CITY"

HERSHEY BEARS

The sport of ice hockey came to Hershey, Pennsylvania, during the depths of the Great Depression in 1931. The first game was played on February 18, 1931, when Penn A.C. faced off against Villanova in the Convention Hall/Ice Palace. The first team officially to call Hershey its home was the Swathmore A.C., playing in the 1931-32 season. They continually played before sellout crowds. Milton S. Hershey and John B. Sollenberger determined that hockey was here to stay. The following season, the Hershey B'ARS joined the Amateur Hockey League and played regularly scheduled games against teams from Baltimore, Atlantic City, and Philadelphia. At the start of the 1936 season, the club was officially renamed because the Hershey B'ARS was considered too commercial. The name BEARS originated from being referred to as "the BEARS from Penn Woods" when the team played at Madison Square Garden. The BEARS were also the first, on December 19, 1936, to skate onto the ice of newly built Hershey Sports Arena, now referred to as the Hershey Park Arena. Since that time, more than 600 men have proudly worn the Hershey BEARS sweater.

NICKNAME: "CHOCOLATE AND WHITE"

HOUSTON AEROS

Playing in the International Hockey League, this Houston franchise was established in 1994-95. The nickname AEROS was not new, as it was also used by Houston's entry in the World Hockey Association, which won league championships in 1974 and 1975. The moniker originally represented the Texas city's connection to the aerospace industry, with Houston being the site of NASA's Johnson Space Center. Today's AEROS incorporate a World War II theme as the logo includes a star found on the wings of WWII bombers. The Houston AEROS are the southernmost team in IHL history.

INDIANA LEGENDS

Joe Newman, co-founder of the American Basketball Association 2000 and one of the owners of the new Indiana club, said that the LEGENDS name was selected because Indiana is truly the home of basketball. "The state lives and dies by it — from grade schools through high schools and colleges and pros," he said. The state's legends are virtually too numerous to mention, including John Wooden, Larry Bird, Oscar Robertson, Damon Bailey, Bobby Knight, and many more. Newman, along with Allan Zukerman and Dick Tinkham, selected the name for that reason. In fact, they intend to create an Indiana LEGENDS Hall of Fame, selecting five individuals a year for inclusion. The team colors are orange, red, white, and blue. Mr. Newman explains, "The original ABA was founded in Indianapolis and the red, white and blue ball, along with the three-point shot, and the slam dunk were created here." From the Gene Hackman movie *Hoosiers*, which featured a history-making true story about a last-minute, game-winning shot, to former Indiana University Hoosiers' head coach Bobby Knight, basketball truly is legend in Indiana.

INDIANAPOLIS ICE

Established in 1988-89, this Central Hockey League franchise in Indianapolis chose the name ICE after a name-the-team contest. "We were happy to see The ICE on top," said team president Ray Compton. Other choices in the final fan balloting included the CAPITOLS, WARRIORS, SILVER STREAKS, TORNADOES, and PURPLE HAZE. Indianapolis was a hockey town long before the arrival of the ICE, including IHL franchises the CHIEFS from 1955 to 1962, and the cleverly nicknamed CHECKERS, who took over in 1984 until 1987.

JOHNSTOWN CHIEFS

Another Hollywood-inspired nickname. The first name to be considered for this hockey team was the JETS after the former Johnston JETS who spent more than 30 years of pro hockey playing in the former Eastern Hockey League and North American Hockey League. After club officials failed to secure the name JETS form the franchise's former owners, they decided on the CHIEFS. This name came form the most famous hockey movie of all time, *Slapshot*, starring Paul Newman, which was filmed in Johnstown in 1977-78. While the club was known as the Charlestown CHIEFS in the movie, it was the Johnstown CHIEFS that took to the ice in what is now the East Coast Hockey League. The CHIEFS are carrying on a tradition of over 55 years of pro hockey in the city of Johnstown.

KALAMAZOO KINGDOM

The city of Kalamazoo, Michigan, waited a couple of years to receive its first outdoor pro soccer franchise. In 1994, the Kalamazoo PRIDE were supposed to play in the USISL (United Systems of International Soccer Leagues), but that never materialized. In 1995, an ownership group formed the Detroit WHEELS and the Grand Rapids EXPLOSION in the USISL. That group also owned the rights to field the Kalamazoo KOSMOS in 1996, but sold those rights. This newest ownership group announced that its team would be called the SPEEDSTERS, but due to negative reactions, hired a marketing firm that produced the Kalamazoo KINGDOM nickname. Other teams playing in the Central Premier Division are: Ann Arbor ELITES, Austin LONE STARS, Colorado Springs STAMPEDE, Detroit DYNAMITE, Des Moines MENACE, Lexington BANDITS, Mid-Michigan BUCKS, Oklahoma City SLICKERS, Omaha FLAMES, Sioux City BREEZE, and Wichita BLUES.

KANSAS CITY BLADES

The moniker BLADES came out of a name-the-team contest, but wasn't the number one choice of Kansas City hockey fans. Their choice was JAZZ, but was rejected in part because the name was already used by the Utah franchise in the National Basketball Association. Ironically, the National Hockey League San Jose SHARKS rejected their fan favorite, the BLADES, because of its "insinuation" of violence. "First of all, we wanted a name with strong hockey connotations. This clearly identifies us as a hockey club," said BLADES owner Russel A. Parker. Established in 1990-91, the BLADES posted the largest single-season turnaround in IHL history in 1991-92, posting 116 regular season points, a 62-point improvement over the previous season.

KANSAS CITY KNIGHTS

Tom Cheatham, general manager of Kansas City's American Basketball Association 2000 franchise, said that the new basketball league was an opportunity to bring affordable, big time b-ball back to Kansas City. The league implemented rule changes that it felt would take the game back to the "true style of basketball," that is, to get the ball up and down the court at a faster pace. Kansas City KNIGHTS was a name voted on by fans from the eight supplied to a local newspaper. The other choices were: BOMBERS, a reference to the former Richards-Gebaur Air Force base; POSSE, which was the owner's first choice; COBRAS, a nod in the direction of the nationally acclaimed Marching Cobras Band; SPITFIRES, from K.C.'s barbecue heritage; FLAMES, also barbecue; RIVERMEN, a reference to the Missouri River; TOR-NADOS, because of the weather known to the area; and of course, the KNIGHTS. The winner is a nod toward the American Royal rodeo, plus it takes into consideration other local big-league teams like the KINGS (the NBA franchise that moved from Kansas City to Sacramento) and ROYALS. Team colors are purple, green and gold. Purple represented royalty, no one else in town was using green, and gold provided a good contrast.

KANSAS CITY WIZARDS

After a month-long campaign in the Kansas City Star asking fans for their ideas, Kansas City, an Adidas-supported franchise in Major League Soccer, had been reduced to five nicknames: RIVERCATS, ROUGHRIDERS, WIZ, TWISTERS, and QUEST. The newspaper received 3,200 responses, six suggesting WIZARDS, which became a variation of the eventual winner, the WIZ. Nine-year-old Sarah Starr, of Lee's Summit, Missouri, was chosen the grand prize winner of the promotion and received two season tickets for the WIZ's premier season at Arrowhead Stadium. General Manager Tim Latta said he liked WIZ for four reasons: flexibility, creative license, visual appeal, and marketability to young audiences. "It was also very important for us to choose a name that was unique," Latta said. "Its biggest strength, aside from its visual appeal, is that it offers us a great creative springboard. Our youth program will be known as the 'WizKids,' our mascot will be some form of Merlin the Magician, and one of our premier giveaway nights may be WIZbees (Frisbees with the WIZ logo). And we have the flexibility of using WIZards when we want to." That flexibility was exercised in November 1996, when the team officially changed its name to the WIZ-ARDS. The change must have helped ... the team won the MLS championship in 2000.

KISSIMMEE COBRAS

Kissimmee ASTROS? Can you imagine the locker room jokes! Houston brought its single-A minor-league club to Kissimmee in the Florida State League in 1988, but decided to use the county name Osceola rather than the city name. In 1995 the team decided to switch back to the city's name, and dropped its parent club's nickname. The Kissimmee COBRAS was chosen for the alliteration and marketing possibilities. In fact, 16 of 21 minor-league teams with new nicknames that

year opted for flash and fun over traditional organization monikers such
as the YANKEES or PIRATES. Why? Big merchandising dollars. "I
think traditional baseball marketing ideas get thrown out the window in
Florida, and especially here in the world of Mickey Mouse and Shamu
the Killer Whale," COBRAS GM Tim Bawmann said. "This seemed an
opportunity to make ends meet and it's been great so far — we've had to
re-order hats and T-shirts." After the 2000 season, the ASTROS ended
their relationship with Kissimmee, and the COBRAS folded when no
other major-league team added the Florida city.

LANSING LUGNUTS

Spawning from the Waterloo DIAMONDS and Springfield SUL-
TANS, the LUGNUTS were moved from Springfield, Illinois, following
the 1995 campaign. Joining the 14-team Midwest League, local residents
of Lansing selected the team name through a contest that brought in over
2,000 entries. In a nutshell, the name LUGNUTS was ultimately chosen
for its tie-in to the Lansing automotive industry and because it was a typically quirky minor-league moniker. In 1999, the LUGNUTS embarked
on a new partnership with the Chicago CUBS.

LAS VEGAS 51s

Strange, creative, and wacky nicknames are nothing out of the
ordinary in minor-league baseball. So when the former Las Vegas
STARS, a member of the Triple-A Pacific Coast League, were in the
midst of changing affiliations from the San Diego PADRES to the Los
Angeles DODGERS in 2000, the idea of changing the nickname was at
the top of their to-do list. What they came up with became the talk
of the minors. The Las Vegas 51s received national attention for their
new name and alien-themed logo. The name is derived from Area 51,
a government-restricted site north of Las Vegas, which has long been
rumored to be where extraterrestrial beings are held. The logo features
an egg-shaped alien head with baseball seams on it; and the mascot,
"Cosmo," features antennae with eyes at the ends. Aaron Artman, the
team's director of creative services, said, "We were looking for something that would stir up attention. We had a bunch of different gambling names, of course — even thought of the Rat Pack connection.
The alien concept just came out of my mouth ... and 51s was what
came out of it." The team's merchandise ranks among the top sellers in
the minors.

LOS ANGELES GALAXY

Playing in the World Soccer League, this Nike-supported franchise sent this information about the team's nickname: The logo system for the Los Angeles GALAXY revolves around the one part of the cosmos that LA can rightfully claim — the sun. Spinning and energetic, the logo not only conveys the warmth and action of the city, but the intensity and movement of the game. The team's colors of orange, yellow, blue and black underscore the theme, while the retro typeface echoes Art Deco LA. As for the mascot/character — well, its creators dubbed it "Twizzle." It's some kind of astral entity, and it means business.

LOUISVILLE RIVERBATS

Jeff Hollis, the Director of Media Relations for the Louisville RIVER-BATS, says that when the time came for someone to name this minor league baseball team, it was a 12-year-old girl who stepped up to the plate. She explained that her choice addressed two major aspects of Louisville — the mighty Ohio River and the world-famous Louisville Slugger bats. This may have been the reason for another, rejected, choice, the Louisville SLUGGERS. COLONELS, the name of Kentucky's former American Basketball Association team, was also under consideration. The RIVER-BATS wear green, purple, and gold as team colors. Their mascot is named Buddy Bat, and this winged mammal stalks the sidelines and entertains the crowds in the color purple.

LOUISVILLE RIVERFROGS

This nickname for Louisville's hockey team was generated from inner-office conversations, which spanned some five months. Assistant General Manager Greg Galiette originally suggested the name FROGS. The name was refined to RIVERFROGS through office brainstorming. Then the nickname was given to Creative Alliance, a local advertising agency, to be included with any other names the agency wanted to suggest. The final three names brought back to the board of directors were RIVERFROGS, VULTURES, and PIRANHAS. RIVERFROGS won out because it was considered "kid-friendly" and would have tremendous across-the-board marketing implications. The name is different, yet not intimidating to kids or adults. Louisville's previous East Coast Hockey League team, the ICE-HAWKS, had become the Jacksonville LIZARD KINGS in 1994, opening the door for the RIVERFROGS.

MACON WHOOPEE

The Macon WHOOPEE Hockey Club came into existence during the 1996-97 season of the Central Hockey League. The name Macon WHOOPEE was taken out of respect for Macon's first pro hockey team, the Macon WHOOPEES, which played in the Southern Hockey League during the 1973-74 season. The Macon WHOOPEES name was originally chosen from the song "Makin' Whoopee," featuring the vocal talents of Doris Day. When the team was brought back into existence in the CHL, the owners of the team wanted to use a name that was already known through-out the community. This one won't be forgotten anytime soon.

MANCHESTER UNITED RED DEVILS

The seeds for Manchester United's future success were sown when workers with the Lancashire and Yorkshire Railway decided to form a team of their own in 1878. It was run by the Dining Room Committee of the Carriage and Wagon Works, and was known as the Newton Heath Lancashire and Yorkshire Cricket and Football Club. Only after Newton Heath went bankrupt did Manchester United emerge from the ashes in 1902. Having joined the Football League in 1892, the club has played in one or other of the top two divisions ever since. During World War II, heavy bomb damage meant Manchester United had to temporarily abandon its Old Trafford ground and play matches at their Manchester rivals' Maine Road stadium. Quickly dominating English football after the war, the new team won the First Division in successive seasons before the 1958 Munich air crash claimed the lives of eight players.

MANITOBA MOOSE

MOOSE season expanded to the city of St. Paul, Minnesota, in the fall of 1994. But, unlike the hunting seasons held in northern Minnesota, this Minnesota MOOSE season is played on ice, and they are targets only for other International Hockey League teams. The MOOSE was the favorite nickname of the fans in the name-the-team contest conducted by the *Pioneer Press* and the favorite of majority owner Kevin MacLean. The MOOSE received 1,031 votes, 57 more than the runner-up, MUSTANGS. Other suggestions included the MALLARDS, WIZARDS, BOBCATS, and TOMCATS. "The people have spoken," MacLean said, happy the fans pre-ferred the same nickname that he did. "This is a name we can have fun with and fun is a big part of the IHL's approach to hockey." In fact, a team executive was heard to say at the time, "We don't know if Bullwinkle will be available for the opener, but we've got a call in for Rocky." The Twin Cities have hosted two previous IHL franchises — the Minneapolis MILLERS and the Saint Paul SAINTS, both from 1959 to 1963. In 1996, the National Hockey League Winnipeg JETS left Manitoba to become the Pheonix COYOTES, and the IHL's MOOSE were moved north to fill the void.

McGILL REDMEN

Montreal's McGill University, founded in 1827, played Harvard in the world's first international intercollegate football game in May of 1874. And it was McGill's students that formed the world's first official hockey team on January 31, 1877. McGill even has a claim in basketball — it was McGill graduate James Naismith who founded the game while a teacher at the Springfield YMCA in Springfield, Massachusetts. Before 1930, the teams operated under a number of colorful monikers reported in the local sports papers. These included the RED-and-WHITE, in reference to the school colors, the McGill HOCKEY CLUB, OLD McGILL, the MEN, the HOCKEYISTS, the RED SQUAD, the RED TEAM, and the BIG RED TEAM. But in the University's 1930 yearbook, and then again in a 1931 *Montreal Gazette* article, the sports teams from McGill were being called the REDMEN. Again, the nickname was a reference to the school colors, worn proudly by all McGill students since the previous decade.

MEDICINE HAT RATTLERS

Prior to 1984, the Medicine Hat College (Canada) athletic teams went by the nicknames ANTELOPE for men, and KUDOS for the women. A Medicine Hat-based junior football team went by the name RATTLERS until that team was disbanded in 1979. After the collapse of that team, Medicine Hat College claimed the RATTLERS nickname for its own. Prior to that time a strong resemblance between the College's ANTELOPE/KUDOS logo and that of nearby University of Lethbridge's PRONGHORNS, another type of antelope, had left the Medicine Hat College without a unique identity for its athletic teams. The Prairie Rattlesnake (*Crotalus viridus*) has a range which extends over much of southeast Alberta and southeast Saskatchewan. In many ways the name RATTLERS, and the symbols, signify attributes that are valuable in athletics. The rattlesnake is a creature of stealth and quickness. It is an efficient and merciless predator. While Medicine Hat College athletes and

coaches do not regard themselves as cold-blooded, they do hope to identi-
fy with the RATTLER'S "killer instinct" — dangerous creatures to be
treated with respect.

MICHIGAN BATTLE CATS

Due to bad field conditions, the Madison HATTERS baseball organization went looking for a new home in 1994. They moved their Single-A
Midwest League club to Battle Creek, Michigan, because of the tremendous popularity of the West Michigan WHITECAPS in Grand Rapids.
They chose "Cereal City" because of the rich tradition in Battle Creek, and
the fine facility in C. O. Brown Stadium. Initially, in order to attract fans
from Kalamazoo, the franchise was named the Battle Creek GOLDEN
KAZOOS. The GOLDEN KAZOOS was a historically significant name to
the area due to a successful ball team by that name in the 1940s and '50s.
But as the premiere season drew closer, an individual came forward claim-
ing that he owned the rights to the GOLDEN KAZOO name. So the club
was renamed the Michigan BATTLE CATS. Though the team ended up
buying the rights to the GOLDEN KAZOOS nickname in June of 1995,
there are still no plans to change the name back. Prior to the BATTLE
CATS, Battle Creek had the CRICKETS, who played in the Southern
Michigan League during the 1910s; and the Battle Creek BELLES, who
competed in the All-American Girls Professional Baseball League from
1951 to 1952.

MICHIGAN K-WINGS

When Kalamazoo joined the International Hockey League in 1974-
75, the team was 40 percent owned by the National Hockey League's
Detroit RED WINGS, a senior club named in memory of the WINGED
WHEELERS, an amateur Montreal Athletic Association team in the
1890s. Local fans became so familiar with the nickname, which is also
used in the arena name, that it remained intact, even though the team was
affiliated with the Dallas STARS (formerly the Minnesota NORTH
STARS) franchise for several years. The K-WINGS, short for
Kalamazoo-WINGS, have the league's most senior owners in Martha and
Ted Parfet. Dallas severed relations with the K-WINGS on April 17, 2000,
and the Michigan franchise has yet to resurface.

NICKNAME: "WINGS"

MILWAUKEE ADMIRALS

Named after a fridge? That's right, and why not for a hockey franchise? Established in 1977-78, the Milwaukee ADMIRALS were actually formed in 1970, playing as an independent amateur team. One of the owners at the time, Erwin Merar, owned an appliance dealership and decided to name the hockey team after his top-selling line, which happened to carry the brand name ADMIRAL. Playing in the International Hockey League for the next 32 years, which folded in 2001, the ADMIRALS then joined the American Hockey League with other former IHL teams the Chicago WOLVES, Grand Rapids GRIFFINS, Houston AEROS, Manitoba MOOSE, and Utah GRIZZLIES.

MINNESOTA ARCTIC BLAST

The Minnesota MOSQUITOS? No. How about the ICE, LOONS, or POLARS? Those were some of the concepts that design and marketing partners Michael Vacanti and Richard Valentine had to work with for Minnesota's new Roller Hockey International franchise before team management decided on the ARCTIC BLAST. "They really liked the idea of the polar bear, so we went with that concept," said Valentine. "Plus it also helps to have an animated character to have as a mascot." "We wanted them to have an NHL-NBA level logo that had durability, and was rather irreverent," added Vacanti. After creating the pencils of the grinning polar bear and blasting puck, the partners put it on the computer, developed the background and came up with the colors silver, black, and BLAST blue. The black and silver combination has been a popular one for both the Chicago White Sox and Los Angeles Kings when they opted for uniform and design changes. "Colors play a big part in merchandising and marketing of a team. Teal has been overdone lately so we wanted to do something different," said Vacanti. Different and fresh is what they came up with, as the ARCTIC BLAST was perceived as a fresh and unique approach to sports franchise identity. The team is presently on sabbatical from the Roller Hockey International League.

NICKNAME: "THE BLAST"

MONTREAL ALOUETTES

In 1946, the Montreal ALOUETTES joined the Canadian Football League. After winning championships and luring top-flight American talent away from the National Football League, including Heisman Trophy winner Johnny Rodgers, the franchise folded in 1981 due to bankruptcy, then was reborn as the CONCORDES in 1982. In 1985 they returned to the ALOUETTES moniker, which means "lark" but here is a fictionalized red bird made popular in a French-Canadian children's song. But again the team was forced to fold in June of 1987. When the South (American) Division of the CFL folded in 1996, the Grey Cup Champion Baltimore STALLIONS moved their franchise up to Montreal, once more resurrecting the ALOUETTES nickname by popular demand.

NICKNAMES: "ALS"
              "RED BIRDS"

NEW BRITAIN ROCK CATS

For more than a decade, this baseball team was known as the Hardware City ROCK CATS. The seemingly odd name stems from a city's nickname. Tool manufacturer Stanley Tools makes its home in New Britain, Connecticut, giving the town the nickname of Hardware City. When the city ended its 12-year affiliation with the Boston RED SOX and welcomed the Minnesota TWINS, a new name was needed. The Double-A club hired Guy Gilchrist, the ultra-hot graphic designer of the Portland SEA DOGS, to come up with a new logo and the Hardware City ROCK CAT was born. He was a cat with sunglasses, an electric guitar, a ponytail, and an earring. Team owner Joe Buzas became concerned that fans wouldn't know where "Hardware City" was. He decided the name would remain Hardware City, but New Britain would appear on the road uniforms. Even the original logo was toned down. "We took out the earring," said director of media relations Chris Whalen, "But the first shipment of T-shirts still had the old logo." Might turn out to be a collector's item someday.

NEWCASTLE UNITED MAGPIES

Founded in 1881, the club — originally known simply as STANLEY — changed its name to Newcastle EAST END before becoming known as Newcastle UNITED in 1892 after a meeting in Bath Lane Hall. By then, rivals Newcastle WEST END had disbanded and the club took over St. James' Park as its home. Elected to the Second Division in 1893, the MAGPIES, which is a diminutive of Margaret, and the name for a genus of chattering birds, was heavily dependent on Scottish players. The club soon won promotion for what turned out to be a 36-year stay in the First

Division, ending relegation in 1934. After a 14-year absence, they returned to the top flight only to be demoted again in 1961. The pattern continued to repeat itself — up in 1965, down in 1978, up in 1984, down in 1989. One hundred years after being elected to the Second Division, the MAGPIES won promotion to the British Premier League.

NICKNAME: "TYNESIDERS"

NORFOLK TIDES

Now playing in the International League, Norfolk had been without professional baseball since the TARS of the Piedmont League folded on July 13, 1955. The Portsmouth MERRIMACS finished that season, but then the league went out of existence. A South Atlantic League exhibition game was held in Portsmouth at Lawrence Stadium and was followed by a study to bring baseball back to the area. A Tidewater franchise in the South Atlantic League was granted in 1961 to William McDonald of Miami. The name TIDES was selected in a contest conducted by the *Virginian-Pilot*. MARINERS was the name of choice, but editor Robert Mason liked the sound and alliteration of Tidewater TIDES. The team operated in the South Atlantic League for two years, then in the Carolina League for another six. In 1969, the METS moved their Triple-A interests to Tidewater, and the TIDES have been a New York affiliate ever since. When the METS sold the franchise in 1992, the new group dropped the Tidewater name in favor of Norfolk, giving the Norfolk TIDES a geographic presence.

NOTTINGHAM FOREST

One of the oldest football (soccer) clubs in the world, Nottingham FOREST of the British Premier League, garners its origins from a meeting at the Clinton Arms in Nottingham in 1865. Founded simply as FOREST Football Club, members had previously met there to play "shinney," an early form of hockey. The FOREST referred to in the club name was FOREST Racecourse or Recreation Ground, where it was originally based. Shortly after its foundation as a football club, players bought themselves RED caps to wear on the field. Hence the team's colors. The Trent Bridge cricket ground was one of a number of temporary homes before FOREST moved to the City Ground in 1898. There is no record of an official badge or crest being in existence before the Second World War, but shortly after that, the club adopted and then adapted the City of Nottingham Coat of Arms, the only difference being the letters NFFC replacing the castle on the original design. The badge first appeared on the club shirts in 1957. By the early 1970s the commercial aspects of the game were beginning to surface, and the need for a new badge became apparent. This is because the club couldn't obtain a copyright for an existing coat of arms, so FOREST decided to change the badge to enable a copyright. The local paper, the *Nottingham Evening Post*, organized a competition in the summer of 1973. The winning entry was chosen from over 800 entries and was submitted by David Lewis. Firsts for FOREST? A referee's whistle was first used in a FOREST game for signalling stoppage, replacing the previous method of waving a white flag. FOREST player Sam Widdowson was the first player to wear shin pads on the outside of his socks, doing so in 1874. Goal posts and crossbar were first used officially at a FOREST ground in 1891.

NICKNAME: "THE REDS"

PEORIA RIVERMEN

Although established in 1982-83, it wasn't until 1984 that the Peoria Civic Center Authority selected RIVERMEN from several entries suggested by citizens through a phone poll conducted by the *Peoria Journal-Star*. It was considered an appropriate moniker by the International Hockey League franchise given that the Illinois River runs next to Peoria's downtown district. The RIVERMEN set a still-standing pro hockey record by putting together an 18-game winning streak early in the 1990-91 season, which would culminate in a Turner Cup championship. The team now plays in the East Coast Hockey League.

PIEDMONT BOLL WEEVILS

Happy for a while just being the PHILLIES, the moniker they brought from Spartanburg, South Carolina, the team held a contest in 1996 to find a new name, something indigenous to the area. BOLL WEEVILS was the choice from among 3,000 entries, which included the TOWELS, the CANNONS, and the LINTHEADS. BOLL WEEVILS as the choice for this Class A South Atlantic League affiliate of the Philadelphia PHILLIES is part of a trend among teams to choose unusual names and just the right logo to draw crowds and increase souvenir sales. Jonathan Frank, licensing director of minor league baseball for Major League Properties, said that in secondary markets, unusual nicknames that relate to the team's region not only promote the team, but promote the game. For instance, the Greensboro HORNETS changed to the BATS, the swinging kind, not the flying variety.

Spartanburg's local press bit deep early, describing the baseball team as "unbollweevible," and nicknaming the stadium the "Cotton Boll."

QUAD CITY RIVER BANDITS

In July of 1991, when word got out of a contest to rename the Quad City ANGELS, suggestions came in from places as far away as Guam and as unusual as the Iowa State Penitentiary. "When people think about the ANGELS," Quad City owner Rick Holtzman said, "they think about the California ANGELS. We wanted to give the franchise more of a Quad City identity." Everyone was thrilled with RIVER BANDITS, RIVER because the one significant aspect of the Quad Cities is the "Mighty" Mississippi, and BANDITS because it has a certain amount of mystery and flair. "The key was to develop a name that is marketable both internally and nationally, and I think we've found that." RIVER BANDITS, a Class A affiliate of the Minnesota TWINS playing in the Midwest League, was selected by the Quad City staff from the more than 1,000 entries and 800 different names suggested by the fans. Bob Heimer of Davenport, Iowa, was the only one to suggest the actual name. "I actually submitted about ten different names," he said. "With RIVER BANDITS I was looking to combine the Mississippi River with the one-armed BANDITS of riverboat gambling." Team colors are red and black.

RANCHO CUCAMONGA QUAKES

The Ventura County GULLS were sold to a group of investors that moved the team to San Bernardino in 1987. The San Bernardino SPIRIT entertained fans at Fiscalini Field until the 1992 season when the city of Rancho Cucamonga told majority owner Hank Stickney of its intention to build a brand new, state-of-the-art ballpark. The rights to the name San Bernardino SPIRIT were sold, and Stickney moved a franchise into temporary trailers just outside the construction of the new ballpark. Fans were asked to select a name for the new team, and on September 30, 1992, it was announced that six people had suggested the nickname QUAKES. Team management chose the very Californian moniker as the winner from over 200 different names. The QUAKES nickname in turn lent some of its theme to the naming of the new stadium. And so the Rancho Cucamonga QUAKES won their first game on April Fools Day, 1993, at the Epicenter! On July 15, 1993, the QUAKES, then a Double-A affiliate of the San Diego PADRES, broke the year-old California League attendance record of 218,444 previously held by the High Desert MAVERICKS. Other nicknames the QUAKES enjoyed over the years include the CRUSHERS, PADRES, ORIONS, LIONS, ORIOLES, and DODGERS. In 2001, the QUAKES became a single-A affiliate for the Anaheim ANGELS.

ROANOKE EXPRESS

The Western Virginia town of Roanoke is proud of its old railway ties, and wanted a nickname that celebrated this fact. Playing in the East Coast Hockey League, it was Jack Bogaczyk of Hockey Roanoke, Inc., who instigated a name-the-team contest through the local newspaper. Finalists included the LOCOMOTIVES and the SHOOTING STARS. At one of the initial EXPRESS organizational meetings, owner Joe Steffen brought along a Barcelona DRAGONS football jersey. The DRAGONS, a member of the once defunct (but now reborn) World League of American Football, presented a dark, forest-green base team color that was immediately accepted. The idea of a train coming out of a star was also uniquely tied in with the history of Roanoke. Considerations of the type of train to be used included going with the history and power of an old steam locomotive, or to take a futuristic approach with a more streamlined, high-speed train. The EXPRESS was the first team in ECHL to utilize a puck in their logo. It's carried in the train's "mouth."

SAN BERNARDINO STAMPEDE

The San Bernardino SPIRIT didn't just want a new name and logo for their baseball team, they wanted an entire theme around which to market themselves. So the SPIRIT name was changed to the STAMPEDE. The move continues the recent trend of singular sports nicknames. It gives the club a more marketable logo — a stampeding horse — and the chance to create a Western theme at its new ballpark. Many fans preferred the nickname SPIRIT, which had represented the team since it joined the California League in 1987. At the time, STAMPEDE general manager Jim Wehmeier said the club wanted to make a clean break, "The SPIRIT went out as 1995 league champions, so we're retiring the name on a winning note. We're also moving to a new stadium, so it's a logical time for the transition to a new name." The team began play in a 5,000-seat stadium, dubbed The Ranch, in 1996. "We were looking for something very wholesome and family-oriented," said co-owner Donna Tuttle. "There is strength to a stampede, mass and energy . . . And instead of picking an animal, we wanted a whole Western theme." In 2001, the STAMPEDE played as an affiliate of the Seattle MARINERS.

SAN JOSE CLASH

A Nike-supported franchise in the World Soccer League, the CLASH media department sent this reason for its name selection: The driving spirit of the San Jose CLASH is the scorpion — quick, lethal, and mean. A striker that hits without warning. An attacker whose defense is just more attack. With shapes and colors that reflect the diverse ethnic make-up and heritage of the Bay Area, the logo system is derived from the soil it represents. And together with the team's name, it promises strong and decisive action in every San Jose match.

SASKATCHEWAN ROUGHRIDERS

Saskatchewan football began on the night of Tuesday, September 6, 1910 with the formation of the Regina RUGBY CLUB, which initially had been intended to be a rowing club. The original colors were old gold and purple. They went to blue and white the following year, and in 1912 turned to red and black — a combination that would remain for the next 36 years. In 1924 the Regina RUGBY CLUB became the Regina ROUGHRIDERS. Ottawa's rugby club had been called the ROUGHRIDERS since the 1890s, but dropped it in favor of calling themselves the SENATORS in 1924. The Saskatchewan RUGBY CLUB jumped at the chance to adopt ROUGHRIDERS as their new nickname. There are two versions of where the name ROUGHRIDERS came from. One states that Saskatchewan got it from the history of the Northwest Mounted Police who were called ROUGH RIDERS because they broke the wild horse broncos used by the force, while Ottawa's ROUGH RIDERS supposedly were Ottawa Valley lumberjacks who rode log booms down the Ottawa River. The other story, which is just as speculative, states there was a Canadian volunteer contingent that once fought with Teddy Roosevelt in the Spanish-American War. His troops became known as ROUGHRIDERS, and following the war, the Canadian volunteers returned to Canada, part of the group settling around Ottawa and the others moving west. Apparently the colors of the infantry unit were red and black. Some of these men became involved in the organization and running of the Ottawa and Regina RUGBY CLUBS, and thus the romance for the ROUGHRIDER nickname — and why both had black and red as their team colors. Ottawa still is black and red. In 1948 the Regina ROUGHRIDERS became a provincially owned and operated club, prompting the name change from Regina to the Saskatchewan ROUGHRIDERS.

NICKNAMES: "THE ROUGHIES"
                    "GREEN RIDERS"

SAVANNAH SAND GNATS

Affiliated with the Texas RANGERS, Savannah's minor-league baseball team has settled on a new nickname, the SAND GNATS. "It's pretty good for us down here," said Director of Marketing Nick Brown. "With all the humid weather, we've got those gnats. Either us or Charleston almost had to grab the nickname." Brown said the name was picked in voting by the public through the news media. Seventy percent of those voting chose SAND GNATS over four other prospective names: HAMMERHEADS, THRASHERS, SHADOW, and SEA TURTLES. SHADOW was a distant second in the results, which were announced February 13, 1996. The Class A team, formerly affiliated with the St. Louis CARDINALS and the Los Angeles DODGERS, switched to the RANGERS in 1998.

SHEFFIELD WEDNESDAY

Few clubs can claim origins as distant as Sheffield WEDNESDAY of the British Premier League. Cricketers who wanted to play during the winter formed the club in the early 19th century. The players, mostly local craftsmen, took a half day off on Wednesdays to play. On a Wednesday evening in 1867, the Sheffield WEDNESDAY Cricket Club was then transformed into the WEDNESDAY Football Club, joining other local football clubs like the Sheffield FC and Hallam FC. The term OWLS, as they are also known, comes from the original home ground at Owlerton — which the OWLS renamed Hillsborough at the start of the First World War. In the 1970s, WEDNESDAY dropped to the Third Division, their reputation damaged by a headline-grabbing bribe scandal. They managed to avoid the ignominy of descending to the Fourth Division by only a single point. So bad was their performance, one fan tried to sue them under the Trades Descriptions Act! (The TDA seeks to control the accuracy of statements made by businesses about goods and services. The prosecution must prove that the defendant made a false statement "knowingly" or "recklessly." Under the circumstances — mostly that a soccer club is not a good or service — the suit seems symbolic. How could Sheffield WEDNESDAY "knowingly" and "recklessly" call themselves a professional football club when their on-field performance was so much less than professional?) In more recent times, the OWLS have restored their pride and built on the success that began with their League Cup victory in 1991. Two years later, only the Arsenal GUNNERS — twice — prevented them from achieving a remarkable League Cup and FA Cup double.

NICKNAME: "OWLS"

SHREVEPORT SWAMP DRAGONS

The city of Shreveport, Louisiana, has had professional baseball since 1895. It has competed under 11 different nicknames, including CREOLES, GRAYS, GASSERS, SPORTS, and then for 30 years as the Shreveport CAPTAINS — after local hero and town founder Captain Henry Miller Shreve. Mandalay Sports Entertainment bought the team in 2000. Mandalay already owned the Dayton DRAGONS in Dayton, Ohio, and went looking for a similar name in Shreveport. The name SWAMP DRAGONS is a reference to Louisiana's famous bogs and bayous, and a dragon named SCORCH that legend has it once lived there! It seems Scorch swam in local Caddo Lake 500 years ago, keeping the Caddo Indians safe from alligators and any other nasty things that meant to bring them harm. Today, a mascot named Scorch patrols the stadium sidelines, protecting his SWAMP DRAGONS. Team colors are green and black, with a hint of red.

TAMPA BAY MUTINY

Shoe manufacturer Nike is supporting this Major League Soccer franchise, and sent this information: The Tampa Bay MUTINY logo system doesn't have any rebellious sailors. No three-masted galleons. No rolling oceans. Just little green winged cybermutants from the dark blue depths of space. Inspired by the futuristic visions of video games, the logos and type suggest a mega-high-tech, ominous force on the field. The logos' designer will even point out that the character isn't controlling the ball with its feet, but with its mind — soccer reaches the fourth dimension! Not your typical pirate story.

TEHRAN PERUZEE

Iran's most popular soccer club is based in the capital city of Tehran, playing in the Iranian National Football League. When the team was formed, it was named in honor of an ancient king named Korosh, who ruled Iran some 2,500 years ago from the capital of his kingdom, the city of Sheraz. The family name Haghamaneshian was the most powerful for many years. They built a magnificent castle, which they called PERSPO-LICE. So, more than two thousand years later, when it came time to name the local soccer franchise, they chose to honor this ancient king by naming their new heroes the PERSPOLICE, after his place of residence. The club's name stayed the PERSPOLICE until the mid-1980s, when nonreligious names honoring Iranian royalty became unpopular. The name was then changed to PERUZEE, which means "winner" in the Persian language.

TOLEDO MUD HENS

Playing in the International League, the Toledo MUD HENS is one of the two most famous teams in all of minor-league baseball (the other being the Durham BULLS), but there's a persistent dilemma with the team's fame — nobody seems to know what a MUD HEN is. This Detroit TIGER Triple-A affiliate says that a MUD HEN is a marsh bird with short wings and long legs that inhabits swamps or marshes. Such birds have been known as marsh hens, rails, or MUD HENS. Teams from Toledo have also been known as the WHITE STOCKINGS, SWAMP ANGELS, BLACK PIRATES, and GLASS SOX. This Toledo baseball club earned its present nickname in 1896, and it has kept it — with those few minor exceptions — ever since. In that year, the team played at Bay View Park, with these strange birds frequenting the marshland outside the field. The abundance of MUD HENS near the park brought about the nickname and the rest, as they say, is history. Alumni of the MUD HENS include Jim Thorpe, Frank Viola, and Kirby Puckett, but the MUD HENS persona is so strong that even famous nonplayers have been seen in a Toledo uniform. Actor Jamie Farr brought the uniform and the MUD HENS nickname nationwide fame in his role as Toledo-born Max Klinger of the hit television series M*A*S*H.

NICKNAME: "HENS"

TORONTO ARGONAUTS

The Canadian Football League's oldest team is also its winningest, with 12 Grey Cup Championships. The ARGONAUTS storybook began in 1872 when a man named Harry O'Brien gathered crews of oarsmen, decked them out in Oxford and Cambridge blues, and formed the ARGONAUT Rowing

Club. The original intent was to give the oarsmen an alternative way of keeping fit. In these early days they were an amateur club, playing a few games a year. In 1873, the first ARGONAUT football club was formed under the guidance of head coach H. T. Glazebrook. The ARGO footballers played one game that year, losing 3-0 to their cross-town rival, the University of Toronto. Still, the game played second fiddle to the water sport. In fact in 1879, the ARGONAUTS didn't play a single football game because many of the players were suffering from stretched stomach muscles sustained in rowing competitions. The sport became more organized when the Ontario Rugby Football Union was formed in 1883. In 1907 the ARGONAUTS, along with the Hamilton TIGERS of the ORFU, joined the Ottawa ROUGH RIDERS and Montreal WINGED WHEELERS of the Quebec Rugby Football Union to form the Interprovincial Rugby Football Union — or the Big Four. It wasn't until 1956 that the Canadian Football Council was formed, and two years later, withdrew from the Rugby Union to become the Canadian Football League. The ARGONAUTS have the distinction of once being owned by former Los Angeles KINGS owner Bruce McNall, hockey superstar Wayne Gretzky, and the much-missed comedian John Candy.

NICKNAMES: "THE BOATMEN"
                "THE ARGOS"

TOTTENHAM HOTSPURS

According to the various publications on the history of the SPURS, this British Premier League club was started by schoolboys — mainly former pupils of Tottenham Grammar School and St. John's Presbyterian School — who were reading Shakespeare and were particularly interested in Henry Percy. The exact date of the first match played is not known but research has established the first recorded match played was on August 30, 1882, when a team called RADICALS beat them 2-0. Unlike many clubs over these last hundred and some years, the SPURS have never moved far from their roots and have always played within one mile of where they first began. Why HOT SPUR? That was the name of the cricket team taken from Harry HOTSPUR, the nickname of Henry Percy (1364-1403), eldest son of the Earl of Northumberland, whose family seat was close to the club's original home, on the rough grass of Tottenham marshes. Percy's nickname was derived from the riding SPURS he wore. In 1898, the HOTSPURS moved to their present world-famous park at White Hart Lane. In 1901 SPUR won the FA Cup. The first game of the final match against Sheffield UNITED at Crystal Palace drew 110,000 fans! The club's world-famous ball-and-cockerel emblem is believed to have its origins in cock-fighting, because combative cocks were fitted with tiny SPURS.

NICKNAME: "SPURS"

TRENT EXCALIBUR

The EXCALIBUR nickname has been used for Trent University of Peterborough, Ontario, athletic teams since 1986. At that time a vote was taken on campus among a number of name suggestions, and this emerged the winner. EXCALIBUR is the name of the legendary sword of King Arthur. The Trent crest consists of the head of a sword surrounded by symbols that represent running water. This design comes from the fact that Trent is located on the banks of the Otonabee River and the sword is depicted in the City of Peterborough crest. Prior to 1986, Trent teams had been called the NATIONALS, but it was decided this moniker did not have the intrigue, interest, and symbolism required.

WEST HAM UNITED HAMMERS

The HAMMERS' wordplay on Ham — also known as the IRONS — began their British Premier League life as the Thames IRONWORKS team formed in 1895 by employees of a shipyard whose managing director, Arnold Hills, came up with the idea of setting up an amateur club. They entered the FA Cup in their inaugural season at Chatham, and the London League in their second year. Although the impoverished club was shut down in June of 1900, it was relaunched a month later as West Ham UNITED. The new club maintained the shipyard connection until 1904, when it moved to Upton Park. Although they never won the First Division, they have had more success in the FA Cup, winning it three times: 1964, 1975, and 1980. In 1965 they added the European Cup-Winner's Cup to their trophy cupboard. Traditionally respected for their stylish play, the best-known of West Ham UNITED HAMMERS stars of recent years were the 1966 World Cup trio of Bobby Moore, Geoff Hurst, and Martin Peters.

NICKNAME: "IRONS"

WINNIPEG BLUE BOMBERS

This Canadian Football League team was the second franchise in pro sports to be named after popular world heavyweight boxing champion Joe

Louis. The first was the Cleveland BROWN BOMBERS (later the BROWNS), a reference to the boxer's nickname, the Brown Bomber. The second franchise was the boys in blue from Winnipeg. It was during the 1936 season that the WINNIPEGS were playing an exhibition game against the University of North Dakota, when a young reporter named Vince Leah remarked, "These are the BLUE BOMBERS of Western Football." He was coining the phrase from a Grantland Rice description of Joe Louis, and with a nod toward the attending American press familiar with it. From that day in 1936, the team has always been known as the Winnipeg BLUE BOMBERS. Founded on June 30, 1930, the team then known as the WINNIPEGS became the first team west of Ontario to win the coveted Grey Cup Trophy. Considering the American connection to the club's nickname, it is perhaps fitting that in 1993, the Winnipeg BLUE-BOMBERS hosted the Sacramento GOLD MINERS in the first-ever Canada-U.S. game in the Canadian Football League.

NICKNAME: "BOMBERS"

WINSTON-SALEM WARTHOGS

Salem, celebrated in literature, film, and song for its infamous witch burnings, would seem the perfect place to field a baseball club called the SPIRITS — the club's name until 1994. But THIS Salem isn't in Massachusetts, it's in North Carolina. In fact, franchise owner Dennis Bastien, who bought the team in 1984, the same year as the Los Angeles Olympic Summer Games, had a completely different reason for selecting the moniker. Bastien, patriotic and very much caught up in the success of those Games, decided to honor the event when he named his team. So, the Winston-Salem baseball team, then a Class A affiliate of the Cincinnati REDS playing in the Carolina League, was named the SPIRITS not because of the dark and mystical history of Salem, but because of the Olympic SPIRIT of the nation at that time. Then a new marketing plan took over, with the new nickname WARTHOGS raised a few eyebrows. But WARTHOGS general manager Peter Fisch has a good track record with this sort of thing — he was assistant GM for both the Carolina MUDCATS and Hickory CRAWDADS when they changed their names with merchandising success. Why the change? "We wanted people here to have something new and exciting to think about whether they liked it or not." In 1997 the WARTHOGS began an affiliation with the Chicago WHITE SOX.